BLOOM'S

HOW TO WRITE ABOUT

Shakespeare's Romances

SUANNA H. DAVIS

Introduction by Harold Bloom

BLOOM'S
LITERARY CRITICISM
An imprint of Infobase Publishing

Bloom's How to Write about Shakespeare's Romances

Bloom's Literary Criticism
An imprint of Infobase Publishing
132 West 31st Street
New York NY 10001

Library of Congress Cataloging-in-Publication Data
Davis, Suanna H.
 Bloom's how to write about Shakespeare's romances / Suanna H. Davis ; introduction by Harold Bloom.
    p. cm. — (Bloom's how to write about literature)
 Includes bibliographical references and index.
 ISBN 978-1-60413-722-4 (hardcover)
 1. Shakespeare, William, 1564–1616—Tragicomedies. 2. Tragicomedy—History and criticism. 3. Criticism—Authorship. I. Bloom, Harold. II. Title. III. Title: How to write about Shakespeare's romances.
 PR2981.5.D37 2010
 822.3'3—dc22

                              2010015949

Bloom's Literary Criticism books are available at special discounts when purchased in bulk quantities for businesses, associations, institutions, or sales promotions. Please call our Special Sales Department in New York at (212)967-8800 or (800)322-8755.

You can find Bloom's Literary Criticism on the World Wide Web
at http://www.chelseahouse.com

Text design by Annie O'Donnell
Cover design by Ben Peterson
Composition by Mary Susan Ryan-Flynn
Cover printed by Art Print Company, Taylor, PA
Book printed and bound by Maple Press, York, PA
Date printed: September 2010
Printed in the United States of America

10 9 8 7 6 5 4 3 2 1

All links and Web addresses were checked and verified to be correct at the time of publication. Because of the dynamic nature of the Web, some addresses and links may have changed since publication and may no longer be valid.

CONTENTS

SERIES INTRODUCTION

BLOOM'S How to Write about Literature series is designed to inspire students to write fine essays on great writers and their works. Each volume in the series begins with an introduction by Harold Bloom, meditating on the challenges and rewards of writing about the volume's subject author. The first chapter then provides detailed instructions on how to write a good essay, including how to find a thesis; how to develop an outline; how to write a good introduction, body text, and conclusions; how to cite sources; and more. The second chapter provides a brief overview of the issues involved in writing about the subject author and then a number of suggestions for paper topics, with accompanying strategies for addressing each topic. Succeeding chapters cover the author's major works.

The paper topics suggested in this book are open ended, and the brief strategies provided are designed to give students a push forward on the writing process rather than a road map to success. The aim of the book is to pose questions, not answer them. Many different kinds of papers could result from each topic. As always, the success of each paper will depend completely on the writer's skill and imagination.

HOW TO WRITE ABOUT SHAKESPEARE'S ROMANCES: INTRODUCTION

by Harold Bloom

THE WORD *genre* means a kind, as in "a kind of literature." Romance is such a kind, though it no longer means what once it did. In France of the twelfth century, the chivalric romance began a mode that continued into the Renaissance. Courtly love and knighthood combined into an adventure genre now ongoing in our science fiction novels and films.

Quest romance continued into the literary romanticism of the nineteenth century and survives in detective fiction today. The novel, from the eighteenth century on, opposed itself to prose romances, a rivalry that has now been absorbed into the general nature of prose fiction.

Shakespeare would have been surprised that we now call his final plays *the late romances.* The Irish critic Edward Dowden first employed that term in his Edwardian book on Shakespeare, and it has held on. It is fairly certain that the dramatist regarded *The Winter's Tale* and *The Tempest* as tragicomedies.

I find it suggestive that the volume I now introduce brings together Shakespeare's "problem plays" or "dark comedies"—*Troilus and Cressida, Measure for Measure, All's Well That Ends Well*—with his five "late romances." All eight plays are tragicomedies, but since this is Shakespeare, they are all beyond genre.

How shall we write about these very accomplished and diverse plays? I urge a centering on their major characters, who differ in mode both from earlier Shakespearean protagonists and from the grand sufferers of his tragedies. Figures such as Thersites, Lucio, and Parolles offer a perspective into the dark comedies that is radically new in Shakespeare. And the enigmatic Leontes and Prospero are even larger departures from Shakespeare's canon. Strangeness and an abrupt, elliptical quality augment in Shakespeare and raise the incitement premium we must respond to in our understanding of psyches deeply allied to our own.

Pragmatically, I advise comparing Shakespeare's later characters with his earlier ones. His influence on himself transcends everything he had absorbed from others. The tragicomedies, whether problematic or replete with romance marvels, are unlike any others and always return us to the abyss of personality that only Shakespeare can irradiate.

HOW TO WRITE
A GOOD ESSAY

by Laurie A. Sterling and Suanna H. Davis

WHILE THERE are many ways to write about literature, most assignments for high school and college English classes call for analytical papers. In these assignments, you are presenting your interpretation of a text to your reader. Your objective is to interpret the text's meaning in order to enhance your reader's understanding and enjoyment of the work. Without exception, strong papers about the meaning of a literary work are built upon a careful, close reading of the text or texts. Careful, analytical reading should always be the first step in your writing process. This volume provides models of such close, analytical reading, and these should help you develop your own skills as a reader and as a writer.

As the examples throughout this book demonstrate, attentive reading entails thinking about and evaluating the formal (textual) aspects of the author's works: theme, character, form, and language. In addition, when writing about a work, many readers choose to move beyond the text itself to consider the work's cultural context. In these instances, writers might explore the historical circumstances of the time period in which the work was written. Alternatively, they might examine the philosophies and ideas that a work addresses. Even in cases where writers explore a work's cultural context, though, papers must still address the more formal aspects of the work itself. A good interpretative essay that evaluates Shakespeare's use of argument in *Cymbeline* cannot simply give a history of the Gallic wars without firmly grounding this discussion in the play itself and using it to show the validity of both Lucius's and the queen's arguments. In other words, any analytical paper about a text, even one that seeks to evaluate the work's cultural context, must also have a firm handle on the work's themes, characters, and language. You must look for and evaluate these aspects of a work, then, as you read a text and as you prepare to write about it.

WRITING ABOUT THEMES

Literary themes are more than just topics or subjects treated in a work; they are attitudes or points about these topics that often structure other elements in a work. Writing about theme therefore requires that you not just identify a topic that a literary work addresses but also discuss what that work says about that topic. For example, if you were writing about the theme of resolutions in *All's Well That Ends Well,* you must not simply discuss the main resolution of the romance between Helena and Bertram but also minor resolutions of issues along the way, such as the king's illness and Parolles's betrayal of his comrades.

When you prepare to write about thematic concerns in a work of literature, you will probably discover that, like most works of literature, your text touches upon other themes in addition to its central theme. These secondary themes also provide rich ground for paper topics. A thematic paper on *All's Well That Ends Well* might consider forgiveness or trickery in the story. While neither of these could be said to be the central theme of the story, they are clearly related to a main theme of nature versus nurture and could provide plenty of good material for papers.

As you prepare to write about themes in literature, you might find a number of strategies helpful. After you identify a theme or themes in the story, you should begin by evaluating how other elements of the story—such as character, point of view, imagery, and symbolism—help develop the theme. You might ask yourself what your own responses are to the author's treatment of the subject matter. Do not neglect the obvious, either: What expectations does the title set up? How does the title help develop thematic concerns? Clearly, the title "A Rose for Emily" says something about the narrator's attitude toward the title character, Emily Grierson, and all she represents.

WRITING ABOUT CHARACTER

Generally, characters are essential components of fiction and drama. (This is not always the case, though; Ray Bradbury's "August 2026: There Will Come Soft Rains" is technically a story without characters, at least any human characters.) Often, you can discuss character in poetry, as in T. S. Eliot's "The Love Song of J. Alfred Prufrock" or Robert Browning's "My Last Duchess." Characters are, however, essential components in Shakespeare's romances. Many writers find that analyzing character is one of the most interesting and engaging ways to work with a piece of literature and to shape a paper. After all, characters generally are human, and we all know something about being human and living in the world. While it is always important to remember that these figures are not real people but creations of the writer's imagination, it can be fruitful to begin evaluating them as you might evaluate a real person. Often you can start with your own response to a character. Did you like or dislike the character? Did you sympathize with the character? Why or why not?

Keep in mind, though, that emotional responses like these are just starting places. To truly explore and evaluate literary characters, you need to return to the formal aspects of the text and evaluate how the author has drawn these characters. The 20th-century writer E. M. Forster coined the terms *flat* characters and *round* characters. Flat characters are static, one-dimensional characters who frequently represent a particular concept or idea. In contrast, round characters are fully drawn and much more realistic characters who frequently change and develop over the course of a work. Are the characters you are studying flat or round? What elements of the characters lead you to this conclusion? Why might the author have drawn characters like this? How does their development affect the meaning of the work? Similarly, you should explore the techniques the author uses to develop characters. Do we hear a character's own words, or do we hear only other characters' assessments of him or her? Or, does the author use an omniscient or limited omniscient narrator to allow us access to the workings of the characters' minds? If so, how does that help develop the characterization? Often you can even evaluate the narrator as a character. How trustworthy are the opinions and assessments of the narrator? You should also think about characters' names. Do they mean anything? If you encounter a hero named Sophia or Sophie, you should probably think about her wisdom (or lack thereof), since *Sophia* means "wisdom" in Greek. Similarly, since the name *Sylvia* is derived from the word *sylvan,* meaning "of the wood," you might want to evaluate that character's relationship with nature. Once again, you might look to the title of the work. Does Herman Melville's "Bartleby, the Scrivener" signal anything about Bartleby himself? Is Bartleby adequately defined by his job as scrivener? Is this part of Melville's point? Pursuing questions like these can help you develop thorough papers about characters from psychological, sociological, or more formalistic perspectives.

WRITING ABOUT FORM AND GENRE

Genre, a word derived from French, means "type" or "class." Literary genres are distinctive classes or categories of literary composition. On the most general level, literary works can be divided into the genres of drama, poetry, fiction, and essays, yet in those genres there are classifications that are also referred to as genres. Tragedy and comedy, for example, are genres of drama. Epic, lyric, and pastoral are genres of poetry. *Form,* on the other hand, generally refers to the shape or structure of a work. There are many clearly defined forms of poetry that follow specific patterns of meter, rhyme, and stanza. Sonnets, for example, are poems that follow a fixed form of 14 lines. Sonnets generally follow one of two basic sonnet forms, each with its own distinct rhyme scheme. Haiku is another example of poetic form, traditionally consisting of three unrhymed lines of five, seven, and five syllables.

While you might think that writing about form or genre might leave little room for argument, many of these forms and genres are very fluid. Remember that literature is evolving and ever changing, and so are its forms. As you study poetry, you may find that poets, especially more modern poets, play with traditional poetic forms, bringing about new effects. Similarly, dramatic tragedy was once quite narrowly defined, but over the centuries playwrights have broadened and challenged traditional definitions, changing the shape of tragedy. When Arthur Miller wrote *Death of a Salesman,* many critics challenged the idea that tragic drama could encompass a common man like Willy Loman.

Evaluating how a work of literature fits into or challenges the boundaries of its form or genre can provide you with fruitful avenues of investigation. You might find it helpful to ask why the work does or does not fit into traditional categories. Why might Miller have thought it fitting to write a tragedy of the common man? Similarly, you might compare the content or theme of a work with its form. How well do they work together? Many of Emily Dickinson's poems, for instance, follow the meter of traditional hymns. While some of her poems seem to express traditional religious doctrines, many seem to challenge or strain against traditional conceptions of God and theology. What is the effect, then, of her use of traditional hymn meter?

WRITING ABOUT LANGUAGE, SYMBOLS, AND IMAGERY

No matter what the genre, writers use words as their most basic tool. Language is the most fundamental building block of literature. It is essential that you pay careful attention to the author's language and word choice as you read, reread, and analyze a text. Imagery is language that appeals to the senses. Most commonly, imagery appeals to our sense of vision, creating a mental picture, but authors also use language that appeals to our other senses. Images can be literal or figurative. Literal images use sensory language to describe an actual thing. In the broadest terms, figurative language uses one thing to speak about something else. For example, if I call my boss a snake, I am not saying that he is literally a reptile. Instead, I am using figurative language to communicate my opinions about him. Since we think of snakes as sneaky, slimy, and sinister, I am using the concrete image of a snake to communicate these abstract opinions and impressions.

The two most common figures of speech are similes and metaphors. Both are comparisons between two apparently dissimilar things. Similes are explicit comparisons using the words *like* or *as;* metaphors are implicit comparisons. To return to the previous example, if I say, "My boss, Bob, was waiting for me when I showed up to work five minutes late today—the snake!" I have constructed a metaphor. Writing about his experiences fighting in World War I, Wilfred Owen begins his poem "Dulce et decorum est," with a string of similes: "Bent double, like old beggars under sacks, / Knock-kneed, coughing like hags, we cursed through sludge." Owen's goal was to undercut clichéd notions that war and dying in battle were glorious. Certainly, comparing soldiers to coughing hags and to beggars underscores his point.

"Fog," a short poem by Carl Sandburg, provides a clear example of a metaphor. Sandburg's poem reads:

> The fog comes
> on little cat feet.
>
> It sits looking
> over harbor and city
> on silent haunches
> and then moves on.

Notice how effectively Sandburg conveys surprising impressions of the fog by comparing two seemingly disparate things—the fog and a cat.

Symbols, by contrast, are things that stand for, or represent, other things. Often they represent something intangible, such as concepts or ideas. In everyday life we use and understand symbols easily. Babies at christenings and brides at weddings wear white to represent purity. Think, too, of a dollar bill. The paper itself has no value in and of itself. Instead, that paper bill is a symbol of something else, the precious metal in a nation's coffers. Symbols in literature work similarly. Authors use symbols to evoke more than a simple, straightforward, literal meaning. Characters, objects, and places can all function as symbols. Famous literary examples of symbols include Moby Dick, the white whale of Herman Melville's novel, and the scarlet *A* of Nathaniel Hawthorne's *The Scarlet Letter.* As both of these symbols suggest, a literary symbol cannot be adequately defined or explained by any one meaning. Hester Prynne's Puritan community clearly intends her scarlet *A* as a symbol of her adultery, but as the novel progresses, even her own community reads the letter as representing not just *adultery,* but *able, angel,* and a host of other meanings.

Writing about imagery and symbols requires close attention to the author's language. To prepare a paper on symbolism or imagery in a work, identify and trace the images and symbols and then try to draw some conclusions about how they function. Ask yourself how any symbols or images help contribute to the themes or meanings of the work. What connotations do they carry? How do they affect your reception of the work? Do they shed light on characters or settings? A strong paper on imagery or symbolism will thoroughly consider the use of figures in the text and will try to reach some conclusions about how or why the author uses them.

WRITING ABOUT HISTORY AND CONTEXT

As previously noted, it is possible to write an analytical paper that also considers the work's context. After all, the text was not created in a vacuum. The author lived and wrote in a specific time period and in a specific cultural context and, like all of us, was shaped by that environment. Learning more about the historical and cultural circumstances that surround the author and the work can help illuminate a text and provide you with productive material for a paper. Remember, though, that when you write analytical papers, you should use the context to illuminate the text. Do not lose sight of your goal—to interpret the meaning of the literary work. Use historical or philosophical research as a tool to develop your textual evaluation.

Thoughtful readers often consider how history and culture affected the author's choice and treatment of his or her subject matter. Investigations into the history and context of a work could examine the work's relation to specific historical events, such as the Salem witch trials in 17th-century Massachusetts or the restoration of Charles to the British throne in 1660. Bear in mind that historical context is not limited to politics and world events. While knowing about the Vietnam War is certainly helpful in interpreting much of Tim O'Brien's fiction, and some knowledge of the French Revolution clearly illuminates the dynamics of Charles Dickens's *A Tale of Two Cities*, historical context also entails the fabric of daily life. Examining a text in light of gender roles, race relations, class boundaries, or working conditions can give rise to thoughtful and compelling papers. Exploring the conditions of the working class in 19th-century England, for example, can provide a particularly effective avenue for writing about Dickens's *Hard Times*.

You can begin thinking about these issues by asking broad questions at first. What do you know about the time period and about the author? What does the editorial apparatus in your text tell you? These might be starting places. Similarly, when specific historical events or dynamics are particularly important to understanding a work but might be somewhat obscure to modern readers, textbooks usually provide notes to explain historical background. These are a good place to start. With this information, ask yourself how these historical facts and circumstances might have affected the author, the presentation of theme, and the presentation of character. How does knowing more about the work's specific historical context illuminate the work? To take a well-known example, understanding the complex attitudes toward slavery during the time Mark Twain wrote *Adventures of Huckleberry Finn* should help you begin to examine issues of race in the text. Additionally, you might compare these attitudes to those of the time in which the novel was set. How might this comparison affect your interpretation of a work written after the abolition of slavery but set before the Civil War?

WRITING ABOUT PHILOSOPHY AND IDEAS

Philosophical concerns are closely related to both historical context and thematic issues. Like historical investigation, philosophical research can provide a useful tool as you analyze a text. For example, an investigation into the working class in Dickens's England might lead you to a topic on the philosophical doctrine of utilitarianism in *Hard Times.* Many other works explore philosophies and ideas quite explicitly. Mary Shelley's famous novel *Frankenstein,* for example, explores John Locke's tabula rasa theory of human knowledge as she portrays the intellectual and emotional development of Victor Frankenstein's creature. As this example indicates, philosophical issues are somewhat more abstract than investigations of theme or historical context. Some other examples of philosophical issues include human free will, the formation of human identity, the nature of sin, or questions of ethics.

Writing about philosophy and ideas might require some outside research, but usually the notes or other material in your text will provide you with basic information, and often footnotes and bibliographies suggest places you can go to read further about the subject. If you have identified a philosophical theme that runs through a text, you might ask yourself how the author develops this theme. Look at character development and the interactions of characters, for example. Similarly, you might examine whether the narrative voice in a work of fiction addresses the philosophical concerns of the text.

WRITING COMPARISON AND CONTRAST ESSAYS

Finally, you might find that comparing and contrasting the works or techniques of an author provides a useful tool for literary analysis. A comparison and contrast essay might compare two characters or themes in a single work, or it might compare the author's treatment of a theme in two works. It might also contrast methods of character development or analyze an author's differing treatment of a philosophical concern in two works. Writing comparison and contrast essays, though, requires some special consideration. While they generally provide you with plenty of material to use, they also come with a built-in trap: the laundry list. These papers often become mere lists of connections between the works. As this chapter will discuss, a strong thesis must make an assertion that you want to prove or validate. A strong comparison/contrast thesis, then, needs to comment on the significance of the similarities and differences you observe. It is not enough merely to assert that the works contain similarities and differences. You might, for example, assert why the similarities and differences are important and explain how they illuminate the works' treatment of theme. Remember, too, that a thesis should not be a statement of the obvious. A comparison/contrast paper that focuses only on very obvious similarities or differences does little to illuminate the connections between the works. Often, an effective method of shaping a strong thesis and argument is to begin your paper by noting the similarities between the works but then to develop a thesis that asserts how these apparently similar elements are different. If, for example, you observe that Emily Dickinson wrote a number of poems about spiders, you might analyze how she uses spider imagery differently in two poems. Similarly, many scholars have noted that Hawthorne created many "mad scientist" characters, men who are so devoted to their science or their art that they lose perspective on all else. A good thesis comparing two of these characters—Aylmer of "The Birth-mark" and Dr. Rappaccini of "Rappaccini's Daughter," for example—might initially identify both characters as examples of Hawthorne's mad scientist type but then argue that their motivations for scientific experimentation differ. If you strive to analyze the similarities or differences, discuss significances, and move beyond the obvious, your paper should move beyond the laundry list trap.

PREPARING TO WRITE

Armed with a clear sense of your task—illuminating the text—and with an understanding of theme, character, language, history, and philosophy, you are ready to approach the writing process. Remember that good writing is grounded in good reading and that close reading takes time, attention, and more than one reading of your text. Read for comprehension first. As you go back and review the work, mark the text to chart the details of the work as well as your reactions. Highlight important passages, repeated words, and image patterns. "Converse" with the text through marginal notes. Mark turns in the plot, ask questions, and make observations about characters, themes, and language. If you are reading from a book that does not belong to you, keep a record of your reactions in a journal or notebook. If you have read a work of literature carefully, paying attention to both the text and the context of the work, you have a leg up on the writing process. Admittedly, at this point, your ideas are probably very broad and undefined, but you have taken an important first step toward writing a strong paper.

Your next step is to focus, to take a broad, perhaps fuzzy, topic and define it more clearly. Even a topic provided by your instructor will need to be focused appropriately. Remember that good writers make the topic their own. There are a number of strategies—often called "invention"— that you can use to develop your own focus. In one such strategy, called *freewriting*, you spend 10 minutes or so just writing about your topic without referring back to the text or your notes. Write whatever comes to mind; the important thing is that you just keep writing. Often this process allows you to develop fresh ideas or approaches to your subject matter. You could also try *brainstorming*: Write down your topic and then list all the related points or ideas you can think of. Include questions, comments, words, important passages or events, and anything else that comes to mind. Let one idea lead to another. In the related technique of *clustering*, or *mapping*, write your topic on a sheet of paper and write related ideas around it. Then list related subpoints under each of these main ideas. Many people then draw arrows to show connections between points. This technique helps you narrow your topic and can also help you organize your ideas. Similarly, asking journalistic questions— Who? What? Where? When? Why? and How?—can develop ideas for topic development.

Thesis Statements

Once you have developed a focused topic, you can begin to think about your thesis statement, the main point or purpose of your paper. It is imperative that you craft a strong thesis, otherwise, your paper will likely be little more than random, disorganized observations about the text.

Think of your thesis statement as a kind of road map for your paper. It tells your reader where you are going and how you are going to get there.

To craft a good thesis, you must keep a number of things in mind. First, as the title of this subsection indicates, your paper's thesis should be a statement, an assertion about the text that you want to prove or validate. Beginning writers often formulate a question that they attempt to use as a thesis. For example, a writer exploring the theme of resolution in Shakespeare's *All's Well That Ends Well* might ask, How does Helena finally secure her marriage with Bertram? While posing questions like this is a good strategy to use in the invention process to help narrow your topic and find your thesis, it cannot serve as the thesis statement because it does not tell your reader what you want to assert about the effect trickery and forgiveness have on the final resolution in the drama. You might shape this question into a thesis by instead proposing an answer to that question: In Shakespeare's *All's Well That Ends Well*, Helena is challenged by Bertram to salvage her marriage in his letter stating that he will be married to her when she has his family ring on her finger and is pregnant with their child. This sets the stage for the ultimate trickery in the play and Bertram's ultimate forgiveness of and love for Helena. Shakespeare leads up to the ultimate trickery and forgiveness with several smaller resolutions in the play. Through the multiplicity of tricks and resolutions, Shakespeare sets up the understanding that the end justifies the means. Notice that this thesis provides an initial plan or structure for the rest of the paper, and notice, too, that the thesis statement does not necessarily have to fit into one sentence. After explaining the philosophy of the end justifies the means, especially through its relationship with the title, you could point out the various small resolutions that happen throughout the play due to trickery and forgiveness. Finally, you could theorize about what the story is saying about the end justifying the means as a philosophy, including its benefits and limitations.

Second, remember that a good thesis makes an assertion that you need to support. In other words, a good thesis does not state the obvious. If you tried to formulate a thesis about the resolution of the drama by saying, Helena and Bertram are married at the end of *All's Well That Ends Well*, you have done nothing but rephrase the obvious.

Since the story is clearly centered on the fact that Helena and Bertram are married, there would be no point in spending three to five pages supporting that assertion. You might try to develop a thesis from that point by asking yourself some further questions: How exactly does Helena get Bertram to recognize their marriage? How is that set up in the play? Do similar things happen along the way? Such a line of questioning might lead you to a more viable thesis, like the one in the preceding paragraph.

As the comparison with the road map also suggests, your thesis should appear near the beginning of the paper. In relatively short papers (three to six pages), the thesis almost always appears in the first paragraph. Some writers fall into the trap of saving their thesis for the end, trying to provide a surprise or a big moment of revelation, as if to say, "TA-DA! I've just proved that Shakespeare in *Pericles, Prince of Tyre* was arguing that beauty is not necessarily good, but that what appears lowly may in fact be most virtuous." Placing a thesis at the end of an essay can seriously mar the essay's effectiveness. If you fail to define your essay's point and purpose clearly at the beginning, your reader will find it difficult to assess the clarity of your argument and understand the points you are making. When your argument comes as a surprise at the end, you force your reader to reread your essay in order to assess its logic and effectiveness.

Finally, you should avoid using the first person ("I") as you present your thesis. Though it is not strictly wrong to write in the first person, it is difficult to do so gracefully. While writing in the first person, beginning writers often fall into the trap of writing self-reflexive prose (writing *about* their paper *in* their paper). Often this leads to the most dreaded of opening lines: "In this paper I am going to discuss . . ." Not only does this self-reflexive voice make for very awkward prose, it frequently allows writers to boldly announce a topic while completely avoiding a thesis statement. An example might be a paper that begins as follows: Shakespeare's *Pericles, Prince of Tyre* tells the story of Pericles, his marriage, and his family. In this paper, I am going to examine the meaning of his suffering in the play. The author of this paper has done little more than announce a general topic for the paper (the philosophical issue of virtue and suffering). While the last sentence might be a thesis, the writer fails to present an opinion about the significance of the virtue and suffering. To improve this "thesis," the writer would need to back up a couple of steps. The writer should examine the work and draw conclusions about the portrayal of suffering before crafting the thesis. After carefully examining key passages in the story, the writer might determine that Nick, having had some disturbing and traumatic experiences in the war, goes out alone into the wilderness in the hope of establishing some kind of control over his environment, and in so doing, of his psyche as well. The writer might then craft a thesis such as this: In *Pericles, Prince of Tyre,* Shakespeare shows that good people suffer. Pericles is a virtuous prince and begins the play by seeking a royal wife. Instead, he loses his sense of safety because of an assassin, his wife in a shipwreck, and his daughter to the betrayal of friendship. Throughout the play, Pericles is always good. Despite his virtue, he suffers one setback after another until, at the conclusion, he is reunited with his lost family through his continued goodness, thus presenting the final judgment that though good people suffer, they are rewarded in the end.

Outlines

While developing a strong, thoughtful thesis early in your writing process should help focus your paper, outlining provides an essential tool for logically shaping that paper. A good outline helps you see—and develop—the relationships among the points in your argument and assures you that your paper flows logically and coherently. Outlining not only helps place your points in a logical order but also helps you subordinate supporting points, weed out any irrelevant points, and decide if there are any necessary points that are missing from your argument. Most of us are familiar with formal outlines that use numerical and letter designations for each point. However, there are different types of outlines; you may find that an informal outline is a more useful tool for you. What is important, though, is that you spend the time to develop some sort of outline—formal or informal.

Remember that an outline is a tool to help you shape and write a strong paper. If you do not spend sufficient time planning your supporting points and shaping the arrangement of those points, you will most likely construct a vague, unfocused outline that provides little, if any, help with the writing of the paper. Consider the following example.

Thesis: Sometimes lost among the list of classics that make up Shakespeare's résumé is the overlooked work *Cymbeline*, certainly one of his more harshly critiqued plays and widely regarded as among the weakest. Perhaps this is due to the ambiguity of villainy in the play. While there is a case to be made that there is a true villain in *Cymbeline*, nearly every character at one point or another exhibits traits of immorality and makes it difficult to separate protagonist from antagonist.

   I.   Introduction and thesis

   II.   Cymbeline sets up sorrow
       A. Cymbeline banishes Posthumus

  III.   Cloten's villainy
       A. Cloten attacks Posthumus
       B. Cloten entreats Imogen, though she is married
       C. Cloten plots to murder Posthumus
       D. Cloten plots to rape Imogen
       E. Cloten attacks an unknown stranger

  IV.   Iachimo tricks Posthumus
       A. Bets with him over Imogen's virtue
       B. Gives him false testimony

   V.   Posthumus orders Imogen's death
       A. Angry at her betrayal, Posthumus orders Imogen's death
       B. He sends her a letter that will isolate her for her murder
       C. He repents

  VI.   Imogen's relationship with her brothers
       A. They meet
       B. They call her brother

```
    C. She is ill and takes the dram from Pisanio
    D. Thinking she is dead, they leave her
       body


  VII. The queen is continually evil


  VIII. Conclusion
```

This outline has a number of flaws. First, the major topics labeled with the Roman numerals are not arranged in a logical order. It makes more sense to discuss Cloten's villainy after Imogen's disappearance because before this he is only a nuisance to her, though after it he plots her rape. The writer should probably move Roman numeral 3 to after Posthumus ordering Imogen's death. In addition, the thesis makes no mention of Imogen's relationship with her brothers, yet the writer includes this as a major topic in the outline. While Imogen and her brothers are an interesting aspect of the story, if they do not relate to the thesis, they should not appear in the outline or in the essay for that matter. Third, the writer includes "He repents" under section V: "Posthumus orders Imogen's death." Letters A and B refer to the circumstances of Posthumus's plotting. Letter C, however, refers to the results of his order and not to the orders themselves. A fourth problem is the inclusion of a section A in section II. An outline should not include an A without a B, a 1 without a 2, and so forth. The final problem with this outline is the overall lack of detail. None of the sections provides much information about the content of the argument, and it seems likely that the writer has not given sufficient thought to the content of the paper.

A better start to this outline might be the following:

```
Thesis: Sometimes lost among the list of classics that
make up Shakespeare's résumé is the overlooked work
Cymbeline, certainly one of his more harshly critiqued
plays and widely regarded as among the weakest. Perhaps
this is due to the ambiguity of villainy in the play.
While there is a case to be made that there is a
true villain in Cymbeline, nearly every character at
one point or another exhibits traits of immorality
```

and makes it difficult to separate protagonist from antagonist.

I.   Introduction and thesis

II.   Cymbeline sets up sorrow
    A. He refuses to recognize his daughter's marriage to Posthumus
    B. He banishes Posthumus

III.   Iachimo sets up Posthumus
    A. He bets with Posthumus
    B. He attempts to seduce Imogen
        1. When she rejects him, he claims it was to test her faithfulness
        2. He asks her to guard a treasure for him and uses this to gather proofs that will convince Posthumus of her infidelity
    C. He lies to Posthumus
        1. He describes Imogen's bedchamber
        2. He describes Imogen's body
        3. He shows him the stolen bracelet as proof of his success

IV.   Posthumus sets up Imogen's murder
    A He writes his servant instructions
    B. He sends a letter calling his wife into the wilderness to meet him
    C. He orders his servant to kill her in the wilderness

V.   Cloten becomes angry
    A. Cloten attempts to win Imogen's hand and is offended when she scorns him
    B. He decides to murder Posthumus and rape Imogen

      C. When he meets her brother, he threatens
         his life

  VI. The queen is completely evil
      A. She schemes to marry the king and set
         her son up as his heir
      B. She schemes against Imogen
        1. She says she will love her but does
          not
        2. She plots to marry Imogen to her son
          Cloten
        3. She attempts to poison Imogen
      C. She plots to overthrow Roman rule

  VII. Conclusion

This new outline would prove much more helpful when it came time to write the paper.

An outline like this could be shaped into an even more useful tool if the writer fleshed out the argument by providing specific examples from the text to support each point. Once you have listed your main point and your supporting ideas, develop this raw material by listing related supporting ideas and material under each of those main headings. From there, arrange the material in subsections and order the material logically.

For example, you might begin with one of the theses cited above: In *Pericles, Prince of Tyre*, Shakespeare shows that good people suffer. Pericles is a virtuous prince and begins the play by seeking for a good wife. Instead he loses his sense of safety because of an assassin, his wife in a shipwreck, and his daughter to the betrayal of friendship. Throughout the play, Pericles is always good. Despite his virtue, he suffers one setback after another until, at the conclusion, he is reunited with his lost family through his continued goodness, thus presenting the final judgment that though good people suffer, they are rewarded in the end. This thesis supplies a framework for how the discussion could be best organized: You might begin by noting Pericles's virtue does not protect him from suffering. You might begin your outline, then, with topic headings such as these: (1) his virtue, (2) his life in jeopardy, (3) his wife lost, (4) his daughter lost, and (5) how his losses are restored. Under each of those headings you could list ideas that support the particular point. Be sure to include references to parts of the text that help build your case.

An informal outline might look like this:

Thesis: In *Pericles, Prince of Tyre,* Shakespeare shows that good people suffer even though they are virtuous, but they are eventually rewarded for their virtue. Pericles is a virtuous prince and begins the play by seeking for a good wife where he would be expected to find one, in the court of a neighboring king. Instead he loses his sense of safety because of the immorality of the king. Pericles's knowledge of that immorality might threaten the king, and so he sends an assassin to kill Pericles. Though Pericles flees from the assassin, he is virtuous enough to find good company in his travels. Even the danger to his life brings him some reward. Cast on a foreign shore, he hears of a contest for the princess's hand and takes part, thus winning for himself a royal wife. When the danger to him is past, he attempts to return home and loses his wife in a shipwreck. Fear for the safety of his newborn child causes him to leave his daughter in Tarsus, where she is lost to the betrayal of friendship. Throughout the play, Pericles remains a good person. Despite his virtue, he suffers one setback after another until he is reunited with his lost family; this suggests that though good people suffer, they are rewarded in the end.

Introduction and thesis

1. Pericles is virtuous.
   - He attempts to find a proper wife.
   - In his search for a royal wife.

- Sails to another kingdom to court a princess.
- Solves the riddle, incest revealed.
  - If doesn't solve riddle, his life is forfeit.
  - If does solve riddle, killed for knowledge.

2. Life in jeopardy.
  - Must escape assassination.
  - Heads home, but that is not far enough.
  - Runs to Tarsus, still not far enough.
  - Is shipwrecked at Pentapolis and loses all his goods.

3. Loses wife.
  - Evil king is dead.
    - Died from evil.
    - Daughter with him.
    - Danger of assassin is now ended.
  - Sets out for home on ship.
  - Encounters a storm.
    - Storm causes premature labor.
    - Baby born.
    - Wife dies.
    - Forced to abandon her body to the sea.

4. Loses daughter.
  - Afraid for his daughter, he leaves her with friends.
    - People who should be grateful to them.
    - He brought them food.
  - Friends are jealous and plot to kill her.
    - Marina is beautiful and accomplished.
    - She shows their daughter up.
    - They pay for her murder.
  - Pirates kidnap her and take her to a brothel.

5. In despair over his losses, Pericles sails away.
   - Lands at Myteline.
   - Governor offers cure for depression.
   - Recognizes his daughter.
   - Receives vision to go to Ephesus.
   - Is reunited with wife.

Conclusion:
   - Pericles is a good person because he follows the social order in seeking a bride.
   - The expectation is that people bring their own fortunes and their goodness or evil brings its own consequences.
   - However, Pericles suffers through no fault of his own. He is a victim of other people and of circumstances.
   - He is constantly being rewarded a little for his virtue and then losing whatever is important. His punishments are greater than his rewards.
   - In the end, he receives his family back. Since they were his in the first place, this is a conundrum of reward. However, the story does end happily.

You would set about writing a formal outline with a similar process, though in the final stages you would label the headings differently. A formal outline for a paper that argues the thesis about *Pericles, Prince of Tyre*—that he is virtuous and eventually is rewarded, even though he suffers, might look like this:

Thesis: In *Pericles, Prince of Tyre*, Shakespeare shows that good people suffer even though they are virtuous, but they are eventually rewarded for their virtue. Pericles is a virtuous prince and begins the play by seeking for a good wife where he would be expected to find one, in the court of a neighboring king. Instead he loses his sense of safety because of the immorality of the king. Pericles's knowledge of that immorality might threaten the king, and so he sends an assassin to kill Pericles. Though Pericles flees from the assassin, he is virtuous enough to find good company in his travels. Even the danger to his life brings him some reward. Cast on a foreign shore, he hears of a contest for the princess's hand and takes part, thus winning for himself a royal wife. When the danger to him is past, he attempts to return home and loses his wife in a shipwreck. Fear for the safety of his newborn child causes him to leave his daughter in Tarsus, where she is lost to the betrayal of friendship. Throughout the play, Pericles remains a good person. Despite his virtue, he suffers one setback after another until he is reunited with his lost family; this suggests that though good people suffer, they are rewarded in the end.

I.   Introduction and thesis

II. Pericles loses his safety in his search for a good wife.
- A. Pericles strives for princess of Antioch.
  1. His search for a wife leads him to solve a riddle.
  2. The riddle's solution shows incest by the king.
  3. The king calls for an assassin.
  4. Pericles runs away and is shipwrecked.
- B. Pericles sets his sights on the princess of Pentapolis.
  1. Pericles has lost all his goods.
  2. He takes part in the contest for Thasia.
  3. He wins and marries Thasia.
- C. The king and princess of Antioch are dead, so his life is safe again.

  III. Pericles loses his wife.
- A. He and his pregnant wife sail for Tyre.
- B. A storm causes Thasia to go into labor early.
- C. The baby is born, but Thasia dies.
- D. The sailors force Pericles to put his wife's body in the sea.

  IV. Pericles loses his daughter.
- A. Out of fear for the baby's life, he leaves Marina with friends.
- B. The friends are jealous and plot to kill her.
- C. Her murder is foiled by pirates who kidnap her.
- D. When Pericles goes to reunite with his daughter, he is informed of her death.

  V. Pericles's virtue is rewarded, and he is reunited with his family.
- A. The musician sent to help his depression is his daughter.
- B. Going to the temple of Diana, as per a vision, he finds his wife.
- C. He and his wife go to reign in Pentapolis, while his daughter and son-in-law reign over Tyre.

  VI. Conclusion.
- A. Pericles is virtuous.
- B. Though he suffers many things, he continues to be virtuous.
- C. Eventually his virtue is rewarded through a restoration of all he had lost.
- D. Shakespeare is offering an alternative explanation for it raining on the just and the unjust and showing that, in the end, the correct judgment will result.

As in the previous sample outline, the thesis provided the seeds of a structure, and the writer was careful to arrange the supporting points in a logical manner, showing the relationships among the ideas in the paper.

Body Paragraphs

Once your outline is complete, you can begin drafting your paper. Paragraphs, units of related sentences, are the building blocks of a good paper, and as you draft you should keep in mind both the function and the qualities of good paragraphs. Paragraphs help you chart and control the shape and content of your essay, and they help the reader see your organization and your logic. You should begin a new paragraph whenever you move from one major point to another. In longer, more complex essays, you might use a group of related paragraphs to support major points. Remember that in addition to being adequately developed, a good paragraph is both unified and coherent.

Unified Paragraphs

Each paragraph must be centered on one idea or point, and a unified paragraph carefully focuses on and develops this central idea without including extraneous ideas or tangents. For beginning writers, the best way to ensure that you are constructing unified paragraphs is to include a topic sentence in each paragraph. This topic sentence should convey the main point of the paragraph, and every sentence in the paragraph should relate to that topic sentence. Any sentence that strays from the central topic does not belong in the paragraph and needs to be revised or deleted. Consider the following paragraph about nationalism in *Cymbeline*. Notice how the paragraph veers away from the main point.

> Cloten also displays a sense of nationalism. Cloten defies Caius Lucius, the Roman ambassador, because he is a nationalist. He is proud of Britain and does not want it to be subservient to Rome. He states that they are not subservient, having British, rather than Roman, noses. "Britain is / A world by itself; and we will nothing pay / For wearing our own noses" (3.1.1424-26). Because Cloten defies the Roman ambassador, he is risking severe consequences for his country. He says they will not pay tribute because there is no reason for

them to pay it. Rome gives them nothing. Everything the
British value, they already owned. He further says that
Caius Lucius may safely stay a few more days, but if he
stays after that, it is war because Cloten is unwilling
to accept the advance of the Roman troops onto English
soil. He agrees that the British are fighting men who
will fight for their freedom. This is one area where
Cloten goes outside his roles of fop and villain. In the
first scene in the play, he is discussing his recent
fight. He fought and lost, though the fight was halted
before he was hurt.

Although the paragraph begins solidly and the first sentence contains
its central idea, the author goes on a tangent in the paragraph's last two
sentences. While the story of the fight is interesting, particularly as the
two lords tell the tale differently, it is not related to the discussion of
nationalism.

Coherent Paragraphs:

In addition to shaping unified paragraphs, you must also craft coherent
paragraphs that develop their points logically with sentences that flow
smoothly into one another. Coherence depends on the order of your sentences, but it is not the only factor that lends the paragraph coherence.
You also need to craft your prose to help the reader see the relationship
among the sentences.

Consider the following paragraph about the queen's nationalism in
Cymbeline. Notice how the writer uses similar ideas as the paragraph
above yet fails to help the reader see the relationships among the points.

The queen in *Cymbeline* also displays a strong sense
of nationalism in the play. The queen does not want to
pay tribute. "That opportunity / Which then they had
to take from 's, to resume / We have again" (3.1.1427–
29). She argues that Caius Lucius's claim to tribute
because of Julius Caesar's conquering is problematic.
She invokes early English nationalism (3.1). This speech
eventually leads to King Cymbeline refusing to pay
tribute and is what starts the war between Britain and

```
Rome. She argues with her husband out of a strong sense
of patriotism and nationalism. Mikalachki suggests that
she embodies Britain's resistance to Rome (303).
```

This paragraph demonstrates that unity alone does not guarantee paragraph effectiveness. The argument is hard to follow because the author fails both to show connections between the sentences and to indicate how they work to support the overall point.

A number of techniques are available to aid paragraph coherence. Careful use of transitional words and phrases is essential. You can use transitional flags to introduce an example or an illustration *(for example, for instance)*, to amplify a point or add another phase of the same idea *(additionally, furthermore, next, similarly, finally, then)*, to indicate a conclusion or a result *(therefore, as a result, thus, in other words)*, to signal a contrast or a qualification *(on the other hand, nevertheless, despite this, on the contrary, still, however, conversely)*, to signal a comparison *(likewise, in comparison, similarly)*, and to indicate a movement in time *(afterward, earlier, eventually, finally, later, subsequently, until)*.

In addition to transitional flags, careful use of pronouns aids coherence and flow. If you were writing about *The Wizard of Oz*, you would not want to keep repeating the phrase *the witch* or the name *Dorothy*. Careful substitution of the pronoun *she* in these instances can aid coherence. A word of warning, though: When you substitute pronouns for proper names, always be sure that your pronoun reference is clear. In a paragraph that discusses both Dorothy and the witch, substituting *she* could lead to confusion. Make sure that it is clear to whom the pronoun refers. Generally, the pronoun refers to the last proper noun you have used.

While repeating the same name over and over again can lead to awkward, boring prose, it is possible to use repetition to help your paragraph's coherence. Careful repetition of important words or phrases can lend coherence to your paragraph by reminding readers of your key points. Admittedly, it takes some practice to use this technique effectively. You may find that reading your prose aloud can help you develop an ear for the effective use of repetition.

To see how helpful transitional aids are, compare the following paragraph to the preceding one about the queen's nationalism in *Cymbeline*. Notice how the author works with the same ideas and quotations but shapes them into a much more coherent paragraph whose point is clearer and easier to follow.

> The queen in *Cymbeline* also displays a strong sense of nationalism in the play. She does not want to pay tribute and says that Britain once more has a choice about its payment. "That opportunity / Which then they had to take from 's, to resume / We have again" (3.1.1427–29). She argues that Caius Lucius's claim to tribute, which rests on Julius Caesar's conquering, is problematic because while Julius Caesar did in fact conquer Britain, it took even that famed leader three attempts and the conquering was not so simple as the famous quote would lead the unaware to believe. In addition, the queen invokes early English nationalism when she appeals to the king to remember his ancestors. She shows her nationalism also when she refers to the "natural bravery of your isle" (3.1.1431). The queen speaks with her husband out of a strong sense of patriotism and nationalism. This speech eventually leads to King Cymbeline refusing to pay tribute and is what starts the war between Britain and Rome. Some scholars take the nationalism of the queen even further. For example, Mikalachki suggests that the queen embodies Britain's resistance to Rome (303), since, while she lives, Britain resists, and once she is dead, though the battle was won, the king agrees to pay the tribute.

Similarly, the following paragraph from a paper on the statue of Hermione and its part in the ending of *The Winter's Tale* demonstrates both unity and coherence. In it, the author argues that the ending is surprising.

> Shakespeare's use of Hermione's statue is unexpected for several reasons. The first reason the living statue is shocking is that the original source for the drama did not restore Hermione; instead she stayed dead and Leontes died as well (Barkan 640). Since the audience

would have been familiar with the original source, their expectations of the drama's resolution would be misleading. A second reason Shakespeare's use of the statue to bring Hermione back to life is unexpected is that the dramatic conventions of the day were overturned. Usually plays with happy endings resolved prior to the final scene, and these resolutions were then reported by minor characters. By saving the restoration of Hermione until the final scene, Shakespeare used this convention to create a surprise ending (Gurr 420). Another reason that the use of Hermione's statue to bring the character back is surprising is that Hermione has been dead for sixteen years. Paulina professes that Hermione is dead, offering to take the body to court so everyone there can judge for themselves. Yet, in the final scene, Paulina uncovers a living statue of Hermione. A final reason that the ending is so unexpected as to be almost shocking is that the king has been tricked. For sixteen years the king has mourned the loss of his wife, and he is amazed at the likeness he sees in the statue. Then the statue moves, and the audience understands that Hermione was alive the entire time not that far from him. That someone would deign to trick a king, with a lie or a statue, adds to the unexpectedness of the ending.

Introductions

Introductions present particular challenges for writers. Generally, your introduction should do two things: capture your reader's attention and explain the main point of your essay. In other words, while your introduction should contain your thesis, it needs to do a bit more work than that. You are likely to find that starting that first paragraph is one of the most difficult parts of the paper. It is hard to face that blank page or screen, and as a result, many beginning writers, in desperation to start somewhere, start with overly broad, general statements. While it is often a good strategy to start with more general subject matter and narrow your focus, do not begin with broad sweeping statements such as There is much evil in the world. Such sentences are nothing but empty filler. They begin to fill the blank page, but they do nothing to advance your argument. Instead, you should try to gain your readers' interest. Some writers like to begin with a pertinent quotation or with a relevant question. Or, you might begin with an introduction of the topic you will discuss. If you are writing about Shakespeare's use of multiple villains in *Cymbeline,* for instance, you might begin by talking about the philosophical reasons that even good people sometimes commit evil action. Another common trap to avoid is depending on your title to introduce the author and the text you are writing about. Always include the work's author and title in your opening paragraph.

Compare the effectiveness of the following introductions:

1. There has always been evil in the world. When even the good people succumb to evil's siren call, there can be confusion as to who is actually the villain. Since people do not like to be confused, usually literature presents a single villain or a cohort of villains in each literary text. This is rather like the serial presentations of the "big bad" on Buffy the Vampire Slayer, where each season there was a new, big, seemingly unstoppable evil. There might be small problems, but there was one "real" bad guy each season. While there is a case to be made that there is a true villain in *Cymbeline,* nearly every character exhibits traits of immorality so that it becomes difficult to separate protagonist from antagonist.

2. Sidonie Gabrielle Colette argued, "As for an authentic villain, the absolute, the artist, one rarely meets him even once in a lifetime. The ordinary bad hat is always in part a decent fellow." Literature, unlike life, usually presents a single villain. One of the most influential and revered playwrights in the history of the English language, William Shakespeare created in his considerable body of work many memorable villains. From Caliban in *The Tempest* to Richard II to *Hamlet's* Claudius,

these characters have become familiar names thanks
to their often inhuman capacity for evil or, at the
very least, malicious mischief. Shakespeare's plays
themselves have also become deeply ingrained in
societal consciousness; even the most uncultured
individual knows the names Romeo and Juliet,
Macbeth, and Othello. Sometimes lost among the list
of classics that make up Shakespeare's résumé are
overlooked works such as *Cymbeline*, certainly one of
his more harshly critiqued plays and widely regarded
as among the weakest. Perhaps this reputation is
due to the ambiguity of villainy in the play. While
there is a case to be made that there is a true
villain in Shakespeare's *Cymbeline*, nearly every
character at one point or another exhibits traits
of immorality and makes it difficult to separate
protagonist from antagonist.

The first introduction begins with a vague, overly broad sentence; cites unclear, undeveloped examples; and then moves abruptly to the thesis. Notice, too, how a reader deprived of the paper's title does not know the title of the story that the paper will analyze. The second introduction works with the same material and thesis but provides more detail and is consequently much more interesting. It begins by discussing villains and the likelihood that evil is done by a regular person. The paragraph ends with the thesis, which includes both the author and the title of the work to be discussed.

The following paragraph provides another example of an opening strategy. It begins by introducing the author and the text it will analyze, and then it moves on to provide some necessary background information before introducing its thesis.

Though Shakespeare's *Cymbeline* was originally titled
The Tragedy of Cymbeline, few would argue today that
it is a tragedy. The dictionary defines a tragedy as "a
drama or literary work in which the main character is
brought to ruin or suffers extreme sorrow, especially as
a consequence of a tragic flaw." While both Imogen and

Posthumus are temporarily brought to ruin by Posthumus's flaw, the ruin is not permanent, as it is in *Oedipus Rex,* and so the play escapes being labeled a tragedy for modern readers. Instead, the argument has moved to whether or not the work is more a comedy or a romance. Comedy, as defined for this course, "emphasizes renewal of human nature" and "celebrates life" while suggesting cynicism and offering "hope of renewal" through a hero who awakens to his better nature after the folly of his actions becomes clear. A romance, on the other hand, is the story of an improbable person, intended for a mixed audience, and "a distinct predilection for love and haphazard adventure" (Griffin, 57). Looking at these two definitions, it is obvious that while Shakespeare's *Cymbeline* has some tragic elements, it can be credibly argued as both a comedy and a romance.

Conclusions

Conclusions present another series of challenges for writers. No doubt you have heard the adage about writing papers: "Tell us what you are going to say, say it, and then tell us what you've said." While this formula does not necessarily result in bad papers, it does not often result in good ones, either. It will almost certainly result in boring papers (especially boring conclusions). If you have done a good job establishing your points in the body of the paper, the reader already knows and understands your argument. There is no need to merely reiterate. Do not just summarize your main points in your conclusion. A boring and mechanical conclusion does nothing to advance your argument or interest your reader. Consider the following conclusion to the paper about Pericles's virtue and his ultimate happy ending:

In conclusion, Pericles was a good person. He was proper and virtuous in all his actions. His search for a proper wife brought him under threat of assassination, which in turn led him to finding the right wife. His restoration of his throne brought about the loss of his wife, and his trust in unworthy friends brought about the ultimate loss of his daughter. Because he remained

> a good and virtuous person, however, he was ultimately
> rewarded with the return of the things he lost. He
> regained both his wife and his daughter.

Besides starting with a mechanical transitional device, this conclusion does little more than summarize the main points of the outline (and it does not even touch on all of them). It is incomplete and uninteresting.

Instead, your conclusion should add something to your paper. A good tactic is to build upon the points you have been arguing. Asking "why?" often helps you draw further conclusions. You might also speculate on other directions in which to take your topic by tying it into larger issues. You might do this by envisioning your paper as just one section of a longer essay. For example, in the paper that argues that *Cymbeline* is both a romance and a comedy, a discussion of the fact that Shakespeare and others were at the time creating a new genre would add interest and resonance to the argument. Along those same lines, you might also touch on aspects of the definitions that were omitted or compare the work to a piece of popular culture that most readers would know. In the following conclusion to a paper on the genre of *Cymbeline,* the author recaps the ways in which the play seems to fit different classifications and then explains the dissonance as requisite to the newly created genre:

> *Cymbeline* includes primarily comical and romantic
> aspects, as can be defended by an examination of
> different parts of the play. While there is the appearance
> of ruin, when Posthumus thinks he has successfully
> ordered the murder of his wife, it is not a permanent
> ruin, and thus the play is not a tragedy. The foolish
> actions of Cloten, the Second Lord's rueful asides,
> and Posthumus's realization of his error strengthen
> the comedy argument, but the love between Posthumus
> and Imogen and the haphazard adventures of both the
> king's sons and Posthumus argue for the work being a
> romance. The confusion the play offers can be reduced
> with the realization that *Cymbeline* was created to fit
> a new genre of drama, referred to as a tragicomedy by
> one of the form's original authors, John Fletcher. The
> play was clearly intended to be a mix of both tragedy

and comedy, which modern readers classify as romance.
It is not a perfect example, as no one should expect
of an early prototype, but it is a good, though thereby
confusing, example.

Similarly, in the following conclusion to a paper on nationalism in *Cymbeline*, the author comments on the implications about the audience's knowledge of history that can be drawn from Shakespeare's portrayal of the Roman-Britain conflict in the play.

Cymbeline is the perfect blend of Roman and English
history (Bergeron 32). The play's incorporation of Roman
history into the story line is important because it
indicates that the story of Britain's struggle with Rome
must have been common knowledge among the members of
the audience. There are no explanations of historical
fact, no asides describing or creating background, and
no other indications of an expectation that the audience
would be confused. Not only were the audience members
aware of the history, but they were also probably proud
of that history. The positive portrayal of Britain in the
play—the single-mindedness of its women, the strength
of its warriors, and the resilience of its royalty—most
likely encouraged the feelings of nationalism already
present among the people who watched. Despite Rome's
growing influence among the citizens of Britain and
Cymbeline's kingdom, they are still able to recognize and
maintain their own cultural beliefs and norms. This is
an important concept in nationalism, because retaining
cultural integrity even when the views of another country
are being forced on the citizens is essential to the
creation of a strong sense of nationhood.

Citations and Formatting
Using Primary Sources:

As the examples included in this chapter indicate, strong papers on literary texts incorporate quotations from the text in order to support their points. It is not enough for you to assert your interpretation without providing support or evidence from the text. Without well-chosen quotations to support your argument, you are, in effect, saying to the reader, "Take my word for it." It is important to use quotations thoughtfully and selectively. Remember that the paper presents *your* argument, so choose quotations that support *your* assertions. Do not let the author's voice overwhelm your own. With that caution in mind, there are some guidelines you should follow to ensure that you use quotations clearly and effectively.

Integrate Quotations:

Quotations should always be integrated into your own prose. Do not just drop them into your paper without introduction or comment. Otherwise, it is unlikely that your reader will see their function. You can integrate textual support easily and clearly with identifying tags, short phrases that identify the speaker. For example:

> The queen's son describes Britain as "a world by itself"
> (3.1.1425).

While this tag appears before the quotation, you can also use tags after or in the middle of the quoted text, as the following examples demonstrate:

> "We will nothing pay / For wearing our own noses," says
> Cloten (3.1.1425–26).

You can also use a colon to formally introduce a quotation:

> Cloten's opinion of the relative worth of the rulers
> of Rome is clear: "There be many Caesars, / Ere such
> another Julius" (3.1.1423–24).

When you quote brief sections of poems or plays (three lines or fewer), use slash marks to indicate the line breaks:

> As the discussion of the statue draws near to an end,
> Paulina offers a hint of the shock that is to come:
> "Quit presently the chapel, or resolve you / For more
> amazement" (5.3.3392–93).

Longer quotations (more than four lines of prose or three lines of poetry) should be set off from the rest of your paper in a block quotation. Double-space before you begin the passage, indent it 10 spaces from your left-hand margin, and double-space the passage itself. Because the indentation signals the inclusion of a quotation, do not use quotation marks around the cited passage. Use a colon to introduce the passage:

In her speech, the queen responds to Caius Lucius with Britain's view of Julius Caesar's conquering:

A kind of conquest
Caesar made here; but made not here his brag
Of 'Came' and 'saw' and 'overcame:' with shame—
That first that ever touch'd him—he was carried
From of our coast, twice beaten; and his
    shipping
Poor ignorant baubles!—upon our terrible seas,
Like egg-shells moved upon their surges,
    crack'd
As easily 'gainst our rocks (3.1.1435-42).

She invokes Britain's heritage and presents it as stronger than the famous conquering hero's exploits against her country.

The whole of Dickinson's poem speaks of the imagination:

To make a prairie it takes a clover and one
    bee,
One clover, and a bee,
And revery.
The revery alone will do,
If bees are few.

Clearly, she argues for the creative power of the mind.

It is also important to interpret quotations after you introduce them and explain how they help advance your point. You cannot assume that your reader will interpret the quotations the same way that you do.

Quote Accurately:
Always quote accurately. Anything in quotation marks must be the author's exact words. There are, however, some rules to follow if you need to modify the quotation to fit into your prose.

1. Use brackets to indicate any material that might have been added to the author's exact wording. For example, if you need to add any words to the quotation or alter it grammatically to allow it to fit into your prose, indicate your changes in brackets:

   "[W]e will nothing pay / For wearing our own noses," Cloten proclaimed (3.1.1425–26).

2. Conversely, if you choose to omit any words from the quotation, use ellipses (three spaced periods) to indicate missing words or phrases:

   The queen reintroduces the ancestor Caius Lucius has invoked, "The famed Casibelan . . . / Made Lud's town with rejoicing fires bright / And Britons strut with courage" (3.1.1442–45).

3. If you delete a sentence or more, use the ellipses after a period:

   Posthumus takes his imprisonment as a just reward and hoping for death, addresses the gods, "Must I repent? . . . For Imogen's dear life take mine" (V.iv.3150,3159).

4. If you omit a line or more of poetry, or more than one paragraph of prose, use a single line of spaced periods to indicate the omission:

```
To make a prairie it takes a clover and
    one bee,
. . . . . . . . . . . . . . . . .
And revery.
The revery alone will do,
If bees are few.
```

Punctuate Properly:

Punctuation of quotations often causes more trouble than it should. Once again, you just need to keep these simple rules in mind.

1. Periods and commas should be placed inside quotation marks, even if they are not part of the original quotation:

   ```
   The doctor informs Cymbeline that his wife died
   "madly."
   ```

   The only exception to this rule is when the quotation is followed by a parenthetical reference. In this case, the period or comma goes after the citation (more on these later in this chapter):

   ```
   The doctor informs Cymbeline that his wife died
   "madly" (V.v.3405).
   ```

2. Other marks of punctuation—colons, semicolons, question marks, and exclamation points—go outside the quotation marks unless they are part of the original quotation:

   ```
   Why does Cornelius call on the witness of "these
   her women"?
   ```

   ```
   Cymbeline makes clear one view of medicine, "Who
   worse than a phsycian / would this report become?"
   ```

Documenting Primary Sources:

Unless you are instructed otherwise, you should provide sufficient information for your reader to locate material you quote. Generally, literature papers follow the rules set forth by the Modern Language Association (MLA). These can be found in the *MLA Handbook for Writers of Research Papers* (seventh edition). You should be able to find this book in the reference section of your library. Additionally, its rules for citing both primary and secondary sources are widely available from reputable online sources. One of these is the Online Writing Lab (OWL) at Purdue University. OWL's guide to MLA style is available at http://owl.english. purdue.edu/owl/resource/557/01/. The Modern Language Association also offers answers to frequently asked questions about MLA style on this helpful Web page: http://www.mla.org/style_faq. Generally, when you are citing from literary works in papers, you should keep a few guidelines in mind.

Parenthetical Citations:

MLA asks for parenthetical references in your text after quotations. When you are working with prose (short stories, novels, or essays), include page numbers in the parentheses:

```
Dr. Adams's remark about completing the caesarian
demonstrates his confidence and pride: "That's one for
the medical journal, George" (18).
```

When you are quoting poetry, include line numbers:

```
Dickinson's speaker tells of the arrival of a fly: "There
interposed a Fly— / With Blue—uncertain stumbling Buzz—
/ Between the light—and Me—" (12-14).
```

When you are quoting plays, include act, scene, and line numbers. Line numbers for plays differ based on whether the edition uses through or scene line-numbering.

An example of through line-numbering:

```
"All the infections that the sun sucks up / From
bogs, fens, flats, on Prosper fall and make him / By
inch-meal a disease!" states Caliban in The Tempest
(2.2.1082-84).
```

An example of scene line-numbering:

> "All the infections that the sun sucks up / From
> bogs, fens, flats, on Prosper fall and make him / By
> inch-meal a disease!" states Caliban in The Tempest
> (2.2.3–5).

Works Cited Page:

These parenthetical citations are linked to a separate works cited page at the end of the paper. The works cited page lists works alphabetically by the authors' last name. An entry for Shakespeare's *Cymbeline* might read:

> Shakespeare, William. *Cymbeline*. Ed. Martin Butler.
> Cambridge, UK: Cambridge UP, 2005.

The *MLA Handbook* includes a full listing of sample entries, as do many of the online explanations of MLA style.

Documenting Secondary Sources:

To ensure that your paper is built entirely upon your own ideas and analysis, instructors often ask that you write interpretative papers without any outside research. If, on the other hand, your paper requires research, you must document any secondary sources you use. You need to document direct quotations, summaries or paraphrases of others' ideas, and factual information that is not common knowledge. Follow the guidelines above for quoting primary sources when you use direct quotations from secondary sources. Keep in mind that MLA style also includes specific guidelines for citing electronic sources. OWL's Web site provides a good summary: http://owl.english.purdue.edu/owl/resource/557/09/.

Parenthetical Citations:

As with the documentation of primary sources, described above, MLA guidelines require in-text parenthetical references to your secondary sources. Unlike the research papers you might write for a history class, literary research papers following MLA style do not use footnotes as a means of documenting sources. Instead, after a quotation, you should cite the author's last name and the page number:

"*Cymbeline* may be considered as a dramatic romance" (Hoeniger 220).

If you include the name of the author in your prose, then you would include only the page number in your citation. For example:

According to Hoeniger, "*Cymbeline* may be considered as a dramatic romance" (220).

If you are including more than one work by the same author, the parenthetical citation should include a shortened yet identifiable version of the title in order to indicate which of the author's works you cite. For example:

According to Jo McMurtry, "'Sirrah,' on the other hand, was used by the Elizabethans in addressing an inferior and may express contempt as well" (*Understanding* 17).

Similarly, and just as important, if you summarize or paraphrase the particular ideas of your source, you must provide documentation:

The Europeans who landed in the New World used Old World names for similar objects, including both flora and fauna (McMurtry *Understanding* 209).

Works Cited Page:

Like the primary sources discussed above, the parenthetical references to secondary sources are keyed to a separate works cited page at the end of your paper. Here is an example of a works cited page that uses the examples cited above. Note that when two or more works by the same author are listed, you should use three hyphens followed by a period in the subsequent entries. You can find a complete list of sample entries in the *MLA Handbook* or from a reputable online summary of MLA style.

WORKS CITED

Barkan, Leonard. "Living Sculptures: Ovid, Michelangelo, and *The Winter's Tale*." 48.4 (Winter 1981): 639–67.

Caesar, Julius. *Commentaries on the Gallic Wars.* Trans. W. A. McDevitte and W. S. Bohn. New York: Harper & Brothers, 1869.

Gurr, Andrew. "The Bear, the Statue, and Hysteria in *The Winter's Tale.*" *Shakespeare Quarterly* 34.4 (Winter 1983): 420–25.

Hoeniger, F. D. "Irony and Romance in *Cymbeline.*" *Studies in English Literature* 2.2 (Spring 1962): 219–28.

McMurtry, Jo. *English Language, English Literature: The Creation of an Academic Discipline.* New Haven, CT: Archon Books, 1985.

———. *Understanding Shakespeare's England: A Companion for the American Reader.* New Haven, CT: Archon Books, 1989.

Plagiarism

Failure to document carefully and thoroughly can leave you open to charges of stealing the ideas of others, which is known as plagiarism, and this is a very serious matter. Remember that it is important to include quotation marks when you use language from your source, even if you use just one or two words. For example, if you wrote, This play has many just sentiments, some natural dialogues, and some pleasing scenes, but they are obtained at the expense of much incongruity, you would be guilty of plagiarism, since you used Hoeniger's distinct language without acknowledging the source. Instead, you should write something like: Cymbeline may include "pleasing scenes" and "natural dialogues," but these do not make up for the confusion caused by the play (Hoeniger 219). In this case, you have properly credited Hoeniger.

Similarly, neither summarizing the ideas of an author nor changing or omitting just a few words means that you can omit a citation. Walter S. H. Lim's article titled "Knowledge and Belief in *The Winter's Tale*" contains the following passage about the connection between the status of Hermione's statue and religious icons:

> What the animation of Hermione's statue does is bring into conjunction conflicting perceptions of the icon in both Reformation and Catholic thought. The idea of the icon is not something associated exclusively

with Catholic thought and practice. Significantly, the icon also occupies an important place in Reformation theology, where it is applied to a definition of the elect, the true *figurae* of Protestant religion."[7] Opposed to this elect is the reprobate, the living image of opposition to God's living image of grace. In Calvinism especially, a powerful interpretation of what constitutes the iconic and the idolatrous emerges in the framework of a sacramental theology built upon the trope of metonymy. False idols are perceived to have the ability to simulate life just as living people are responded to as material shapes. According to the logic of this Calvinistic emphasis, the elect—those whom God, in his sovereign pleasure, had chosen for himself from all eternity—are given the means of grace outside of the capabilities of human agency and free will. Grace is God given and totally independent of the sinner who is dead in sin. . . . In *The Winter's Tale,* the statue of Hermione occupies the analogous position of the dead text, subsequently infused with quickening power.

There is no question that the differences between Catholic and Protestant theology were well known during Shakespeare's time. The adaptation of the language of the icon to represent those Christians who have been chosen by God makes the spiritual aspects of Paulina's presentation of the statue more poignant. The fact that the statue of Hermione is in the chapel should hint to modern readers of the place of religion in the play. There is further invocation of the statue as icon when Perdita asks to kneel and kiss the statue's hand.

Below are two examples of plagiarized passages:

Shakespeare's use of the statue of Hermione as a type of icon refers to both Catholic and Protestant views of iconography. The statue is both the symbol of Hermione and a representation of her salvation, as becomes clear when the statue comes to life.

The animation of the statue of Hermione brings up conflicting perceptions of the icon in Catholic and Protestant thought, where the icon is seen as either a symbolic representation of the person or a representation of her salvation (Lim 320).

While the first passage does not use Lim's exact language, it does list the same ideas he proposes as the critical themes without citing his work. Since this interpretation is Lim's distinct idea, this constitutes plagiarism. The second passage has shortened his passage, changed some wording, and included a citation, but some of the phrasing is Lim's. The first passage could be fixed with a parenthetical citation. Because some of the wording in the second remains the same, though, it would require the use of quotation marks, in addition to a parenthetical citation. The passage below represents an honestly and adequately documented use of the original passage:

> According to Walter S. H. Lim, when Shakespeare brings the statue of Hermione to life, he brings up "conflicting perceptions of the icon" in Catholic and Protestant thought where the icon is seen as either a symbolic representation of the person or a representation of her salvation (320).

This passage acknowledges that the interpretation is derived from Lim while appropriately using quotations to indicate his precise language.

While it is not necessary to document well-known facts, often referred to as common knowledge, any ideas or language that you take from someone else must be properly documented. Common knowledge generally includes the birth and death dates of authors or other well-documented facts of their lives. An often-cited guideline is that if you can find the information in three sources, it is common knowledge. Despite this guideline, it is, admittedly, often difficult to know if the facts you uncover are common knowledge or not. When in doubt, document your source.

Sample Essay

Dennis Dowthitt
Dr. Davis
Early British Literature
May 26, 2010

Villainy in *Cymbeline*

Sidonie Gabrielle Colette argued, "As for an authentic villain, the absolute, the artist, one rarely meets him even once in a lifetime. The ordinary bad hat is always in part a decent fellow." Literature, unlike life, usually presents a single villain. One of the most influential and revered playwrights in the history of the English language, William Shakespeare created in his considerable body of work many memorable villains. From Caliban in *The Tempest* to Richard II to *Hamlet*'s Claudius, these characters have become household names thanks to their often inhuman capacity for evil or, at the very least, malicious mischief. Shakespeare's plays themselves have also become deeply ingrained in societal consciousness; even those individuals unexposed to literature know the names Romeo and Juliet, Macbeth, and Othello. Sometimes lost among the list of classics that make up Shakespeare's résumé are overlooked works such as *Cymbeline,* certainly one of his more harshly critiqued plays and widely regarded as among the weakest. Perhaps this reputation is due to the ambiguity of villainy in the play. While there is a case to be made that there is a true villain in Shakespeare's *Cymbeline,* nearly every character at one point or another exhibits traits of immorality and makes it difficult to separate protagonist from antagonist.

The title character is the king of Britain and, from his first appearance, he seems set to cause sorrow and hardship. By banning Posthumus Leonatus, the newly wed husband of his daughter, Imogen, and ordering his daughter's incarceration, Cymbeline offers a highly negative impression of himself. This is compounded when he explains the logic behind his banishment; he considers Posthumus of lowly birth and thinks their marriage will "have made my throne a seat for baseness" (1.1.178–79). Here the king shows a stubbornness and arrogance as well as a condescension toward the class of people that doubtless makes up the audience that may well set him up to be the villain. This perception, however, is tempered by the knowledge that Imogen is his only remaining child, his two sons having been kidnapped at a young age and taken away by what is, at that point, an unknown party. This gives Cymbeline an almost sympathetic aspect, and his notable absence from most of the play's important scenes reduces the likelihood of Shakespeare's intention to present him as the villain.

The next suspect for the play's villain is Iachimo, an Italian womanizer and braggart whom Posthumus encounters in his exile. Through subversive taunting and mockery, Iachimo convinces Posthumus to enter into a bet concerning Imogen's chastity, which he sets out to compromise. It is at this point that Iachimo seems to become the knave of the tale by sneaking into Imogen's bedchamber and noting details that convince Posthumus of her infidelity. This trickery can certainly be seen as an expression of evil, as it appears that Iachimo's sole agenda is to defame Imogen and destroy Posthumus, actions motivated by jealousy. Iachimo possesses all the traits of a villain. He is crafty and clever, of quick wit and devious intelligence, the "shrewd destructive force we had been cozened out of anticipating" (Kay 39). Taken on their own, however, Iachimo's actions are not criminal. He is certainly dishonorable in his methods and vindictive in his jealousy, but Iachimo kills no one; he is essentially a lying homewrecker. His later shame and regret at these actions further distance him from villainy; he carries a "heaviness and guilt in [his] bosom" that he gives voice to in the final act, thereby earning Posthumus's forgiveness (5.2.2993). The severity of his actions, his repentance, and his ultimate forgiveness by those he had wronged keep Iachimo from succumbing to complete villainy, though he is certainly villainous.

It is Posthumus himself, initially presented as the hero of the story and described as a gentleman, who commits the first act that can be labeled murderous.

Even before he does, though, his acceptance of the bet with Iachimo has been widely criticized and offered as proof that there is "beneath Posthumus's apparently perfect gestures, an essential meanness in the man himself and in the conventional virtue that he embodies" (Swander 260). Whether or not the terms of the wager cast Posthumus in an unfavorable light is debatable, but there can be no argument that what he does next is villainous. After Iachimo convinces him that Imogen is no longer chaste, Posthumus becomes enraged and orders his servant, Pisanio, to kill her. Here the protagonist becomes the antagonist, and perhaps the most wicked deed of the entire play is committed by the character who to this point had been a "blameless hero" whose "procedure is entirely in accord with the ethics of romance" (Lawrence 428). This is the best example of the merging of good and evil in the play and may well present a case for classifying Posthumus as a villain. However, his eventual reunion with Imogen and his forgiving of Iachimo, all after having been driven suicidally mad with guilt, serve as a redemption of sorts and once again present him in an almost heroic light. Thus his villainy, while extreme, is limited in scope of both time and action.

One figure that is often perceived as a villain in Cymbeline is Cloten, son to the queen and misguided suitor of Imogen. Immediately unlikable, Cloten has no redeeming value and makes absolutely no claim on the audience's sympathy or concern. He is a conceited and spoiled milksop who goes on to declare the vilest of intentions after Imogen repeatedly rejects him; he sets out to kill Posthumus before Imogen's eyes and then rape her. Unlike the other characters, he exudes no hesitation or reluctance in this goal; rather, he says that "I'll be merry in my revenge" (3.5.2123). These are the motives and intentions of a criminal, but up to this point Cloten has been portrayed as an arrogant oaf, one who is "not a villain so much as a fool" (Hoeniger 222). Carol Kay points out that "we seldom fear what we find amusing, and Scene III creates a highly amusing half-buffoon, half-bully whose potential threat is consistently eradicated by the Second Lord's jibes" (38). It is for this reason that, despite the fact that he has evil characteristics, Cloten does not exactly fit the role of villain, at least not to such a degree that he should be considered the story's chief scoundrel.

The sole character who is universally recognized as a villain and who offers no exceptions to that label is Cloten's mother, the queen. From the beginning, Imogen knows, and informs the audience, that she is duplicitous at best. After the queen insists that she is on Posthumus and Imogen's side, Imogen observes, "how fine this tyrant can tickle where she wounds" (1.1.103). In short order, it is made clear just how evil the queen is, as "the queen's attempt to poison her stepdaughter is a profoundly treacherous act," which cements her wretched position of villainess of the play (Glasov-Corrigan 391). The queen then goes to great lengths to convince Cymbeline that Britain should go to war with Rome, a testament to the fact that her manipulative treachery extends to every aspect of hers and the king's lives. It is in the play's final act, though, that her true nature is brought to light and revealed to the king and all other involved parties, when the doctor reveals her dying words were marked with hatred and cruelty. Her confession that she never loved Cymbeline and attempted more than once to kill Imogen may be a last-minute attempt at spiritual absolution, but the audience still sees in an otherwise insouciant denouement the villain that had been there all along.

The queen is almost certainly the main antagonist, and arguably her son joins her as a villain, but the lack of a real heroic figure in Cymbeline is what makes the distinction between villain and nonvillain difficult. Belarius and Arviragus might be seen as heroic, but their nearly ancillary roles during the bulk of the play reduce their significance. The only truly innocent major characters throughout the play are Imogen and Pisanio, as everyone else engages in some form of criminal behavior. Even Belarius, the unjustly banished lord who is presented as respectable in character, is a kidnapper. This ambiguity and lack of rigid archetypes contributes to the effectiveness of the play and adds a philosophical angle to an otherwise standard plot. Instead of being presented with a mustache-twirling malicious malefactor, the audience is left to decide for itself who is the real villain. That perhaps is part of the reason why Cymbeline is so widely disregarded.

WORKS CITED

Colette, Sidonie Gabrielle. "Villain quotes." *ThinkExist. com.* 2006. <http://thinkexist.com/quotes/with/keyword/villain/>. Web. 21 May 2009.

Glazov-Corrigan, Elena. "Speech Acts, Generic Difference, and the Curious Case of *Cymbeline.*" *Studies in English Literature, 1500–1900* 34(1994): 379–99. Web. 17 May 2009.

Hoeniger, F. D. "Iron and Romance in *Cymbeline.*" *Studies in English Literature, 1500–1900* 2(1962): 219–28. *JSTOR.* Web. 17 May 2009.

Kay, Carol McGinnis. "Generic Sleight-of-Hand in *Cymbeline.*" *South Atlantic Review* 46 (November 1981): 34–40. *JSTOR.* Web. 17 May 2009.

Lawrence, William Witherle. "The Wager in *Cymbeline.*" *PMLA* 35 (1920): 391–431. *JSTOR.* Web. 15 May 2009.

Mikalachki, Jodi. "The Masculine Romance of Roman Britain: *Cymbeline* and Early Modern English Nationalism." *Shakespeare Quarterly* 46.3 (Autumn 1995): 301–22. *JSTOR.* Web. 20 May 2009.

Shakespeare, William. *The Tragedy of Cymbeline*. *The Yale Shakespeare*. Ed. Wilbur L. Cross. New York: Barnes & Noble, 1993. 1321–63. Print.

Swander, Homer. "*Cymbeline* and the 'Blameless Hero.'" *ELH* 31 (September 1964): 259–70. *JSTOR*. Web. 20 May 2009.

HOW TO WRITE ABOUT SHAKESPEARE'S ROMANCES

WILLIAM SHAKESPEARE (1564–1616) is widely considered the preeminent playwright in the English language. His writings for the stage are among the most commonly read works of literature in classrooms and are frequently performed. For the last two centuries, one of the requirements for great actors was that they become accomplished performers and interpreters of the Bard of Avon's plays.

Shakespeare married at the age of eighteen in a hurried ceremony. His oldest daughter was born six months later. He and his wife then had twins, but only the daughter of the pair survived. After the birth of the twins in 1585, there is nothing known about Shakespeare until 1592, when references to his plays begin to appear in London. Whatever he was doing, it brought him to work as a successful playwright in London.

A popular playwright, Shakespeare continued to write and see his works performed for years. His earlier plays were primarily histories and comedies; his later works were mostly tragedies and romances, also known as tragicomedies.

Many of his plays appeared in various publishing forms throughout his lifetime, but the first compilation of the works was published in 1623, after his death, and is referred to as the First Folio. It is a first in at least two ways. It is the first collection of Shakespeare's works. It is also the first folio printed that contained only plays. Though it was not titled First Folio when it initially appeared, it is traditionally referred to by that name instead of its published title, *Mr William Shakespeare's Comedies, Histories And Tragedies. Published According To The True Originall Copies.* The First Folio was a collection of his plays, thirty-six of them, half of which had not been previously published. The two plays excluded from the First Folio are both romances, *Pericles, Prince of Tyre* and *The Two Noble Kinsmen.* These plays are both of contested authorship, though most scholars now agree that at least part of each play was written by Shakespeare. The publishers of the First Folio might have regarded the works as not exclusively Shakespeare's, since they clearly are not, and excluded them for this reason. Or, possibly, the right to print them rested with someone else. This appears to have been the problem with *Troilus and Cressida,* and the resolution of printing issues is the explanation for its inclusion in the First Folio, though it is not in the table of contents. Citations of the plays discussed in this volume are from the online *Open Source Shakespeare,* except for citations of *The Two Noble Kinsmen.* This work was not included in the *Open Source Shakespeare,* so the Norton edition was used.

In order to write about Shakespeare's life in his work, you will need to read some Shakespearean biographies. Because Shakespeare is the reigning English author, there are thousands of books that deal with his life and works. There are some particular authors and works, however, that have gained critical primacy. One of these works is the reprinted and shortened version of an earlier volume. S. Schoenbaum's *William Shakespeare: A Compact Documentary Life* covers Shakespeare's family and includes copies of primary documents. A slightly older work is by Gerald Eades Bentley, *Shakespeare: A Biographical Handbook.* The oldest biography that remains an essential resource is by E. K. Chambers, *William Shakespeare: A Study of Facts and Problems.* Consulting any of these three biographies will give you a strong sense of Shakespeare as both a person and a playwright. Examining all three of them will give you essential background from which to write about Shakespeare's life as it is reflected in his plays.

From the little background given here, you might consider writing about Shakespeare's presentation of father-daughter relationships and how these could be an indication of his experience with his daughters. You might look at his emphasis on chastity in view of his premarital relationship with Anne and his role as a father of two daughters. His family's religious history appears to have influenced his plays as well, and learning more about that would allow you to examine the plays with this in mind more successfully. Shakespeare's experience with politics is also evident in the romances; thus, reading more about life in Elizabethan England would help you see those elements as they were incorporated in the plays. There is a range of aspects of Shakespeare's life that significantly influenced his plays.

Because of the multiple influences that bear on the romances, familiarity with Shakespeare's life would make you more able to comment on the plays, having drawn accurate and interesting conclusions from your analysis. Understanding the historical and cultural context in which Shakespeare wrote also adds valuable references to your search for a unique claim to make about his plays. In addition, looking at what previous scholars have said about the plays you will be dealing with is useful. Their ideas may give you other perspectives from which to examine the plays. Your understanding of the works of previous critics will help you to constructively enter the critical conversation. After you have grounded your reading in biographical, historical, and critical research, you will be better able to write an insightful essay.

TOPICS AND STRATEGIES

In the following pages, you will find suggestions for how you can begin writing a critical analysis essay about Shakespeare. Choosing a specific play or plays to concentrate on is important since you will be unable to cover all of Shakespeare's work in a single paper. From the sample topics, you can mine ideas regarding which texts would be particularly useful for that specific essay; however, you should not limit yourself to these. Using an idea you have come up with to develop your essay, as long as there is evidence to support your argument, will potentially make your paper more compelling to the person evaluating your work. Considering the required length for your essay, the length of the plays, and the number of plays you want to examine can help you plan your paper. Make sure you have enough time to adequately consider the play(s) you have selected. Also be sure to provide a rationale in your essay for your choice of plays. Sometimes the basis of selection is obvious to you, but it needs to be clear to your reader as well. As an example, you might indicate that you have chosen to examine all the romances dealing with parental input about marriage partners. When you are clear in your own mind about the reasons for choosing the play(s) you did and the essay makes those reasons obvious to your readers, then your selection appears thoughtful and your argument stronger as a result.

Themes

Shakespeare deals with some common themes in the romances. While not every play deals with all of the themes, many of them discuss the themes of the nature of romantic love, honor, and the question of the dominance of nature or nurture. Included in this section are suggestions as to which plays you might use for a specific topic, but again the lists are by no means exhaustive. If you see a topic's connection to another work, that will simply make your paper better. When you have selected the plays you want to study, you will want to read each of them again, paying particular attention to any passages that pertain to your topic, analyzing those passages, and keeping careful notes. After that, the creative part of crafting an essay begins: comparing your notes on each play and attempting to come up with original arguments.

Sample Topics:

1. **The nature of romantic love:** How does Shakespeare describe and illustrate the nature of romantic love in his romance plays?

   Obviously you will want to work with the plays that discuss romantic love. Since all of the romances touch on that topic, you might want to limit your choices to the plays that empha-size the nature of romantic love. Some of the texts particularly useful for this topic would include *The Tempest, Cymbeline, Two Noble Kinsmen,* and *Troilus and Cressida.* The first two plays include parental involvement, one positive and one nega-tive. How are the parents involved in the situation? How do they test the love of the young couple? What does Shakespeare show about love through the responses to adversity in the play? What does Shakespeare specifically say about adversity and romantic love? The second two works include unsuccessful examples of romantic love. What is Shakespeare explicitly, through the words, and implicitly, through the action, saying about romantic love? How is it defined? How does it act? What are the results? Look at the positive aspects of romantic love detailed in these two works. What do they offer in perspective on the topic?

2. **Honor:** What does Shakespeare say about honor in his romances?

Working with honor as a topic, you might focus on *All's Well That Ends Well; Pericles, Prince of Tyre;* and *Measure for Measure.* In all three of these plays, Shakespeare has his characters discuss honor. Beginning in the first act of *All's Well That Ends Well,* the king of France discusses honor most specifically. Others throughout the play mention it and either display or fail to show honor. Who is the most honorable character? Who is the least honorable? How do you view those characters in the play? Is one more likable than the other? In *Pericles,* Antiochus is the first to mention it. Look at what he says. Is there a difference between perceived and actual honor based on his speech? In the second scene, Pericles discusses honor and dishonor. Later in the play, Simonides describes honor and its place in the cosmos. What is Shakespeare saying about honor in this play? In *Measure for Measure,* there is also much discussion of honor. Shakespeare takes advantage in this play of the habit of calling the nobility "your honor." The play also contains myriad references that can be read in very different ways. When Isabella says, "Heaven keep your honor" (2.4.1056), is she asking God to watch over Angelo or to give him honor? Isabella and the duke most often discuss honor in the play. Are they honorable? If so, in what way? How is honor used ironically in the play? What might Shakespeare think about honor, based on this play?

3. **Nature versus nurture:** Shakespeare discusses both explicitly and implicitly the still-common question of which is more

dominant, nature or nurture. What seems to be Shakespeare's opinion based on the romances?

Shakespeare offers several different approaches to this topic. In two plays, he specifically shows people who are raised apart from their royal families whose actions nevertheless show their nobility. The first example is Cymbeline's sons, who are raised in the mountains of Wales yet are true to their noble heritage. The second example is in *The Winter's Tale* when Perdita is raised by a shepherd yet retains the expected grace and beauty of the nobility. In *Cymbeline,* however, Shakespeare also provides an example of nurture providing nobility in the character of Posthumus. Being raised in the royal household has given Posthumus sufficient character to cause Imogen to love him. Is he a noble character in the play? How is his character portrayed? In what way is he good/heroic, and in what way is he faulty/base? How can nature or nurture be ascribed to these differences? Finally in that same play, Shakespeare provides an example of nurture in the royal household losing out to the nature of the character's mother, through the king's stepson Cloten. What is Shakespeare arguing through the presentation of this character?

Another play that touches on the nature versus nurture debate is *The Tempest,* in which the characters of Caliban and Miranda are both raised by Prospero, but only one exhibits noble virtues, while the other acts evilly. How are these two, raised by the same man but responding so differently, evidence of Shakespeare's argument for the power of nature over the influence of nurture? For further illumination, you might examine the character of Ferdinand in the play. He has been raised by a dishonorable but noble father. What are the results as evident in his character? What is Shakespeare saying by portraying him as such?

Character

None of the characters in Shakespeare's romances appear in multiple plays. To write about character in the romances, then, you will need to choose a certain kind of character to analyze in order to develop your essay. Because Shakespeare uses the same classes of characters over and over again, you have multiple groups to choose from. You might examine what Shakespeare says about queens. Another group common in the romance plays are soldiers. Or you might examine the high-level deputies of the various leaders. Examining the daughters in various plays might also offer compelling insights. Daughters are main characters in most of the romances. Is Shakespeare saying something about daughters specifically through this, or is he arguing for a particular kind of daughter? Irrespective of the type of character you decide to focus on, you will want to reread all the plays you intend to discuss, creating careful and full notes on the character types. Through comparison and contrast of the characters in the different plays, you will be able to offer potentially exciting conclusions. Using your examination of several soldier, deputy, wife, or daughter characters, what claim can you make concerning Shakespeare's presentation and, presumably by extension, opinion of these various groups?

Sample Topics:

1. **Queens:** Because the romances deal with royalty quite often, there are multiple portrayals of queens. These are wives of kings, not heads of state in their own right. What points does Shakespeare make about these women through his characterizations of them?

   Contrasts can be revealed by examining the queen in *Cymbeline* and Hermione in *The Winter's Tale.* Reread these plays to see how Shakespeare presented the two women. Look at what they say and what is said about them. Look at how they act and how others react to them. They are very different women despite their shared title of queen. Are there any similarities between the two women other than their rank? Do their husbands rely on them? Adding the queens of *Pericles, Prince of Tyre* to your study increases the possibility of making generalizations in your essay. Thaisa, the wife of Pericles, and Dionyza, the wife of Cleon, are also portrayed in their own light. Even in adversity, Thaisa is faithful to her vows, while Dionyza, having been rescued from adversity, breaks her vows in prosperity. Is there a point to Shakespeare's presentation of the queens who are in negative situations being good and queens whose lives are easy being evil? Why might he have chosen to portray them as such? What could he be saying about the benefits of adversity? When is inner goodness or evil revealed in a person?

2. **Soldiers:** Shakespeare's time, as many before and since, was concerned with the possibility of war. Critic Eric Mallin notes that England was constantly in fear of invasion during Shakespeare's lifetime (145). What does Shakespeare's portrayal of soldiers tell us of his attitude toward them?

In the romances, there are several plays that include soldiers among the characters. Of all of them, *Troilus and Cressida* and *All's Well That Ends Well* have the most carefully developed soldiers. Looking at these two plays and examining Shakespeare's portrayal of the various soldiers in them offers significant opportunities for drawing provocative conclusions. You might even limit your examination to the soldiers in one of the plays. Who are the soldiers in *Troilus and Cressida* most worthy of closer analysis? You may, of course, begin with Troilus. Since he is a title character, Shakespeare's presentation of him might be particularly significant. At the beginning of the work, Shakespeare presents Troilus and his brother Hector, the champion of Troy. (Hector would be another strong soldierly presence to examine.) In addition, the Greek camp has two important soldiers whose battles are discussed in the play, Ajax and Achilles. What does Shakespeare have these soldiers say and do? How does he have others react to them and speak about them? Looking at these four warriors in particular, what does it appear that Shakespeare says about soldiers in general? How do they act nobly? When do they act ignobly? What circumstances influence them? In *All's Well That Ends Well*, Bertram runs away to be a soldier. He is not, however, seeking to achieve an esteemed goal, becoming an officer, but fleeing a situation he wants no part of, his marriage. What does this say about soldiers? When Bertram runs away, he goes with Parolles, who is quickly shown to be a coward and a liar. What point might Shakespeare be making with this character? The Captains Dumaine are also soldiers in the play. Are these two men more honorable than the others? What do they say and what is said about them to make you think so? Is Shakespeare arguing for or against soldiers, or is he making some other point with his varied soldier characters? If you decide to take the two plays together, you have at a minimum eight important soldiers to analyze. Are there any ways in which all eight are similar besides their association with militaristic roles? What is significant about the eight? Why? Is Shakespeare making the point that war brings out the worst in people, or is he making a different point? Based on your reading and your notes, what do you think Shakespeare is saying about soldiers?

3. **Deputies:** Shakespeare has several leaders pass their responsibilities on to deputies. These men may be acting with or without honor in following the orders they are given. This issue became a major argument after World War II in the trials of Nazi soldiers whose defense was that they were simply following orders. Long before that war, Shakespeare had examined the role of deputies or followers. What does Shakespeare say about the responsibility of followers in the romances?

Measure for Measure offers Angelo, a supposedly honorable deputy offered the opportunity to rule Vienna in his duke's stead. Was he following his orders when he called for the arrest and execution of Claudio? At what point does he become at fault? Is this an example of the corrupting force of power? If it is, what does it say about Angelo versus what it says about the duke? Escalus was also given great responsibilities. Does he fulfill them well? Does he let the power corrupt him? What is Shakespeare saying in this play about following orders and having power? *Cymbeline* includes a deputy who refuses to follow his orders. Pisanio does not kill Imogen, as Posthumus orders, though he tells Posthumus he did so. When Posthumus comes to his senses, what argument does he make about Pisanio's responsibilities in terms of following orders? Is this significant? Why? Does it make any difference to think about the fact that Posthumus was not following the king's orders to leave Imogen alone? What point is Shakespeare making here? If you wanted to look at it that way, *The Winter's Tale* is a contrast between two men who obeyed and disobeyed evil orders. In the play, when Leontes orders Antigonus to abandon Perdita, he does so. The gods repay this careful though sorrowful following of orders with a horrific death. When Leontes orders Camillo to murder Polixenes, even though Leontes is Camillo's king, Camillo instead goes to Polixenes and tells him of the plot, and the two flee Sicilia together. Despite not following the orders Leontes gave him, Camillo ends up rewarded with a powerful position in Bohemia. What is Shakespeare saying with this contrast? Does it solidify or weaken this point if you examine Leonine and Dionyza in *Pericles, Prince of Tyre?* Was Dionyza right to order Leonine to kill Marina? When Leonine reports he has carried out his orders, what is his reward? Is this a case of poetic justice? In these four plays, six men are charged with responsibilities by their rightful leaders. Looking at all six of them, what is Shakespeare arguing about following orders? Doing the right thing? Responsibility?

History and Context

Shakespeare wrote his romances more than 400 years ago. This fact creates some significant cultural shock for readers. The language is different, customs are confusing, and allusions are unclear. All of these factors potentially frustrate students in their desire to master Shakespeare's plays. While far more study would be required to fully understand Shakespeare and his work than most people are willing to engage in, some historical or contextual background can illuminate many of the romances.

Sample Topics:

1. **Roman mythology:** How does Shakespeare take advantage of Roman mythology to develop his romances?

Beginning with a solid understanding of Roman mythology is essential to understanding many of Shakespeare's romances. Two seminal works in mythology are Edith Hamilton's *Mythology,* which covers Greek, Roman, and Norse mythos, and Bulfinch's *Mythology: The Age of Fable or Stories of Gods and Heroes.* Once you understand the general Roman pantheon of gods, you will be in a much better position to discuss the romances.

In *The Winter's Tale,* Florizel waxes eloquent about romantic love, describing what the Roman gods did for the sake of love. Did the gods take love seriously? What did love mean to them? How did love usually work out in Roman mythology?

In *Pericles, Prince of Tyre,* several different goddesses are invoked, all of whom are aspects of a single goddess. How does knowing that shape your understanding of the play? Why is Diana a fitting goddess for this play? What aspects of Diana that are not described impact the story nonetheless? Was Shakespeare making additional allusions?

Roman gods are not only invoked, but one makes an appearance in *Cymbeline.* What is the significance of the three gods discussed in the play? Why is Jupiter appearing as a character in the play particularly shocking? Why is his inclusion necessary to the play? What is Shakespeare trying to say with this appearance? Does it add weight to the discussions of the other gods?

The Tempest includes the appearance of three goddesses of Roman mythology who discuss two other Roman deities. Why is it significant that the two discussed are not also included in the work? What do the three who appear have in common? Why might Shakespeare be invoking them? How do they add to the complexity of the play?

In *The Two Noble Kinsmen,* Hymen, the god of marriage, walks onstage in the first scene. Multiple gods are invoked, and three are specifically asked to take a hand in the plot: Mars, Venus, and Diana. What is the significance of these three gods? How do they relate to the characters that pray to them?

Which is the most significant in the play? The play mentions many other members of the Roman pantheon. Why might Shakespeare use so many? What do they add to the play?

Looking at these plays, you can see the Roman gods as active participants, even when they do not physically appear. What is Shakespeare implying by that? Is he arguing for a particular stance about Roman gods? Is it a parallel argument for something else? Is he simply trying to show off his education, or would his audience also have understood the allusions and emphases added through the Roman mythology?

2. **Classical history:** Shakespeare invokes Greek and Roman history, as well as early British history, in the romances. Is there a particular point to his adaptation of classical history in the plays?

A general familiarity with the history Shakespeare recalls in the various plays would be a good starting place for an essay. An introduction to Shakespeare's use of Roman history might begin with Kahn's *Roman Shakespeare: Warriors, Wounds, and Women,* though there are several other fine works on the topic. Or individual plays might lead you to other sources. For *Troilus and Cressida,* the best preparation you could have for a discussion of the history in the play would be having read Homer's *The Iliad* and Ovid's *Metamorphoses.* However, a simpler introduction from a good online site, such as Lomio's *The Trojan War,* can provide you with sufficient background to be able to write intelligently on the topic. How does Shakespeare use the Trojan War in the play? Does knowing that England was associated with Troy in earlier British literature, such as Geoffrey of Monmouth's *History* or the Arthurian romance *Sir Gawain and the Green Knight,* change your perspective of the play? What might Shakespeare have been saying, knowing that? Why might Shakespeare have used this story, which he adapted from Chaucer? What did this history specifically provide to the British audience? Shakespeare adapts another ancient story in the play *Pericles, Prince of Tyre.* This story originates in history, where the main character was Apollonius. Because it is so old, no one has been able to locate the original tale, though linguistic evidence supports a Greek origin.

The tale is mentioned in Roman works, but it is most likely from Gower's story that the tale came to Shakespeare.

Examining how book 8 of the *Confessio Amantis*, the play's primary source, differs from Shakespeare's *Pericles* is yet another useful historical analysis. Is the name change of the main character significant? Look at where the original name would have come from and which god is hailed in the play. Is there a relationship? In the story there are various place names. All of these places exist. The only unclear reference is Pentapolis, though historically there are multiple citations of this location. Why would Shakespeare have included real place names? What does he gain from it? Is there obfuscation in his use of Pentapolis, or was its origin clear from the play?

In *Cymbeline*, Shakespeare uses actual Roman historical interaction with Britain, through Julius Caesar, to set up the play. The BBC offers an online description of Roman Britain by Mike Ibeji that might help you understand the historical context to which Shakespeare refers in this play. What part did the Caesars play in England's history? How does Shakespeare incorporate that history into the play? What other historical implications might have been essential to the audience's understanding of the work? Having read through the introduction to Roman Britain, go back and reread *Cymbeline*. What other insights can you gain from the play? Other examples of English history are included in *Cymbeline*, through the naming of actual English kings. What part did those men play in England's nationhood? What is the relevance of referencing them? How does their invocation add to the play? Can you see a similarity in Shakespeare's use of history in *Cymbeline; Pericles, Prince of Tyre;* and *Troilus and Cressida?*

3. **Contemporaneous history:** Though Shakespeare wrote 400 years ago, even older tales were modern for him. His parents lived through Henry VIII's reign and the religious changes that ensued as England switched from a Catholic nation to a Protestant one. He himself lived under Gloriana, Queen Elizabeth I, and James I. Where does he reference this contemporaneous history in his romance plays?

Looking through the romances, you will find multiple references to the events and history of Shakespeare's day. The development of the theory of the divine right of kings came from James I and is referenced by Shakespeare in *Cymbeline.* When does the play discuss kings? What is it saying about them, and how does Shakespeare's use of a flawed king affect or influence this viewpoint? Where does Cymbeline's concern for his kingdom overcome his care for his daughter? Is this a discussion of the limitations of kingship or a show of the devotion of kings? What view does Shakespeare present on the divine right of kings?

Elizabeth I was queen of England until 1603. Since her father made a great effort to produce a son as heir, it is clear that male succession and male rule was expected. In many literary and artistic works, Elizabeth I was associated with the Roman goddess Diana, so seeing a reciprocal association of Diana with the queen is reasonable. In *Pericles, Prince of Tyre,* Shakespeare changed the associated deity from Apollo to Diana. How is this change significant? What about Diana in the play is similar to Elizabeth? How can the play be said to support Elizabeth's reign? Examining *All's Well That Ends Well* leads to a discussion of the religious history of England. In 1.3, Clown speaks, referencing a papist and a puritan and saying they are the same. Is this an argument on Shakespeare's part about the religious schism? What might he be saying to argue that they have one head and that they are like deer in the same herd? Is there any sense to his using a French word for coal for the young Puritan's name? What might Shakespeare have meant by that?

Referencing the history of Shakespeare's time in the plays was deliberate, since the strength of a great writer is that everything in the work is carefully chosen. Some have seen in *The Winter's Tale* reference to Anne Boleyn, one of Henry VIII's wives. A reference to Henry VIII and Anne Boleyn's relationship may be noted in Isabella's rejection of Angelo in *Measure for Measure.* Anne Boleyn's sister was a mistress of Henry VIII, but Anne refused his advances unless he married her. Anne was wrongly imprisoned, like Hermione, for an alleged affair with a friend of the king.

Anne Boleyn's only daughter, Elizabeth I, eventually assumed the throne from Henry VIII. How might a work sympathetic toward a character reminiscent of the queen's mother be a political stroke of genius? Perdita becomes the only heir to her father's throne, as eventually Elizabeth does as well. Is this a fairy tale version of the story of Elizabeth I's rise to power? What is "cleaned up" from the historical tale? Are there any other parallels in the play with Elizabeth I and Anne Boleyn?

What other historical references are there in the romances? *Measure for Measure* offers a view of religion in a state in which the secular leader rules the church. How does this match the England of Shakespeare's day? What political point might Shakespeare have been making by his inclusion of a convent, a novitiate, and a false friar?

Philosophy and Ideas

When you decide to write an essay concerning the philosophy and ideas Shakespeare presents in his romances, there are various approaches you might take. Many of the romances deal with the issue of the use and abuse of power. What philosophy of rule encourages the indulgence of the whims of the leaders? How is this philosophy shown to be faulty in the romances? Many of the romances also deal with the status of women. This is a topic of particular interest to modern readers, since women have equal rights under the law now but did not then. When does Shakespeare present positive portrayals of women? Where does his work argue that equal rights cause overwhelming difficulties? What aspects of womanhood were essential in Shakespeare's day? Many of the works also describe father-daughter relationships. Knowing that Shakespeare was the father of two daughters who survived to adulthood and eventually got married, this is an interesting aspect of the later plays to examine. How does Shakespeare portray the fathers? When do they make good choices? Is there a timing difference from when they make bad choices? The realm of philosophy and ideas offers a revealing entryway into Shakespeare's works. The following suggestions are not the only topics by a considerable margin. If some point of philosophy that Shakespeare applied in his work catches your attention, you might find pursuing that topic far more fruitful.

Sample Topics:

1. **Use and abuse of power:** What does Shakespeare show about the use and abuse of power through the romances?

As you examine this topic, several of the plays will come to mind. *Measure for Measure* focuses on the use and abuse of power. *The Tempest* is a revenge tale that happens because of a lack of use and an abuse of power. In *The Winter's Tale*, a king abuses his family without reason and loses them all. Even *Troilus and Cressida* can be seen as a discussion of the use and abuse of power as those who have gained power move the other characters as they will.

Looking at *Measure for Measure,* what do you think Shakespeare is saying about good government? Is he promoting mercy over justice every time? What have been the results of that use of power previously in Vienna? When there is a change, is it a positive one? After Angelo is removed, what abuses of power continue? Is Shakespeare saying that even individually positive actions might be harmful for an entire kingdom? Does he show how power can harm individuals? Do not look just at Angelo, but at others in the play. How does Shakespeare use them to develop this idea?

In *The Tempest*, Prospero had lost his position of duke because he failed to exercise his power. Is this an abuse of power, according to Shakespeare? What actions on Prospero's part indicate that it might be? While the king of Naples has dethroned Prospero, his actions lead to other potential abuses. What are they? Why do they flow naturally from Alonso's earlier decisions? Because Leontes is king in *The Winter's Tale,* his ability to abuse his family and followers is increased. What would Leontes have had to do if he had not been a king, if he suspected his wife of adultery? What multiple abuses do his inaccurate suspicions bring about? How does Leontes take advantage of and abuse Antigonus? There are multiple deaths in the play; which of these are related to the use and abuse of power? What is Shakespeare saying when you examine the play from that perspective?

Troilus and Cressida offers another perspective on the use and abuse of power. When Calchas takes advantage of his power in the Greek camp to negotiate for the release of his daughter, what is the result? How might this be seen as an abuse of power? Remember that fathers had control of their daughters until they were married, but after their marriage, they were under the governance of their husbands. By agreeing to the trade, the Trojans have gone against the cultural norms. How can this be seen as an abuse of the power of a ruler and a husband?

2. **Status of women:** What commentary is Shakespeare making about the status of women and the cultural expectations placed on them?

Since Shakespeare uses women characters throughout the romances, any of them could be examined for this topic. Particularly strong choices would be *All's Well That Ends Well*, since Helena takes an active part in creating the future she desires, and *The Winter's Tale*, since Paulina assumes a powerful role in the play.

Helena is in love with Bertram and uses her inheritance from her father to secure marriage to him in *All's Well That Ends Well*. In the bulk of the play, Bertram runs from Helena, avoiding the responsibilities of his marriage and acting like a well-to-do bachelor. When Helena finds that Bertram is plotting a seduction, she arranges to be the one seduced, thus tricking her husband into sleeping with her. What is Shakespeare showing about the status of women in this play? What does he say about their power? About their intelligence? About their persistence and patience?

Throughout *The Winter's Tale*, Paulina transcends the conventional behaviors expected of women in her day. She approaches the prison guard, takes the baby to the king, refuses to be silenced by her husband, makes the king swear to follow her decisions, and either hides the queen for years or brings a statue to life. (Shakespeare leaves this latter plot point deliberately ambiguous.) Clearly, Paulina does not match our expectations of a downtrodden woman. Is anyone in the play surprised by her actions? Who is opposed to them? Why? How does she sidestep or avoid societal expectations?

Looking at these plays, and several others as well, is it possible that Shakespeare is suggesting that women have greater power than is granted them under the law? Are they more active and involved than we might expect, based on our understanding of the times? Are Shakespeare's strong women the exceptions that prove the rule, or are they evidence that women wielded far more power than has previously been supposed?

3. **Father-daughter relationships:** Identify and evaluate the multiple models of father-daughter relationships in Shakespeare's romances.

For this topic, you might focus on *The Tempest* and *Pericles, Prince of Tyre.* In *Pericles,* Shakespeare presents four different father-daughter relationships: Antiochus and his daughter, Simonides and Thaisa, Cleon and his daughter, and Pericles and Marina. Examining these four relationships can lead to an understanding of Shakespeare's views of father-daughter interaction. Who has a good relationship? How is this evidenced? Who has a bad relationship? How is it presented or characterized? In *The Tempest,* Shakespeare presents the story not only of a duke who has lost his kingdom but of a father trying to take care of his daughter. What dangers has their exile brought to Marina? What limitations? How does Prospero deal with these difficulties? What is his goal in dealing with them? What is Shakespeare intimating about father-daughter relationships?

Form and Genre

When considering form and genre, you are examining the way a text is put together and the type of work it is. Shakespeare's romances have also been described as problem plays, because they seem to include partial examples of other genres or resist assignment to or association with a single genre. Look at the definitions of romance and examine how the plays you focus on match those definitions. Alternately, you can look at the descriptions of comedies and tragedies and describe how the plays fall in those genres. In addition, other earlier types of works are used in the plays, so you can examine how morality plays or fairy tales may have influenced or been included in the romances. Form would involve primarily looking at the structure of the play, its component parts and overall presentation. However, you might also examine possible limitations of the form and how Shakespeare overcame these.

Sample Topics:

1. **Comic and tragic elements:** The romances have also been called tragicomedies. Examine how Shakespeare employs the different conventions associated with tragedy and comedy in the plays.

   John Fletcher described a specific genre of dramatic writing, which he helped develop, as tragic-comedy, because the works blended elements of both. The romances resemble comedy in that romantic escapades take place and the plays end happily, while they bear elements of tragedy in that they are darker and more serious in plot, tone, and themes. Though different romances emphasize different aspects of tragedy and comedy, all of them relate to both genres. Look at the differences between the two genres and see how these are manifested and exploited in the romances. *The Tempest, Troilus and Cressida,* and *The Winter's Tale* are excellent for examining the comic and tragic elements of Shakespeare's romances.

2. **Romance:** To what extent do the later plays match various definitions of the romance?

   While tragedy often deals with revenge, and several of the plays touch on that aspect of the tragic, romance is more often involved with forgiveness. *The Tempest, Measure for Measure,* and *The Winter's Tale* clearly deal with the triumph of forgiveness over revenge. Looking at these plays, who could have taken revenge? How? What did they choose to do instead? Why? Did this decision result in a positive outcome for them?

Northrop Frye's definition of romance places the hero/ heroine in a series of adventures and pits her/him against an adversary. *Pericles, Prince of Tyre* is most clearly a romance by this definition, but so is *All's Well That Ends Well*. Compare the lead character's adventures and adversaries in these two plays. How does Shakespeare use the quest trope and the rivalry of the main character and an adversary in these plays?

Barbara Fuchs suggests that "romance associates female figures in particular with both treacherousness" and sexual intrigue (16). Clearly, *Cymbeline* fits the first definition, as do the suspicions Leontes harbors about Hermione in *The Winter's Tale*. In *The Tempest*, Shakespeare deflects the treacherousness onto Sycorax, Caliban's absent mother, while warning Ferdinand against involving Miranda in any sexual activity. In *Measure for Measure*, the expectations are turned upside down as Isabella can be seen as personifying honor, while Angelo is involved in treachery, though he attempts to blame Isabella for his reaction to her. *Pericles, Prince of Tyre* assigns different roles to different women in the play, since the princess of Antioch is involved in an incestuous relationship with her father and Dionyza resorts to murder to eliminate her daughter's competition. Which of the other romances lend themselves to a discussion of this description of the genre?

Symbols, Imagery, and Language

Ralph Waldo Emerson wrote, "Put the argument into a concrete shape, into an image, round and solid as a ball, which they can see and handle and carry home with them, and the cause is half won" (267). While it was written long after Shakespeare's time, the quote offers an approach to exploring Shakespeare's use of symbol and imagery; discuss them in terms of the argument each makes. What argument would be advanced by the symbols and imagery Shakespeare used?

Sample Topics:

1. **Storms:** Shakespeare employs storms frequently in his plays. What was their purpose? What did they signify?

As you make note of the presence of storms in the plays, you might begin to see a pattern to them. If you do not see one immediately, a closer examination might be in order. Consider the title of *The Tempest*. Why did Shakespeare choose it as the name of his work? How is the play about a literal storm? How is it about an allegorical storm? In *The Winter's Tale*, a storm claims the life of which character? Why did Shakespeare choose a storm as the instrument of death, and what does it signify? Storms are also a major feature of *Pericles, Prince of Tyre*. A storm brings Pericles to Pentapolis, deprives Thaisa of her life, and marks the beginning of Marina's life. Marina says that life is like a storm, "Whirring me from my friends" (4.1.1556). What do all the storms have in common? What argument might Shakespeare be intending by their use?

2. **Sea:** What is the symbolic import of the many references to the sea? What argument might Shakespeare be fashioning by using bodies of water in such a manner?

The sea is a major element in several of the romances: *The Tempest, The Winter's Tale, Pericles,* and *Cymbeline*. In *Cymbeline*, the sea is discussed in terms of its defense of England against the conquerors. Yet that same sea brings demands for tribute. What is the intention of this juxtaposition? *The Tempest* uses the sea as a vehicle for exile and for reconciliation. Again, we have a symbol of both creation and destruction. In *The Winter's Tale*, the sea carries Perdita away, avenges her abandonment, and brings her home again. How much does the sea add to the play? In *Pericles*, the title character sails from place to place searching for a wife and later for an escape from or a balm to his grief. What does he find in his sea journeys? What is the point of the sea in the plays? Are the sea and storms inexorably linked in Shakespeare? What is the meaning of that?

3. **Metaphors:** Shakespeare's romances are full of metaphors, which add to the depth and resonance of the play's language

and themes. Examine some of the metaphors to see what arguments Shakespeare makes through their judicious placement.

In *Pericles,* Shakespeare portrays "life as a journey" through the various voyages and trips the title character undertakes. How are the various sea journeys equivalent to new stages in the life of Pericles? In the first scene of the play, Pericles states, "Kings are earth's gods" (1.1.152). How does Shakespeare show the accuracy of that metaphor throughout the play? In *Troilus and Cressida,* the language of food is employed as a metaphor for consumption in general. What does it mean when Troilus says, "Sweet love is food for fortune's tooth" (4.5.2927)? Is food portrayed as sustenance to be consumed and then excreted after digestion? How does Shakespeare use this metaphor in the discussion? In *The Tempest,* how does Stephano employ the metaphor of the man in the moon to enslave Caliban? Shakespeare incorporates a tree metaphor twice in *Cymbeline;* once it is used by Belarius and once by Posthumus. Examining these or other metaphors, what argument might Shakespeare be making with them?

Compare and Contrast Essays

Remember to do more in your compare and contrast essays than simply point out the ways in which your plays are different or similar. Part of the essay is to frame and explain the significance of the comparisons and contrasts, using your notes to turn reflections and glimmers of thought into an illuminating analysis. If you begin with a point of comparison, it may be easier to explain its resonance and ramifications. For example, if you decide to compare *Troilus and Cressida* to *The Tempest* because they each partially hinge on the interactions of brothers, then your analysis will allow you to make conclusions about Shakespeare's portrayal of sibling relationships.

Sample Topics:

1. **Elements present throughout various Shakespeare works:** Using several of Shakespeare's romances, compare and contrast a single aspect, such as a theme or a character type.

Begin by choosing two or more plays that seem to have important similarities. If you want to look at sibling relationships, you might examine *Troilus and Cressida* and *The Tempest*. Both of these works offer the interactions of brothers. If you want to expand your essay to look at brother-sister relationships, you can add *Measure for Measure* and compare Cassandra and Hector's relationship in *The Tempest* to Isabella and Claudio's relationship. Troilus, Hector, and Paris seem to have good relationships. The impetus for ousting Prospero from his position was to give it to his brother. How is their relationship described in the play? How does that relationship impair the interplay of Alonso and Sebastian? Both Cassandra and Isabella love their brothers and attempt to help them. Why are their attempts unsuccessful? What are their brothers' reactions? What do the reactions say about their relationships? How does Shakespeare present sibling relationships in the romances? Other examples are marriage relationships, father-daughter relationships, and the roles of sex and chastity.

2. **Compare Shakespeare's work to that of another author:** Choose another author of the same time period, preferably also a playwright, and compare and contrast the playwright's romances or tragicomedies to Shakespeare's.

A good author to choose would be John Fletcher, since he created the tragicomedy and during the period after Shakespeare's death had a reputation rivaling the Bard's. He is also the most likely co-author of *The Two Noble Kinsmen*. Thus, two works that could be fruitfully compared might be *The Night Walker* by Fletcher and *Measure for Measure*. Both include a broken marriage contract, multiple deceptions, a supposed death, and a reconciliation between the originally betrothed couple at the end. *Measure for Measure* deals with the highest social class, while *The Night Walker* offers the same topic in a lower social order. Comparisons and contrasts between who begins the deceptions, how the rejected fiancées react, and the level of reconciliation at the end are all strong subjects for discussion. How does Wildbrain compare with the false friar? Which character, Lurcher or Lucio, increases the inequity of the judges? Is Snap the equivalent of Isabella? How do Maria and Mariana differ? Both works are romances. Are they about reconciliation? Do they deal with serious subjects in serious language?

Bibliography and Online Resources

Bentley, Gerald Eades. *Shakespeare: A Biographical Handbook.* Westport, Conn.: Greenwood Press, 1986. Print.

Bulfinch, Thomas. *Mythology: The Age of Fable or Stories of Gods and Heroes.* 1855. Web. 21 July 2009.

Chambers, E. K. *William Shakespeare: A Study of Facts and Problems.* London: Oxford UP, 1930. Print.

Chaucer, Geoffrey. *Troilus and Cressida: A Modernized Version.* Trans. A. S. Kline. 22 June 2001. <http://www.poetryintranslation.com/PITBR/English/Chaucerhome.htm>. Web. 21 July 2009.

Emerson, Ralph Waldo. "Eloquence." *The Works of Ralph Waldo Emerson, Vol. 3.* Ed. Chester Noyes Greenough. 1914. Web. 9 August 2009.

Frye, Northrop. *Anatomy of Criticism.* Princeton, NJ: Princeton UP, 1957. Print.

Fuchs, Barbara. *Romance.* New York: Routledge, 2004. Print.

Hamilton, Edith. *Mythology.* New York: Back Bay Books, 1998. Print.

Homer. *The Iliad.* Trans. Samuel Butler. 1898. *The Literature Network.* 2009. Web. 21 July 2009.

Ibeji, Mike. *An Overview of Roman Britain. BBC.* 2001. Web. 21 July 2009.

Kahn, Coppelia. *Roman Shakespeare: Warriors, Wounds, and Women.* New York: Routledge, 1997. Print.

Lomio, Paul. "The Trojan War." *History of the Trojan War.* <http://www.stanford.edu/~plomio/history.html>. Web. 21 July 2009.

Mallin, Eric S. "Emulous Factions and the Collapse of Chivalry: *Troilus and Cressida." Representations* 29 (Winter 1990): 145–179. *JSTOR.* Web. 21 July 2009.

Ovid. *Metamorphoses.* Trans. Samuel Garth, John Dryden. *Internet Classics Archive.* 2009. Web. 21 July 2009.

Schoenbaum, S. *William Shakespeare: A Compact Documentary Life.* New York: Oxford UP, 1987. Print.

Schwartz, Debora B. "Shakespeare's Four Final Plays: The Romances." *English 204/339*. 2005. Web. 21 July 2009.

Shakespeare, William. *Open Source Shakespeare.* Ed. Eric M. Johnson. George Mason U, 2003. Web. 1 July 2009.

Wheeler, L. Kip. "Some Distinctions Between Classical Tragedy and Comedy." *Carson-Newman College: Dr. Wheeler's Website.* 2008. Web. 21 July 2009.

TROILUS AND CRESSIDA

READING TO WRITE

*T*ROILUS *AND* Cressida (1601–03) tells the story of a small part of the Trojan War. The conflict was set in motion when Helen, the wife of the Greek king Menelaus, went to Troy with Paris, son of the Trojan king, Priam. There is some argument about whether Helen went willingly or not. The Greeks, nonetheless, felt their honor was impugned and banded together against Troy. The story told in *Troilus and Cressida* reflects the culmination of the soldiers' experiences and presents the refusal of Achilles to fight and the ultimate reason for his battle, as it is told in *The Iliad.* Because of its subject matter and the way it was described and identified when initially published, the play is often regarded as a history. However, while it is based on the story of the war, there are significant additions to the work, including the love story of Troilus and Cressida, which was not included in the original versions of the Trojan War's history but was added during the medieval era. Chaucer's *Troilus and Criseyde* is the best-known source of the various ones Shakespeare most likely consulted. Since Shakespeare wrote of many different love stories in his plays and his is an English version of stories associated with the Trojan War, the relationship of Troilus and Cressida is a good venue for examining the play.

In approaching the work, it will be helpful to reread the sections at the beginning in which the partners speak of and to one another. Troilus talks to Cressida's uncle Pandarus about his impatience in winning Cressida and says, "And when fair Cressid comes into my thoughts,—/ So, traitor!

'When she comes!' When is she thence?" (1.1.61–62). He is obsessed with her. He even admits to being irrational in his feelings: "I tell thee I am mad / In Cressid's love" (1.1.81–82). Are there any other indications that Troilus is irrational in his response to Cressida? Or is his response simply the euphoria of newfound fascination? Look through his discussions with Pandarus and Cressida. One to examine is his conversation with Pandarus about Cressida just before Troilus and Cressida meet to talk:

> Pandarus: Have you seen my cousin?
> Troilus: No, Pandarus: I stalk about her door,
> Like a strange soul upon the Stygian banks
> Staying for waftage. O, be thou my Charon,
> And give me swift transportance to those fields
> Where I may wallow in the lily-beds
> Proposed for the deserver! O gentle Pandarus,
> From Cupid's shoulder pluck his painted wings
> And fly with me to Cressid!
> Pandarus: Walk here i' the orchard, I'll bring her straight.
> *[Exit]*
> Troilus: I am giddy; expectation whirls me round.
> The imaginary relish is so sweet
> That it enchants my sense: what will it be,
> When that the watery palate tastes indeed
> Love's thrice repured nectar? death, I fear me,
> Swooning destruction, or some joy too fine,
> Too subtle-potent, tuned too sharp in sweetness,
> For the capacity of my ruder powers:
> I fear it much; and I do fear besides,
> That I shall lose distinction in my joys;
> As doth a battle, when they charge on heaps
> The enemy flying. (3.2.1656–78)

How does Troilus describe his attraction to Cressida? How does he speak about it? Is it a powerful thing? Is it rational? Is it frightening? What is Shakespeare saying about the relationship of Troilus and Cressida with this description of Troilus's feelings? Is he supportive of their relationship, or does he think it is problematic? How can you tell?

For a better understanding, examine Troilus and Cressida's relationship-related discussions, especially when they are talking to or about each other. Do those comments and conversations add anything to your understanding of the conversation? Shakespeare developed the relationship in the play by integrating these additional discussions.

TOPICS AND STRATEGIES

Suggested topics are included here to help you determine how you might approach writing about *Troilus and Cressida*. The suggestions certainly do not form a complete list of all possible topics. You might well come up with a topic that is of more interest to you and therefore better for you to pursue after looking at some of the examples. If, however, you decide to use one of the suggestions, refer to the questions primarily in the early stages of writing your paper, as you are brainstorming, generating ideas, and planning. They are insufficient on their own to form a complete essay. You will still need to develop additional questions of your own about the topic and look at additional passages in the text that inform your topic. Each will help you determine your own thesis and support it with reasonable evidence from the play. Remember that developing a strong essay requires that you have a thesis statement, show support from the play, and argue for your claim persuasively.

Themes

Romantic love, homosexual relations, and the conflict between personal and governmental issues are important in the play, and each of them offers a viable avenue for approaching *Troilus and Cressida.* You do not want to simply show that the text deals with the topic you chose. Instead, you need to make an argument about what the play has to say about that particular aspect you are examining. You might, for example, argue that the play suggests that romantic love causes problems, as it does for Troilus and Cressida, Helen and Paris, and Hector and Andromache. Or you might argue that it is not true love that is the problem in the play but the fact that people misunderstand what love actually is. In that case, you might look at Troilus and Cressida's speeches and actions to show that their relationship is based on lust. Then you would want to look at the other romances shown in the play, noting similar situations or dynamics in those relationships. Whatever you choose as your argument, you need to make sure you support it with textual evidence from the play.

Sample Topics:

1. **Romantic love:** The play takes its title from the main romantic characters, the Trojan prince Troilus and Cressida, the daughter of a Trojan priest. This immediately emphasizes the romance in the play.

   Read through and take notes on each of the romantic relationships in the play. How would you describe them? Look particularly at the romance of the title characters. What brings them together? What is it that keeps them from being a couple? How are their actions indicative of the level of their commitment to each other? Though the title characters are the work's main presentation of romantic love, they are not the only couple included in the play. The relationship of Helen and Paris was the impetus behind the entire Trojan War. Many other relationships are shown, discussed, or hinted at. Whose romantic histories are hinted at in the play?

   Are there any positive examples of romantic love in the play? According to the play, what might a good romantic relationship look like? Is such a thing possible? What kind of situation would create a positive and stable relationship?

2. **Homosexuality:** Shakespeare clearly shows that Patroclus and Achilles are in a sexual relationship. Though they are also emotionally involved with women, they are also involved with each other.

   Examine the descriptions of the relationship of Patroclus and Achilles. Look at what various people say about Achilles and how Theristes describes Patroclus. What is Shakespeare saying here? Does he decry homosexuality? Is it presented as a problem for the other characters in the play? Is it accepted? Is it sanctioned? How is it viewed? How does Shakespeare present it? Does the relationship happen between two outcasts? Is it a problem for the two characters involved?

To some extent, the play relies on the audience's understanding that physical relationships between older and younger men were acceptable in ancient Greece. The sexual relationship had to be made explicit to the audience, because men during Shakespeare's time were typically closer, emotionally and physically, than is common today. The audience might not have realized Shakespeare was presenting a sexual relationship between the two men, as opposed to a close platonic friendship, if it were not spelled out. How does this affect the presentation of homosexuality in the play? Is it acceptable? Is it shown as normal? Who talks about it? How do they speak of it?

3. **Personal versus governmental interests:** Shakespeare presents conflicting levels of interest in the play. For example, Helen is sought by Menelaus and the Greeks for different reasons. Menelaus has a personal stake; his wife has been taken from him. The Greeks want her returned for governmental reasons; their honor has been compromised and must be reestablished.

How does *Troilus and Cressida* present conflicts between personal and governmental interests? Who are involved in these conflicts? While the entire war is predicated on these differing and sometimes opposing interests, many characters are affected by these different concerns. They include Troilus and Cressida, Achilles, Hector and Andromache, and Helen and Paris. Look at an example of Paris discussing his differing interests and how they played out; one example is 2.2.1126–39. What does Paris say was his primary motive? Was it in conflict with governmental interests? If it was, what would he do? Since the two interests are not in conflict, how is the situation Paris is in significantly different from that of other people in the play?

Do personal or governmental interests prevail among the Greeks? Among the Trojans? Do personal interests succeed for some characters while the government triumphs over other individuals' desires? What does this say about the people? About their importance? Who is more important in the various conflicts? How can you tell? Since Cressida has been abandoned to the Greeks by the government, she seeks personal protection. How is this different from Helen's relationship with Paris? Why is this seen as betrayal by Troilus? How did Shakespeare intend the audience to view the situation?

Character

Troilus and Cressida has a large cast of characters to choose from as you prepare to write your essay on the play. A paper focusing on Troilus, Cressida, Achilles, Theristes, Ulysses, or any one of the other central characters could easily be written. If you decide to write a character analysis for your essay, you will want to examine all you know about the personage you choose. Pay attention to her or his behavior, speech, and relationships. You should not only note these aspects but also be aware of what other characters say about your chosen character. For example, if you are looking at Cressida, how important is Ulysses's opinion of her? What does her uncle say of her? How does that reflect on Cressida and on her uncle? How does her father's demand for her exchange indicate her inherent value? How does the Greeks' agreement to trade a trusted counselor for her indicate Cressida's value? Remember to use these questions as you develop and strengthen your argument.

Sample Topics:

1. **Troilus:** Troilus is a title character of the play, a Trojan prince, and the husband of Cressida. What is Troilus doing when he is first introduced in the play? With whom is he speaking? About whom is he speaking? What does he say? What personality traits does he display in the conversation? Is he patient or impatient? Is he articulate? Is he aggressive? Is he sympathetic? Do you like Troilus having only read his first conversation with Pandarus? What did you notice about him? Why did you respond to his character the way you did? What was it in the scene that made you like or dislike him?

   Read through the sections detailing the relationship of Troilus and Cressida. How does that romantic interest develop in the play? What does it tell you about Troilus's character? How does it end up? What does that tell you about Troilus?

Troilus is a prince of Troy. How is this position developed in the play? Is he respected? Are his opinions solicited or followed? What do his opinions show about his character? What do his arguments show about him? Does he develop the arguments well? If you have studied logical fallacies before, you might look to see if any of these creep into his arguments about policy.

When Cressida is going to be turned over to the Greeks in return for a Trojan counselor, how does Troilus react? Does he attempt to stop this? Why or why not? What does it tell us about him? What is his priority in his response? How does that impact your understanding of his character?

2. **Achilles:** Achilles is a Greek prince and their greatest warrior, but he is not fully engaged in this war due to conflicts of interest. The first mention of Achilles is by Cressida. She says, "There is among the Greeks Achilles, a better man than Troilus" (1.2.397). How is Achilles a better man than Troilus? Is this a true statement, or is it more a reflection on Cressida and her nature than on the relative goodness of Troilus and Achilles? How do you know?

In the Greek camp, Ulysses goes into a rant about Achilles before the audience even meets Achilles. Read this passage (1.3.595ff), and look at how Achilles is described. Is Ulysses a reliable narrator? Should you trust what he says? Is Ulysses's description an accurate one? Ulysses manipulates the situation in the Greek camp to get Achilles to do what he wants; how does his ability to do this impact your understanding of Achilles?

How is Achilles as a character introduced? What is he doing and saying when the audience first sees him onstage? What does this introduction tell us about Achilles? Is he a smart man? Patient? Aggressive? Annoying? Read through the first scene in which he appears and determine how Shakespeare was introducing him (2.1).

Achilles has two romantic interests in the play: Patroclus and a Trojan woman. What does this tell you about Achilles? What do his reactions to the two reveal about his character? How does he treat them? Are they important to him?

Achilles eventually goes to war. What is his impetus? Are his actions in the death of Hector just? Are they honorable? Are they the actions of a champion of Greece? Do they show the Greeks in a positive or negative light? Is Achilles truthful in his account? How do others react to his slaying Hector? Do they think that he has fulfilled his position as Greek champion?

3. **Hector:** Hector is a Trojan prince, the Trojan champion, and the husband of Andromache. He is first mentioned by Troilus in the same breath as Priam (1.1.67). Troilus seems to feel that Hector is in charge of his life. Why would Hector have such power? What does this say about him?

Alexander speaks of Hector next, saying that he "chid Andromache and struck his armourer" (1.2.160). What does this description tell us about Hector? Does Shakespeare intend for us to like him? To respect him?

Hector is a deciding voice in the Trojan councils. During their meetings, what does he say? With whom does he agree? With whom does he disagree? Does he change his mind? Is he rational or irrational in these decisions?

As the Trojan champion, it is Hector's responsibility to end the war with the Greeks without further bloodshed. How does his fight with Ajax help or hurt his position? Why does he not kill Ajax? Is mercy typical of Hector? In what other ways does he display mercy? Look closely at his conversations with Troilus. Is Hector honorable in his fights? Are others equally honorable? What does this say about Hector?

Hector disregards his wife Andromache's warning. He rejects her words and sends her inside. What do their interactions tell us about Hector? Does he respect his wife? Does he disagree with her? Are his final words ones you would want to exchange with your spouse right before you died? What does his attitude reveal about the role of women in his life?

History and Context

Troilus and Cressida takes place during the Trojan War. Being familiar with the war, its great heroes, and its conclusion would help you better understand the play. Knowledge of the Trojan War can also offer you strong ideas for essay topics. Much of what we know about the Trojan War comes from Greek and Roman poets, especially Homer's *The Iliad* and Ovid's *Metamorphoses.*

Sample Topics:

1. **The Trojan War background and story:** The Trojan War began as a result of various difficulties. Look through an online discussion of the Trojan War, such as Paul Lomio's. How are these difficulties expressed or dramatized in Shakespeare's *Troilus and Cressida*? How does Shakespeare present the Trojan War? Does he favor one side over the other? The history of the Trojan War was written by the Greeks, which would likely result in a bias in their representation and characterization of the conflict. Is this bias evident in Shakespeare?

   How does Shakespeare present both sides of the conflict? Does he give voice to speakers from both the Greeks and the Trojans? Are they given about the same amount of time and credibility? Are the champions of both sides equally flawed? Do they have fatal flaws, as is expected in tragedies? If so, what are these flaws? How does Shakespeare introduce them? If not, why would Shakespeare leave these out?

2. **Differences between *The Iliad, Metamorphoses,* and the history in *Troilus and Cressida:*** The story of Troilus and Cressida is a medieval addition to the Trojan tale, probably coming from Chaucer. Read or search through the poems, and look for other differences between Shakespeare's play and the original poem.

   Peter Levi suggested that Shakespeare produced *Troilus and Cressida* in response to an audience request for a play about the Trojan War (234). Looking at what the audience would have known about the war, from other sources, might open up an interesting perspective on Shakespeare's presentations.

The play presents the major heroes of the epic as dullards. Look at Shakespeare's descriptions of Achilles, Agamemnon, and Ajax, for example. This characterization of the soldiers and warriors is more in line with Ovid's presentation than Homer's. What is this negative depiction supposed to add to the story? Does it make the play more comedic? If so, how? Does it reduce the distance between the audience and the characters, in portraying the characters as more human and flawed? If so, how? What other impacts might the unflattering portraits have?

How does the addition of the story of Troilus and Cressida impact the play? Is it a foil to the Helen-Paris story? If so, how? If not, why not? Does the lovers' situation offer a commentary on the war? Do the two characters offer a commentary on the war itself? Are they symbols?

3. **Sexual mores during the Greek period:** Male citizens of Greece could have multiple sexual partners and pursue many different relationships. Men were expected to marry, and their wives were supposed to be chaste, as they were expected to bear the next generation of Greeks. However, the men also permitted themselves multiple sexual partners and extramarital relationships. It was generally accepted that older men might have a younger male partner; since men had far more power than women, these relationships were usually more equitable. In addition, sex could be had with others, both slave and free, for a price. Because of this, an individual's sexual relationships were often complex.

How are sexual relationships presented in the play? Whose sex life is referenced or represented the most onstage? What other characters' relationships are also emphasized in the play? How do the various sexual connections reveal aspects of Shakespeare's understanding of both Trojan history and Greek sexual mores? Are there any indications that some relationships were less acceptable to Shakespeare's audience than others? What are the indications? Does Shakespeare present the relationships in an evenhanded way, or are some relationships privileged over others? How is that privileging shown?

4. **England's military history:** According to Eric S. Mallin, at the end of the sixteenth and beginning of the seventeenth centuries, England was constantly in fear of invasion from both the Irish and the Spanish, which fostered a preoccupation with war (145). How does this knowledge potentially transform your reading of *Troilus and Cressida*?

If Troy is representative of England in the play, as it often was in earlier British literature, how might the play be read differently? Since the audience would already be aware of Troy's eventual fall, why would Shakespeare choose to present their lives before the fall? What warnings are included in the play that might be intended for England and English viewers to heed instead? How does, for example, Hector's nobility lead to his downfall? What course should he have adopted instead? How might the fight between Ajax and Hector, since they are cousins, be related to England and one of its warring partners? What other instances of this potential duality are included in the play?

If the English are represented by the Greeks, with their various members of royalty and competing groups of soldiers, what does this say about England? Does the presentation of the Greeks mimic the typical factionalism of a royal court? Could it be extrapolated to refer to England? Are there any hints in the play that lead to this reading? How would your answer be changed if you knew that, around the time the play was composed, the Earl of Essex was often referred to as Achilles, in reference to the Greek hero (Mallin 150)? You might want to read up on the Earl of Essex, during Elizabeth I's reign, and see if there are any parallels between him and Shakespeare's presentation of Achilles.

Philosophy and Ideas

If you choose to write on philosophy and ideas, you are writing about the philosophical or ideological positioning of *Troilus and Cressida*. For the play, you might focus on questions of value, the place and use of women, or the concept of honor. In any case, your essay should focus on and discuss the play's relationship to the philosophical framework you decide to analyze. In the case of value, for example, you might want to determine whether the play presents a single view of value or a multiplicity of views in regard to value. If you note a variety of viewpoints on value, which one is favored by Shakespeare based on the textual evidence in the play? You might decide, for example, that Shakespeare felt that multiple ways of determining value existed but that the subjective view of value was the most important. In that case, your essay would investigate the different discussions of value and then show how the subjective view was reserved for the strongest arguments in the play.

Sample Topics:

1. **Value:** What does *Troilus and Cressida* present as valuable? How does it show conflicts of value? Gayle Greene wrote:

> Various ideas of value are expressed and debated in the play, but it is the relativistic assumptions stated by Troilus in the Trojan council scene . . . and elaborated in the exchange between Ulysses and Achilles . . . that motivate character and action. The value of a person, object, or event is subjective and relative to will and "opinion"—conferred by the "prizer," rather than inherent in the "prize." (272)

Greene asserts that during this period there was a "crisis of values" (272), which could account for the various views portrayed in the play. Locate and analyze passages that comment on values, such as the exchanges Greene mentioned. First, look at the debate between Troilus and Hector (2.2.1045–53) and then look at the statement on honor that Achilles gives (3.3.1946–59).

How does Shakespeare present the different views of value in the play? Who represents each view? Does he give greater weight to one? How does he do so? What does this mean? Is a central character supporting one argument over the other? Is a more likeable character supporting one? What arguments are most persuasively supported in the play and how?

2. **Status of women:** Cressida, Helen, Andromache, and Cassandra are the female characters in the play. Female characters make up less than 14 percent of the cast. What is the play's view of these various women?

Cressida is the daughter of Calchas, the niece of Pandarus, and the wife of Troilus. As such, she is an expendable aspect of the Greek-Trojan conflict. Her status as the wife of a Trojan prince is trumped by Antenor's place as counselor. She is given no choice in being traded to the Greeks. What does this say about the status of Cressida in the play? Does it reflect the status of women in the play overall? If she has been cast out from Troy, why should she not attempt to gain status among the Greeks? How could she do this? What is the response to her doing this?

Helen was the wife of Menelaus originally but was stolen from the Greeks and married to Paris. She had no say in her situation either. At one point, the men argue over whether she should be returned to end the war, just as they debate her relative value. What is her value? How is it determined and by whom? While she is described as beautiful, is this a benefit to her or a liability? Does she have any ability to make decisions in the play? What do other people say about Helen? Which of these are positive? Which negative? Which description do you think most closely reflected Shakespeare's opinion?

Andromache is Hector's wife. As such, she is a princess of Troy. Her husband is their greatest warrior. Look at how Hector treats her. Analyze what he says to her and about her. Is this the proper reaction to someone of high status? What do his statements indicate about Andromache's status? Is she listened to? By whom? When? Why or why not?

Cassandra is Hector's sister. She comes to warn him of his impending doom. He does not believe her because, though she can tell the future, she was cursed by Apollo for not loving him and permanently discredited as a result. Does Cassandra have any status in the family? In the city? Look at what people say about her. Is there anything positive about their commentary? Her royalty counts for less than nothing. Why? What does this say about the status of women in the play?

Form and Genre

Troilus and Cressida has been described as a tragedy. It has also been called a "dark comedy." Joyce Carol Oates agrees with the former, while virulently rejecting the latter, despite the unconventional approach Shakespeare takes in the work: "*Troilus and Cressida* is a tragedy that calls into question the very pretensions of tragedy itself." In its first publication in 1609, the play is identified as a history, but in its 1623 publication, the play was inserted between the histories and the tragedies. In this volume it is categorized as a romance, since it engages and reflects both early and modern definitions of romance. The fact that the play can be associated with multiple genres indicates that its ambiguous or difficult-to-classify nature would be a productive line of inquiry that could be developed into an excellent paper.

Sample Topics:

1. **Tragedy:** Some have defined the play as a tragedy. Look up several discussions of tragedy and note what elements *Troilus and Cressida* has in common with tragedy. In what ways does it match the definitions? In what ways does it diverge from or resist such a characterization? The emotions most commonly associated with tragedy are fear and pity. Examine the title characters of the play for these associated emotions. Usually tragedies end with death. Who dies in the play? How much of the play is taken up with their stories?

   Usually a tragedy has a balance of good and evil. Is this evident in *Troilus and Cressida*? Who are the good characters? Who are the evil ones? Can the characters be divided evenly between these two poles? Does it seem like good and evil are contending in the play, or is one mode clearly dominant or ascendant? While a play can have tragic elements and still not be a tragedy, if the majority of the play focuses on the tragedy, it is usually considered one. Would you define *Troilus and Cressida* as a tragedy? Why or why not?

2. **Comedy:** The play has also been identified as a comedy. What makes it comedic? The characters can be comedic. Who in the play is comic? Is Theristes a major figure in the play? How does Pandarus potentially transform the play into a comedy? Are these characters the important ones? Are they an integral part of the stories? Are they reconciled to society at the end of the play?

Sometimes in comedy, the theme of life, enjoying life and living it well, is central. Comedies often emphasize the triumph of good times over bad. In the play, do you see this happening? When does it occur? Does it happen throughout the play or only in isolated parts? At the end, does the play present itself as a celebration of life?

Comedies commonly have little or no motivation underlying the actions presented. The characters are involved in coincidental affairs that rarely require or show thought, being almost entirely arrived at through impulsivity. Does the play match this perspective of comedy?

3. **History:** The play was originally classified as a history, as it is set during the Trojan War. Can such an interpretation of the play be sustained?

Look at which parts of the play are history related. These would include the sections on fighting and on the different camps. Then look at those parts that are not reflective of the historical backdrop. These are primarily the romantic and domestic scenes. Which aspect is treated the fullest or at greatest length? Which section is more integral to the play? How does

Shakespeare indicate the importance of the historical aspect of the play? Were the characters mostly considered to be historical? Is this play an example of creative nonfiction? How does this history impact the audience? Are there any explanations of the historical aspects of the play for those who are not aware of the history? Why or why not?

4. **Romance:** The play is classified as a romance as well. In what ways does *Troilus and Cressida* match the definition of a romance?

Do the title characters contribute to a modern romantic reading of the play? How important is this understanding of romance to the play? In addition, the play is clearly set in a foreign locale. How important is this locale to the play? Is it an incidental addition, intended to create a romance, or is it integral to the play? Why is that relevant? Romance also emphasizes reconciliation and restoration. Who is reconciled in the play? How are they reconciled? To what or whom are they reconciled? Who undergoes a form of restoration in the play? How are they restored? To what are they restored? Romance usually includes a muted form of happiness, presenting joy mixed with sorrow. How does joy factor in the play? What about sorrow? Which dominates? Which is emphasized? How are the two parts of joy and sorrow emphasized? For example, the title might indicate a joyous coupling, but if the audience members already knew the history of Troilus and Cressida, they might expect instead a tragedy. Romances can also be unrealistic or fantastical. In what ways is the play unrealistic? Are there any supernatural elements?

Language, Symbols, and Imagery

Language, symbols, and imagery are foundational elements of literature. As you might expect, a strong analysis of these elements can lead to compelling discoveries about a text. These revelations can eventually become part of the argument of your essay. Looking at the play's title, its chivalric language, or its food imagery might be strong starting

points for your examination. While the analysis ought to be compre-
hensive, you may not use all of it when you draft the final essay. That is
to be expected. It is far better to find out you have too much material to
cover than too little. Having more analysis than you can use also makes
it more likely that your paper will be stronger because you can leave out
the weaker arguments. Use your analyses to create an interpretation
that will be the focus of your essay. Then you can select the best supporting material for that interpretation from your notes and use that
material to write the essay.

Sample Topics:

1. **The title:** What kind of commentary is the play making with its
   title?

   Troilus and Cressida were medieval additions to Greek history.
   How does that fact influence an understanding of the title and
   the expectations it potentially sets up? Why is this important?
   How does this factor help explain the structure of the play?
   Many people argue that the play is problematic because it has
   two different story lines that are not satisfactorily resolved.
   Is the title sufficient explanation for the problematic presentation of the play? Knowing that the love story is a medieval
   addition, would you be surprised to find that there is chivalric
   language in the play?

2. **Chivalric language:** Discuss the chivalric aspects of the play.
   Where are some medieval elements contained in the play?
   Reread the speech in which Aeneas is delivering Hector's challenge. How is this similar to how knights behaved in tourna-
   ments? In what ways is the speech similar to courtly love
   language?

   How do the Trojan princes show knightly aspects? How do
   they speak of honor? Courage? Their determination to stay the
   course? How is the medieval ideal evidenced through the Trojans? Through their language? Their actions? Is there any indication of the glorification of war in the play? Who is glorifying

it? The glorification of war is a possible reading of knighthood, since the primary function of knights was to fight. Passages glorifying battles and battle strength would also be part of the chivalric language. Look particularly at descriptions of Hector and Achilles for this.

3. **Food imagery:** Shakespeare introduces food imagery immediately in the play.

Clearly in the context of the play, the cake metaphor (1.1) stands for sexual relations and for marriage. Cake is traditionally associated with weddings and is often the main focus of wedding receptions. What does the metaphor of cake making say about relationships? How can the verbs mentioned apply to sex and marriage? What other associations does cake making have? For this, think of leavening. What does it do?

"Sweet love is food for fortune's tooth," Troilus says (4.5.2927). What does this quotation say about love? Will it be consumed? Why? How is this shown in the play? Appetite represented as a wolf, eating eggs and meat, one's pride being eaten up, wit in the belly, and overeaten faith are also referenced in the play. Look at how the language of food is used as a metaphor in the play. Does the appropriation of this imagery by Shakespeare say something about consumption? Is the point of the food metaphors to make the discussions more accessible to the average member of the audience?

In addition, eating together plays a part in the play. Look at which characters eat together, who is expected at meals, and how absences are treated. Why are meals important? What do communal meals say about a group? Why is eating together a symbol for agreement? How is that shown in the play?

4. **Speech and style language:** T. McAlindon states that "*Troilus and Cressida* contains a high proportion of words referring to speech and style. Yet most of these go unnoticed" (30). What role do these aspects play in the work?

Look at how Ajax is described, by Ulysses and by Theristes. How do these descriptions relate to speaking ability and style of language? What do they tell us about Ajax, and how do they develop the idea that eloquence is important?

Vows are often important, in both love and war. They are clearly emphasized in the play, as *oath* is used four times, a form of *swear* nine times, and *word* thirty-six times. Read through these uses and look for the point behind them. Who is swearing and giving oaths? To whom? Are these kept? Who is giving his word or speaking? Who is doing so wisely? Who is speaking foolishly? What is the impact of the discussion of words? How is it subsumed in the story?

Compare and Contrast Essays

Comparing and contrasting two aspects or elements of a work helps you identify features that you might not have noticed otherwise. For *Troilus and Cressida,* for example, you might compare and contrast Hector and Achilles. Determining how they are alike and how they are different might help you see what constitutes a hero in the play. It might also help show how evenly matched the two opposing forces were. You do not have to limit your comparisons to the text, however. You might compare Chaucer's *Troilus and Criseyde* with Shakespeare's version of the tale. Some scholars think the poem is Chaucer's best work, so the way in which Shakespeare adapted and changed the story is particularly interesting and potentially significant. Once you have compared and contrasted the texts or elements you have chosen, you must determine what argument you wish to make about the texts or elements and develop them into an essay.

Sample Topics:

1. **Hector and Achilles:** Comparing the two heroes of the warring factions provides an in-depth look at what a hero is. Examine the descriptions of both characters. Note what others say of them, particularly Ulysses's description of Achilles and Alexander's description of Hector. What do they each say? How are those heroic attributes? How are they heroic values? Do the Greeks and the Trojans differ in regard to their conception of heroism? If so, how? If not, what might be the reason?

How does Pandarus describe Hector, particularly in comparison to Troilus? Was this a legitimate description or the result of his role in the wooing of Cressida? What does Aeneas say of Hector when he announces his challenge? How does this increase your understanding of Hector's character? Troilus scolds Hector for something he has done. What is it, and how does it increase Hector's standing as a hero? Why does it prompt such heroic advancement? Examine other discussions of Hector, as well as his own actions and words. For example, he treats his wife poorly. Is this part of being a hero? Or is heroism isolated from personal relationships?

How does Ulysses describe Achilles? How does he use Achilles's weaknesses against him to manipulate him? Why is Achilles pouting? Why does Achilles agree to fight Hector? Why does he retract his agreement? Why does Achilles eventually attack Hector nonetheless? Does this happen in an honorable duel or even in an honorable way? How does that reflect on Achilles? What does it say about heroes in general?

2. **Achilles and Ajax:** Since Ajax was the Greek's "runner-up" as hero, both his strengths and his weaknesses can reveal much about the view of heroes and heroism supported in the play. Achilles, as the Greek's champion, has other strengths and weaknesses, which can also inform a discussion of heroism.

Return to the questions about Achilles posed in the preceding topic description. Use them to compare Achilles to Ajax. How does Theristes describe Ajax? How does Ulysses describe him? What do these descriptions have in common? What does that say about Ajax? How is Ajax used against Achilles? What about Ajax makes this possible? What happens when Ajax goes out to fight Hector? Who wins? Who stops the fight? How does Ajax react to that? How is Ajax not portrayed as a hero in the play? What does this say about being a hero? Why is this important or relevant to a study of the play?

3. **Troilus and Cressida in Chaucer and Shakespeare:** Chaucer's poem is one of the primary sources for the love story in the play. Looking at differences in the two works may help illuminate

Shakespeare's particular goals for the play. If you wish to limit your additional reading, you could examine only "Book V: The Betrayal" and compare it to Shakespeare's presentation of Cressida's unfaithfulness.

The two presentations of the end of the relationship locate Cressida in the Greek camp. How did she get there? Why was she there? What was Diomedes's motivation? What parts are taken by different people in the two versions? Why would this be necessary? Does Chaucer's version illuminate Shakespeare's or lend it additional resonance? In Chaucer, Cressida wrote Troilus regularly. This is only mentioned in terms of the final letter in Shakespeare. What does Shakespeare's version lose or gain by altering that detail? Continue through the two works looking for how Chaucer's is a more complete telling of the tale and Shakespeare's assumes the reader or audience member has knowledge of Chaucer's rendering. What other indications of this can you find? What do they mean to the modern reader?

Bibliography and Online Resources for *Troilus and Cressida*

Greene, Gayle. "Language and Value in Shakespeare's *Troilus and Cressida*." *Studies in English Literature 1500–1900* 21.2 (Spring 1981): 271–85. Print.

Homer. *The Iliad*. Trans. Samuel Butler. 1898. *The Literature Network*. 2009. Web. 1 May 2009.

Kitteredge, George Lyman. *Chaucer and His Poetry*. Whitefish, MT: Kessinger Publishing, 2004. Print.

Levi, Peter. *The Life and Times of William Shakespeare*. New York: Henry Holt and Co., 1998. Print.

Lomio, Paul. "The Trojan War." *History of the Trojan War*. <http://www.stanford.edu/~plomio/history.html>. Web. 1 May 2009.

Mallin, Eric S. "Emulous Factions and the Collapse of Chivalry: *Troilus and Cressida*." *Representations* 29 (Winter 1990): 145–79. JSTOR. Web. 1 May 2009.

McAlindon, T. "Language, Style, and Meaning in 'Troilus and Cressida.'" *PMLA* 84.1 (January 1969): 29–43. *JSTOR*. Web. 1 May 2009.

Oates, Joyce Carol. "The Tragedy of Existence: Shakespeare's 'Troilus and Cressida.'" *Joyce Carol Oates on Shakespeare.* 1999. < http://www.usfca.edu/fac-staff/southerr/shakespeare.html>. Web. 1 May 2009.

Ovid. *Metamorphoses.* Trans. Samuel Garth, John Dryden. *Internet Classics Archive.* 2009. Web. 1 May 2009.

Rossetti, William M. *Chaucer's Troylus and Criseyde Compared with Boccaccio's Filostrato.* Chaucer Society, 1873. Print.

Rowland, Beryl. "A Cake-Making Image in *Troilus and Cressida.*" *Shakespeare Quarterly* 21.2 (Spring 1970): 191–94. *JSTOR.* Web. 1 May 2009.

Shakespeare, William. *Open Source Shakespeare.* Ed. Eric M. Johnson. George Mason U, 2003. Web. 1 May 2009.

Tate, Eleanor. "*Troilus and Cressida:* A Matter of Form." <http://sunzi1.lib.hku.hk/hkjo/view/34/3400207.pdf>. Web. 1 May 2009.

MEASURE FOR MEASURE

READING TO WRITE

EVEN THOUGH Shakespeare's *Measure for Measure* is one of the most famous of his romances, you might still find yourself unsure about how to choose an essay topic. A close reading of passages in the play can offer a focus for an essay.

Read through the passage in which the duke of Vienna, Vincentio, offers his rationale for the need to enforce the laws of Vienna.

> We have strict statutes and most biting laws.
> The needful bits and curbs to headstrong weeds,
> Which for this nineteen years we have let slip;
> Even like an o'ergrown lion in a cave,
> That goes not out to prey. Now, as fond fathers,
> Having bound up the threatening twigs of birch,
> Only to stick it in their children's sight
> For terror, not to use, in time the rod
> Becomes more mock'd than fear'd; so our decrees,
> Dead to infliction, to themselves are dead;
> And liberty plucks justice by the nose;
> The baby beats the nurse, and quite athwart
> Goes all decorum. (1.3.309–21)

The duke uses various images to discuss the Viennese people. He says the laws are "bits and curbs." What are bits usually used on? What does Vincentio say they are for? How do those two things relate? How are they different? Why is he mixing his metaphor here? Who becomes the overgrown lion in his speech? Why is it important that it does not go out hunting? The next part of the speech refers to the common disciplinary action of making switches from tree branches and spanking children with them. Why would just the sight of the switches be an effective deterrent? Why does the duke say they have quit being effective? What does he say happens as a result? Why would it be considered harmful, as far as the duke is concerned? What does Friar Peter say in response to the duke's comment? How does that negate or influence the audience's response? What is the duke's argument in this passage? How is it shown throughout the play? Is it accurate or inaccurate?

Using this passage as a starting point, you could write an essay about law in the play, about the duke's role, or about the language of the play and the function of imagery and metaphor. A close reading can also generate an entire essay from a single passage. Decide what point you think Shakespeare is trying to make through the presence of the duke and argue that claim with evidence from the play as support. Such a close reading is often a fruitful approach to writing on a literary text, although there are many others as well.

TOPICS AND STRATEGIES

The sample essay topics that follow suggest possible avenues of discovery as you work toward producing a fully fleshed essay. These suggestions might spark your interest or they might help you generate a topic of your own. Looking them over is a good way to start work on your essay, even if you do not eventually choose to write on the suggestions in this chapter. These are suggestions and are not exhaustive. There are plenty of other topics that can be pursued. Use the suggested topic strands as ways to expand on your ideas and better organize them. Not all of the questions need to be answered in order to produce an excellent essay; they may best be viewed as initial prompts in the writing process.

Themes

Measure for Measure explores and presents various themes, including love, responsibility, honor, and the issue of right and wrong. If you decide to write your essay on a particular theme, clearly distinguish what the play is arguing or suggesting about that theme. As an example, if you choose to look at what the play says about love, you might point out that *Measure for Measure* looks at both filial love and romantic love and concludes, ultimately, that romantic love is weak. Shakespeare has Angelo fall in love with Isabella. Angelo only wants her to satisfy his physical desires. Isabella loves her brother Claudio enough to work for his release but not enough to give in to a dishonorable request. She says Claudio would be better off dead, since he will be in heaven. Angelo, for his part, makes it clear that he killed Claudio simply because, if Claudio were left alive after his sister's dishonor, he would kill Angelo. No one else would believe Isabella's story about Angelo, but Claudio would have, indicating that filial love is a strong force in the play.

Alternately, you might choose to look at the fleeting nature of romantic love in the play. Angelo is betrothed to Marina, but when her dowry is lost, he abandons her; his love for her is as lost as her dowry. Angelo is enamored of Isabella, but as soon as he thinks he has taken her virginity, his love turns to scorn. You might argue that in the play Shakespeare is suggesting that love is not a good basis for a marriage and that something else, a strong dowry or a sharp wit, is a better one.

Sample Topics:

1. **Love:** According to the play, how is love defined?

> Various characters in the play represent different views of love. The duke says that he loves his people, yet he leaves them to the ministrations of Angelo. How is this considered loving them? What does the duke mean by saying he loves them? How do his actions support or negate this statement?
>
> Angelo says that he loves Isabella. What does this mean? Pay attention to his words and actions in the second act, particularly scenes 2 and 4. How does Angelo define love? Is his love selfish or selfless? Does it persist once he thinks he has attained what he desired? What does that say about his love?
>
> Isabella asserts that her brother cares for her. What does she expect him to do? How does she expect him to act? Claudio states that if Isabella does as Angelo asks, it will be counted as a virtue of her love for her brother. How is Claudio defining love? After being rebuked by the duke in his aspect as the false

friar, Claudio says he will ask his sister's pardon. Is this a display of love? Why or why not?

Marina loved Angelo and continues to pine for him even after he has falsely rejected her. What kind of love does Marina represent? When she has achieved her goal of sleeping with her betrothed, what more does she want? Why does she argue for Angelo's life? Is this love? Why or why not?

Lucio says he knows and loves the duke. What has he said about the duke before this? How does he say he knows the duke? Do his comments exemplify love? How? The duke suggests that love and knowledge go together (3.2). What does he mean by this pairing? What does it say about love? Is this a comment on other characters' views of love in the play? Of whom might it be a criticism?

At the end of the play, twice the duke admonishes Angelo to love Marina. Does Angelo know what this means? What is the duke commanding of him? Is that love? Why or why not?

2. **Responsibility:** One theme the play focuses on is the issue of responsibility. How does this consideration factor in *Measure for Measure*?

Duke Vincentio places Escalus and Angelo in charge of Vienna as he leaves. Is this a good use of the duke's responsibility? Are they ready for the responsibility? Do they think they are ready for it? Does this present a positive view of them or a negative one? The duke, when he is masquerading as the friar, asks Juliet if she loves Claudio. She says she does and she loves the woman who wronged him. Vincentio then asserts that she has the greater responsibility for their sin and guilt. What does this indicate about responsibility in a physical relationship? With whom does it lie and why?

3. **Honor:** What is the play's view of honor and the meaning of honor? Honor is an issue that surfaces throughout the play. The duke feels that his honor would be compromised if he enforced laws long ignored, so he chooses someone honorable to enforce them.

Listen to what is said about Angelo in the play. Escalus says, about the choice of Angelo to rule in the duke's absence, "If any of Vienna be of worth / To undergo such ample grace and honour / It is Lord Angelo" (1.1.26–28). Here the honor is imputed to Angelo in that the duke chose him. Escalus believes the duke chose well. Angelo defends the honor in his decision to execute Claudio, saying that if Angelo likewise offends, let him also be executed (2.1.481ff). Even when Angelo has become enamored of Isabella, he still refers to himself as a saint (2.2.954). After he suggests the trade of Isabella's virginity for Claudio's life, she appeals to this sense of honor, saying, "little honour to be much believed / And most pernicious purpose!" (2.4.1179–80). When she promises to inform everyone of his evil suggestion, he says no one will believe her because of the honor others associate with him. He has an unsoiled name and a high position in the government (2.4.1185ff). What is Shakespeare saying about honor here? Does Angelo deserve the honor the duke bestows on him? Does he act honorably to fulfill his responsibilities? How does Isabella regard his honor? How does Angelo defend his honor? If Angelo is seen as honorable, how likely is it that honor exists? Is Shakespeare arguing against the possibility of honor given Angelo's true nature? Or is Shakespeare arguing that honor may appear to reside somewhere it does not?

Isabella contends that Claudio possesses honor. When Angelo asks her to trade sexual favors for her brother's life, she says Claudio would not ask her to do that because his honor is so great. Isabella informs Claudio of Angelo's request by saying, "In such a one as you consenting to't, / Would bark your honor from that trunk you bear" (3.1.1299–1300). When Claudio first hears of the offer, he echoes his sister's view of the matter, saying his sister should not agree. However, immediately after, he tells her that it is not such a great sin to give up her virginity, that it would in fact be a virtue because it would spare his life. She tells him that mercy would become a pimp, to trade her for Claudio. Is Claudio honorable? Why is he in jail in the first place? Does it concern an issue of honor? Note that Shakespeare married his wife when she was pregnant with their first child. What might this say about his lingering feelings of doubt about his own honor?

4. **Judgment:** The play offers various views of judgment. Which one does Shakespeare support?

The duke leaves because it is too hard to enforce the once ignored or overlooked laws (1.3.309ff). He leaves Angelo in charge but remains close by disguised as the false friar to see how the shift of power works out. Angelo asserts, "We must not make a scarecrow of the law" (2.1.453). So the laws begin to be enforced. Claudio says that Angelo chose to enforce the laws against him out of a need to create a name for himself (1.2.248–64). Is that a correct assessment? What else does this view say about the judging of Claudio? What does it say about the rightness of the judgment? Lucio believes that Claudio should be thanked, as he has impregnated Isabella's friend (1.4.378–80). Is this a judgment that the play supports? At the end of the play, the duke says that Angelo may be the judge of his own cause (5.1.2572). How useful is this? Why is it problematic? What does modern U.S. law say about this? How does Angelo judge? Are his judgments good ones?

Character

The play's characters can serve as a lens clarifying and bringing into focus the work's various themes and meanings. When analyzing characters, remember to look at what they say, what is said about them, how they act, and how others react to them. Always a particularly telling aspect of a character is what Shakespeare has him or her say as an aside or to the audience, once the stage is empty of everyone but that character. Make sure you pay special attention to those particular moments. Is the character you chose to examine dynamic; that is, does she or he change in the play? If she or he does, part of your analysis should include a discussion and evaluation of the transformation. Also look to see if the character supports a particular viewpoint or idea. Is the character defending the idea of sticking to the letter of the law? If the character is, is Shakespeare subscribing to that viewpoint as well? You can sometimes surmise Shakespeare's possible view of the character by how he or she acts throughout the play or how others talk about the character. What are other indications as presented in the work?

Sample Topics:

1. **Angelo:** When considering Angelo, listen to what he has to say and what is said about him. Examine the character from all sides in order to produce a fully fleshed analysis.

   Record what you know about Angelo. What does he say about himself? What do others say about him? Do his actions match his words? How do others act around Angelo? How do others react directly to him? Do they feel free to argue with his viewpoint? What does this suggest about him and his position in the play's social world? He says that he should be judged with the same measure that he judges, but when the play ends, this golden rule of judgment does not transpire. What is Shakespeare saying about justice and mercy with this character? Does Angelo want to be judged as he is judged? Why or why not? How does he feel about taking responsibility for his actions? What does this indicate about his character? Angelo calls himself a saint. Is he? What does a saint do, and how does a saint act? Do Angelo's actions reflect this model? Is Angelo a good judge? Is he an honorable man? Is he truthful? How do you know? What is Shakespeare's overall intention in creating the character of Angelo? Is Shakespeare warning against pride? Is he warning against hypocritical judges? Is he saying to be careful what you ask for? Or is he suggesting that responsibility is a difficult burden?

2. **Duke Vincentio:** Analyze and evaluate the character of the duke.

   What do you know about the duke? Why does he choose to "leave" Vienna? What is his motive? Is this a good motive for a leader? Why do you think he chose to stay in Vienna disguised as a friar? What does he do as a friar that he could not do as duke? What does he learn as a friar? How does that change his attitude? What does he do for Claudio? For Isabella? For Marina? How does he treat Isabella when she makes a formal complaint against Angelo? Is there a good reason for this? What reason does he give? Why do you think he does it? Is it an effective choice? A moral one? The duke says that he confessed Marina, meaning he acted as her priest and, in the privacy of the confessional, heard what she had to say. This is a privilege or function reserved only for priests. What does it say about the duke that he had no compunction in filling his position with a replacement? What does it say about him that he almost brags of it? Is he trustworthy? What is his final judgment for Angelo and Claudio? Why is this ironic? Think about why he left town in the first place. What does it say about the duke? Why does the duke pardon Barnardine? How does the pardon work in the play to reinforce or reintroduce an idea? What is the duke's final request? How do you think it will be met? Is the duke a weak man? A strong one? A foolish one? What was Shakespeare trying to say with Vincentio? What do you think of that?

3. **Isabella:** Analyze Isabella's role in the play. What kind of character has Shakespeare created her to be?

The first and the last things that we learn about Isabella are in contradiction. Which do you think was her choice? Why do you think she might choose one over the other? Why does Isabella agree to meet with Angelo? Is Isabella responsible for Angelo's reaction to her? Does she do anything to encourage his interest? What is her response to his attempted assignation? What does she expect her brother to do? How does she tell him? What does this suggest about her? Is her character consistent? Why does she listen to the friar's suggestion? How does she feel about it? Why does his suggestion appear legitimate to her while Angelo's is not? What does she do? Is this a form of lying? Has she done something evil in order to bring about a greater good? How is this different from what Angelo was asking of her? What is her reaction when she learns of Claudio's death? Is her response to Angelo, then, in keeping with her character? How will she answer the duke? Will it be a free choice? Why or why not? Does Isabella change in the play? If so, how?

4. **Lucio:** What is Shakespeare possibly saying through the inclusion of Lucio in the play?

Shakespeare uses Lucio as comic relief. How is this fact reflected in the presentation of his character? Is Lucio reliable? How do we know? When do we first get a glimpse of Lucio as an unreliable narrator? What proof of Lucio taking liberty with the truth does Shakespeare provide? Why is it relevant that Mistress Overdone is caring for Lucio's illegitimate child? What is Shakespeare saying about Lucio by including this detail? Why does Lucio tell the friar he knows the duke well? Does he? Why does Lucio tell the tales he does about the duke? What is the possible psychology behind it? How does the play end for Lucio? Is this a just ending or a merciful one? How does he feel about it? What point is Shakespeare potentially making in choosing this course for Lucio?

History and Context

Often the historical, cultural, and social context of a literary text affects and influences a reader's understanding of that work. *Measure for Measure* was written in England in the early years of the seventeenth century. The author grew up just after a turbulent period in English religious history. Each of these considerations, and many more, can add to our understanding of the text. You might do some reading about Shakespeare's life or his time period and see what other contexts you see presented in the play. Or you could choose one of the starting suggestions here to develop your argument and essay.

Sample Topics:

1. **Power of nobility:** How does Shakespeare portray the relative power of the nobility?

The nobility of Shakespeare's day enjoyed a great deal of power. Only someone high in the social order could order the arrest of someone in the nobility. Usually the nobility received light sentences, if they received any at all, for the same sorts of things that would lead to the death of commoners. Where is the issue of the power of the nobility made manifest in the play? Look at Angelo's condemnation of Claudio. Examine Escalus's argument for clemency for Claudio. Look at Angelo's argument for denying the veracity of Isabella or at the duke's orders to the provost and Friar Peter. What does this say about his power, both religious and secular? As a commoner watching the play, the representative audience member would have recognized the vast social gulf between him and the characters being portrayed. How did Shakespeare indicate that gulf in the play? How did he use it to make points, and what specific observations do you think he was trying to make?

2. **Catholic religious orders:** Shakespeare uses Catholicism in the play to make several statements. How do you see him appropriating religion to suit his purposes in the work?

At the beginning of the play, Isabella is in a convent, preparing to become a nun. As a novice, she would be a part of the community in the convent but would not have taken the final vows. This fact arises in the discussion about who must open the door and speak to Lucio when he comes to the convent in search of Isabella. Isabella would not have been required to become a nun, though she had been a novice. Once she had become a nun, though, she would not have been able to leave the convent to plead for her brother without permission. How do we know this? Look at her discussion with Lucio (1.4). How is it made clear in her discussion with the false friar (3.1)? Why might Shakespeare have chosen as a main character a woman who was planning to enter the convent? What does it say about respect for the church that the duke posed as a friar? Why was the duke able to command Friar Peter? What does this say about the separation of church and state? Confessions were supposed to be heard only by ordained priests in the Catholic church. What does the duke do that makes it clear he does not respect the church rules? Why can he get away with this? What might Shakespeare have been saying about the English monarchy with this part of the play?

3. **History of religious changes:** Just before Shakespeare's time, there was a shift from Catholicism to Anglicanism in England.

The religious differences between the two were significant. Why does Shakespeare invoke a Catholic community in the play?

It appears that Isabella wanted to become a nun. She was not sent to the convent by her family but had chosen to go there. At the end of the play, her wishes are overridden by the duke, when he asks her to marry him. He has the power to decide what she may or may not do. Many modern critics think that Isabella is a weak character, because it appears that she will marry the duke. However, the duke had power over both the government and the church. Look at his commanding of the friar, his listening to Marina's confession, and his absolving of the prisoners' sins in jail. The English church was created by Henry VIII when he broke away from the Catholic church. The British people had no choice but to convert from Catholicism and become Anglicans. Was Shakespeare using Isabella to say that the average person had no choice in his or her religious election, just as Isabella had none? Was the play a commentary on the secular powers' control over the religious leaders? What other aspects of the play indicate that this was one of Shakespeare's preoccupations in the work?

Philosophy and Ideas

To write about the philosophy and ideas of *Measure for Measure,* or any text in literature, you must examine the philosophy and the social ideals portrayed in the work. For *Measure for Measure,* you might notice that the work engages the biblical admonition of "Judge not, lest ye be judged. . . . [W]hat measure ye mete, it shall be measured to you again" (Matthew 7:1, 2b). Having found a philosophical presentation of this idea, in the duke's sense of the term, you can look at the play for examples of judging and judgment, the withholding of judgment, and requests for leniency in judgment. Think also about what Shakespeare is saying by the fact that the measure with which Angelo judged was not then used to judge him. After identifying an idea to study in the play, locate passages that deal with this idea and analyze them carefully. You might also look at the characters that are associated with the particular idea and consider them as well. Having analyzed the relevant passages, such as all the ones related to judging and not judging, use your analysis to create a thesis for your essay that will clarify for your reader what Shakespeare was trying to say about the concept of judging in the play. There is no right or wrong interpretation. Instead, there are interpretations supported by the text and those that are not. Clearly you want to show that your interpretation is derived directly from the textual evidence. However, you do not want to simply make a statement about the text; make sure that you also make a conclusive and tautly argued point.

Sample Topics:

1. **Justice and mercy:** What commentary does *Measure for Measure* offer about the relative value of justice and mercy?

   The play begins with the premise of the duke leaving. He feels like his city is suffering because he has not been enforcing the laws, so he decides to leave and let his deputies enforce the laws. Examine the speech in which he addresses Escalus and Angelo (1.1.33ff). Is the duke giving one of these a higher value? If so, which one? Have Vincentio's actions been all about mercy? Look at the passages in which the duke says why he is leaving (1.3). Is justice the point of his actions? Or is there something else? Claudio speaks of the laws and their lack of enforcement in act 1, scene 2. How do the two discussions differ? Why does Angelo say he can only offer justice? How does he discuss the concepts of justice and mercy? What does Isabella say about mercy? How will heaven react to it? What was Shakespeare saying about the relative value of these two concepts?

2. **Pride and humility:** What does Shakespeare say about these two opposing characteristics?

   Who is prideful in the play? Is pride represented as a positive characteristic? Is the character's sense of pride useful or profitable? What does he do as a result of his pride that harms others? What does he do that harms himself? Who in the play is humble? Is this seen as a positive characteristic as well? How does Shakespeare contrast the two? Escalus remarks, "Some rise by sin, and some by virtue fall" (2.1.494). Who rose by sin? Who fell from virtue? Was the proud character still in a strong position at the end of the play? Was the humble person in a lower position? What does this movement say about pride and humility?

3. **Truth:** Truth is an important concept in the play. How is it integrated into the work, and why is it given prominent thematic treatment?

The first person to mention truth, several times, is Lucio. Why is this ironic? Is Shakespeare trying to suggest something in this? Shakespeare has Vincentio say, "There is scarce / truth enough alive to make societies secure" (3.2.1735–36). Why is this statement ironic? Who is Vincentio masquerading as when he says this?

Angelo says no one will believe Isabella if she reveals what has happened to her. Why would Angelo be so sure of this? There are two indicators. How are they relevant? How does the duke's attitude when Isabella comes to accuse Angelo seem to support Angelo's belief? Why is the duke behaving as he does? What does it say about truth that the romantic male protagonist lies throughout most of the play? What does it say about truth that the higher ranks are believed before the lower social orders? Is Shakespeare making a particular point about this inequality or imbalance? Why?

4. **Law:** One of the main conceptual concerns in the play is the notion of law. Having not enforced the laws yet allowing them to remain on the books has caused problems for the duke. His attempts to remedy this are the impetus for the play's action.

Read the first discussion of the newly enforced law (1.2.236ff). What is the issue Claudio is concerned with? Read the duke's discussion of the need to enforce the law (1.3.309ff). What is the duke concerned about? Angelo also discusses this same need to enforce the law (2.1.453–56). What is the point of this repetition? What is Shakespeare emphasizing? Why? In Isabella's discussions with Angelo (2.2), she speaks of the law, the reception of mercy, and the ultimate lawgiver, God. What is Isabella's perspective on the law? Is Shakespeare supporting her approach or not? During the play, we learn that Angelo has broken the legal agreement he made to marry Marina. Why is this law not seen as important? The duke masquerades as a friar, thus breaking church law. Why is that significant? How is the duke's final disposition of Barnardine's case an argument for or against the law? What about his sentence to Angelo? What point is Shakespeare making about the law? Who is above the law? What is the law's proposed function in the play? Does the law succeed in fulfilling this function?

Language, Symbols, and Imagery

The careful use of language, symbols, and imagery are integral parts of good literature. Shakespeare's works are still read today partially because he proved himself a master of the English language. If you choose to analyze these aspects of *Measure for Measure,* you will be joining a long literary conversation. An analysis of these literary elements can help you create an argument that can serve as the centerpiece of your essay. You might choose to address the title of the work, for example, and discuss whether measure was given for measure. Or you might look at the language of Elbow and how his saying the opposite of what he means leads to rhetorical irony and comic effect. Alternately, you might look at the metaphors contained in the play and examine what they add to the experience of the work. Analyzing language, symbols, and imagery requires careful and precise attention to language and the appreciation of subtle differences in meaning, but it can also be one of the most rewarding and enriching ways of approaching a work of literature.

Sample Topics:

1. **The title of the play:** What is the significance of the title?

Does Shakespeare follow through on the implicit promise he makes in the title to the biblically literate audience in naming the play *Measure for Measure?* Look to the Bible and the book of Matthew, the first two verses of the seventh chapter, for the original reference the title is derived from. Who is the recipient of the judgment? Who received a worse judgment? Who received a lighter judgment? What does this tell us? What was Shakespeare trying to point out by establishing these differences in the measurement of judgment? Note the characters who received these judgments. Are they fair or not? Is there an irony proposed in the title in that the audience would be expecting a certain kind of judgment of the characters only to have this expectation overturned? Who in the play invokes the title? What is his position in the play? Who in the Bible story would be the equivalent figure to the duke? What does that say about the play?

2. **Elbow's opposites:** Read Elbow's scenes. What language usage issues are presented?

Elbow provides comic relief to the play by saying the opposite of what he means. How might Shakespeare be employing Elbow for rhetorical irony? Why does his continued misuse of words lead to a comic effect? What words does Elbow misuse? Are these particularly difficult words? Would the audience have known what he meant immediately or would it have been the repetition of various misuses that clued them in to the comedy? If Elbow had said what he meant, what difference would that have made in his scenes? By saying the opposite, did he sometimes say more than he meant to? Does his misuse of language reveal something about his character besides his inability to know the meaning of words? What other point might Shakespeare be making through the character of Elbow and his language? Is it significant that the elbow is the site of the funny bone, which when forcibly struck is not a pleasant or enjoyable experience? Why did Shakespeare name the character as he did?

3. **Metaphors:** What role do metaphors play in *Measure for Measure?*

In the play, Shakespeare invokes metaphors often in order to say more with fewer words. Isolate some of those metaphors and determine what purpose Shakespeare might have had in employing them. In act 1, scene 2, Lucio and the First Gentleman disagree with each other, the latter using a cloth metaphor to differentiate between the two of them. What would the cloth metaphor tell the audience about the two characters? Which is the fancier cloth? Which is the more expensive? Which cloth would be more familiar to the audience? A second metaphor about cloth involves gentlemen's clothes used to outfit thieves (4.2.1926–30). Read through the passage and determine what you think it means. Why would an apparel metaphor fit here? Why the emphasis on cloth? Is it a reference to the words of the title, measuring for clothing? Look at other metaphors in the play. What is their relevance? Why would Shakespeare engage his audience with those metaphors? Are they easily understood? Are they confusing? What deeper meaning do they add that simply expressing the concept would not convey?

4. **Names:** Shakespeare employs some specific and intentional name choices in the play. Why and what are the ramifications of identifying a character with a name of particular metaphoric or symbolic import?

Look at the significance of the assigned character names in the play. When are they accurate, and when are they ironic? Are there any indications beforehand about which are which? Vincentio comes from the Latin "to conquer." How is this appropriate for the duke? How is it inappropriate in the context of the play? Isabella means "pretty" or can be parsed phonetically to mean "is a bella" or is an attractive woman. Is it an accurate naming? How do others respond to her physical appearance? Is that the only attribute that is commented on? Angelo means "angel." How does this descriptor fit Angelo? If the name is not appropriate, at which point does it become apparent that it is not? When is Angelo compared to a devil? Who calls him a devil? Angels are also messengers of heaven. How does Isabella play with that designation when she speaks to Claudio in prison? Claudio is derived from a name meaning "lame" or "crippled." Is this how Shakespeare views Claudio's character? How is the concept of lameness expressed in the play? Why might Shakespeare have chosen this name for his character? Mariana is a mix of two important Christian names: Mary, the mother of Jesus, and her mother, Anne. Both were said to have virgin births. How does this fit her? Why is that her main association in the play? How might it have a symbolic meaning beyond the obvious? Is there any indication that Shakespeare had that intention? If so, where in the text is it found? Lucio is a name meaning "from light." The appellation is also related to Lucifer, a name for the devil or the fallen angel of light. What might Shakespeare have been intending by including that name? Did he intend his names to mean something more than just a means of identifying his creations for the audience? Were the names meant to have the meanings attributed here? Note also that all the names are Latinate, meaning they are from the Latin-derived languages, such as Spanish or Italian. Yet the city the play takes place in is Vienna, an Austrian city. What is the significance of the names coming from Latin in a German-speaking city?

Compare and Contrast Essays

Compare and contrast essays offer students a different way of approaching the text. A good compare and contrast essay might examine elements in the text, such as two characters from the play, or elements present in multiple pieces, such as the duke in *Measure for Measure* and the duke in *The Tempest*. By comparing and contrasting, you will be able to speak about the play from a wider perspective. This, in turn, may enable you to see and make sense of subtler meanings found in the text. As you write your essay, be sure not to limit it to a mere list of similarities and differences. Instead use that list to generate an argument that will help your audience to view the play in a different way.

Sample Topics:

1. **The dukes from *The Tempest* and *Measure for Measure:*** Read both of these romances. Compare the dukes. Do not simply look for surface differences, though. For example, Prospero was married and is a father, while Vincentio is single. That observation is, in itself, not significant. Instead look for how those differences manifest themselves in the play.

   In *The Tempest*, Prospero is most concerned for his daughter, Miranda. Who is Vincentio most concerned for? How are their concerns manifested? Consider the differences between the two dukes abandoning their responsibilities. What was the reasoning behind each, and how successful was each in escaping or sidestepping duty? Did Prospero and Vincentio get what they were searching for? If they did, once it was attained, did they value it? How do the two men act outside the traditional role of a nobleman in their respective plays? What is the significance of that? What do the two men have in common at the end of their respective plays? How is what they actually gained different from what they had originally envisioned? Are they happy with their situation? Is Shakespeare more sympathetic toward one of the dukes than the other? What makes you think that? How might that be significant?

2. *Measure for Measure* **and** *All's Well That Ends Well:* These two plays are both romances, involve issues of sex and the order of society, and involve bed tricks, the originally medieval trope in which an individual is duped into sleeping with a partner. Despite these similarities, though, they are very different plays.

To pursue this topic, you might compare the situation of Helena and Bertram with that of Claudio and Juliet or even Angelo and Isabella. Which of these pairings feels compelled to be a couple? Which of these couples seems to want to be together? Who will be separated and why? In addition, you can explore the implementation of the bed tricks in each of the works. The bed trick was typically employed to compel reluctant husbands into fulfilling their conjugal duties. Angelo almost loses his life over his situation, while Bertram seems resigned to his. Why would these experiences make them content with a marriage they both sought to avoid? How were their avoidance strategies similar? How were their respective approaches to Isabella and Diana similar? Why would Shakespeare repeat such a unique strategy? How are the plots different from each other? Did Shakespeare change his emphasis from one to the other? Or is it a case of repetition for the sake of reinforcement?

3. **Escalus and Angelo:** Compare these two characters. What are the ramifications of their similarities, differences, or both?

Escalus is a foil to Angelo. He, too, has been appointed by the duke a judge in the city of Vienna. He does not succumb to temptation in the play, however. He argues for clemency. He supports Claudio's case. Yet he does not have the power of Angelo and so, in the end, his position is more precarious and he is not able to convince Angelo to follow his plans. Is he a better man than Angelo? Or is it a case of power corrupting and absolute power corrupting absolutely? What negative things do we learn about Escalus during the play? How does this compare to what we learn about Angelo? Why might Angelo have been given more power than Escalus? Which of the two men changes over the course of the play? Do you think this is a relevant change? Will it become permanent?

4. **Lucio and Elbow:** These two characters offer comic relief. Are their humorous purposes achieved through similar or diverse means?

Both Lucio and Elbow provide comic relief through their words. The humor Lucio brings to the work comes from his maligning the duke's character in the presence of the duke in disguise. Elbow's comic relief is generated more through his use of words that mean the opposite of how he intends them. The audience knows that Elbow does not mean what he thinks he means, and this linguistic tension allows a serious scene to be funny. These two characters are the main reason that *Measure for Measure* is often classified as a comedy. What do they have in common? How does Shakespeare use them to relieve the seriousness of a judgment scene? Which is more admirable? Which is more engaging? Why? What point does Shakespeare make with each? What about the two characters was different enough that Shakespeare included both of them instead of combining their respective functions and roles? How are they similar?

Bibliography and Online Resources for *Measure for Measure*

Campbell, Oscar James. *Shakespeare's Satire.* 2008. Web. 1 June 2009.

Chambers, E. K. *William Shakespeare: A Study of Facts and Problems.* New York: Oxford UP, 1989. Print.

Holland, Norman N. *Psychoanalysis and Shakespeare.* New York: McGraw-Hill, 1966. Print.

Lawrence, William Witherle. *Shakespeare's Problem Comedies.* New York: Macmillan, 1930. Print.

Shakespeare, William. *Open Source Shakespeare.* Ed. Eric M. Johnson. George Mason U, 2003. Web. 1 June 2009.

Shakespeare, William, and Brian Gibbons. *Measure for Measure: The New Cambridge Shakespeare.* New York: Cambridge UP, 2006. Print.

Shell, Marc. *The End of Kinship: "Measure for Measure," Incest, and the Ideal of Universal Siblinghood.* Stanford: Stanford UP, 1988. Print.

Shuger, Deborah Kuller. *Political Theologies in Shakespeare's England: The Sacred and State in "Measure for Measure."* New York: Palgrave Macmillan, 2001. Print.

Skura, Meredith Anne. *The Literary Use of the Psychoanalytic Process.* 1981. Web. 1 June 2009.

ALL'S WELL
THAT ENDS WELL

READING TO WRITE

SHAKESPEARE'S *ALL'S Well That Ends Well* (1601–08) presents the story of Helena, an orphan who falls in love with Bertram, the son of her foster mother. The play takes place in France, where Helena was born, and in Florence, where a war offered many Frenchmen the opportunity to obtain glory. The story is about love, sex, and marriage and how these concepts and institutions fuse and intersect. One technique you can use to identify a topic or to provide evidence for a claim you have already formulated is close reading. When you closely read a passage, you read it multiple times slowly, paying careful attention to the language. Ask yourself why Shakespeare selected and arranged the words in the precise way that he did. Imagine how the sense of the passage would change if you replaced any of the words with a synonym or reordered the sentences. Choose a passage of interest to you, perhaps one of the king's long speeches, such as this one:

> 'Tis only title thou disdain'st in her, the which
> I can build up. Strange is it that our bloods,
> Of colour, weight, and heat, pour'd all together,
> Would quite confound distinction, yet stand off
> In differences so mighty. If she be
> All that is virtuous, save what thou dislikest,
> A poor physician's daughter, thou dislikest
> Of virtue for the name: but do not so:

From lowest place when virtuous things proceed,
The place is dignified by the doer's deed:
Where great additions swell's, and virtue none,
It is a dropsied honour. Good alone
Is good without a name. Vileness is so:
The property by what it is should go,
Not by the title. She is young, wise, fair;
In these to nature she's immediate heir,
And these breed honour: that is honour's scorn,
Which challenges itself as honour's born
And is not like the sire: honours thrive,
When rather from our acts we them derive
Than our foregoers: the mere word's a slave
Debosh'd on every tomb, on every grave
A lying trophy, and as oft is dumb
Where dust and damn'd oblivion is the tomb
Of honour'd bones indeed. What should be said?
If thou canst like this creature as a maid,
I can create the rest: virtue and she
Is her own dower; honour and wealth from me. (2.3.1018–45)

The references in this passage to social class make it a particularly strong choice for analysis. The play was written in a time of growing strictness in the delineation of social class. In the play, Bertram has objected to marrying Helena on the grounds that she is a commoner. The king responds in this passage in a surprising manner. He says that all blood, noble and commoner alike, is the same when mixed or commingled. The king states that Helena is virtuous, an important designation. He also argues that virtue, found among commoners, is still virtue. In general, he is suggesting that since Helena is clearly good, wise, and physically attractive, her origins or commoner's status should be immaterial. This is an older view of nobility, that it arises as the result of virtue. Following this view, the king can create or arrange for her nobility by giving her a title. She is naturally virtuous, and the king can endow her with wealth and honor. What does this imply about the king? Is Shakespeare speaking through the king to present a radical change in politics? How could this passage be used to argue that? How accurate is the science in the passage? Are all bloods alike? Based on the quotation, what can be said about virtue? About social class?

This speech is significant in its view of social class. In the play, Bertram is clearly the gatekeeper of social class. He believes in those who are noble, until it is proved to him that they are liars and cheats. He looks down on anyone whose class is lower than his own. He might admire Diana and be attracted to her, but when she comes to claim her position as his wife, as he has promised her, Bertram labels her a camp follower. The king, the highest level of social class, is not ruled by a strict understanding of aristocracy. He believes that virtue, service to the king, and virginity are important aspects that show a more elevated nature than birth and social rank might have afforded a person. How is this a twist on expectations of social class? Why is it important that it is the king who supports this view? What does Bertram's support of the opposite imply about Shakespeare's view? Do Diana and Helena offer support for the king's beliefs or Bertram's? What about Parolles and Bertram?

As you can see, a close reading of one passage can generate ideas for several essays. If you have analyzed a passage and generated various questions and ideas, you should then identify other passages that you think will lead you to a more sophisticated argument or help you to refine your thoughts. Analyze these subsequent passages as you did the first and continue the process until you feel as though you have reached a conclusion that might function as a claim on which you can base your essay.

TOPICS AND STRATEGIES

The topic suggestions included here, rather than limit or constrict you, should spark your imagination. Do not approach these essay topics as a series of questions to be answered in sequence. Instead, use the questions to help generate your own ideas about a given topic. Or use the questions to generate your own lines of inquiry. What can you ask that relates to the questions posed? Record your ideas and formulate your claim, the argument you wish to make. Then go back to your notes and begin to marshal the evidence for your claim, organizing and arranging your thoughts into a persuasive essay.

Themes

When you think about a play's theme, you are attempting to determine what major ideas or issues it is concerned with relating. Many works share the same or similar themes, as there are central questions that humans have consistently grappled with and explored through literature. Each work will have its own perspective on the themes with which it deals, and it is your job as a writer to discover and articulate this perspective in your essay. *All's Well That Ends Well* deals with such themes as love, marriage, and integrity. By isolating the most significant passages pertaining to one of these themes and then reading them closely with an aim to analyzing the language employed, you can discover what the play is arguing or suggesting about that particular issue; in doing so, you will have formulated a thesis that can serve as the centerpiece of your essay.

Sample Topics:

1. **Love:** What is the play's message about romantic love in the context of marriage? Can the two exist together?

   Analyze the scenes between Helena and Bertram. What is their relationship based on? What does it provide them? How does Bertram's relationship with Helena affect his ideas about the war and his thoughts about the future? Does the play view these thoughts as reflecting well or poorly on Bertram? Analyze the scenes in which Bertram interacts with or corresponds with Helena and Diana. What do these show about Bertram's view of love and sex? Is lust synonymous with love for Bertram? When lust is quenched, is the desire quenched as well?

2. **Integrity:** How are honesty and faithfulness rewarded in the play? What part does integrity hold in the play?

   Reread the play, paying careful attention to discussions of honesty, truthfulness, faithfulness, and honor. What do the different characters believe? Bertram flees his marriage bed for war. He hopes to gain honor in the fight with Florence.

What does this say about the role of honor in domestic and international relations? Parolles is believed by Bertram to have integrity, but when he is exposed as a liar and a traitor, Bertram rejects him. Bertram pledges his marriage vows to Helena, his vow of fidelity to Diana, and he swears to the king that he loved Helena after all. What does this say about Bertram's integrity and decisiveness? Helena loves Bertram and, after his rejection, she leaves France so that he may, in time, return to his home. What does this say about her integrity? When she finds that her husband has been courting another woman, Diana, and she tricks him into bed with her, how does this reveal or conceal integrity on Helena's part? Diana agrees to a subterfuge. How does her tricking Bertram reflect on her honor?

3. **Power:** What does *All's Well That Ends Well* articulate about power and its place in relationships?

Power is displayed on many levels in the play. The countess calls Helena daughter and says she is adopting her. The king promises her anything in his power, including a noble marriage. Bertram is a count, a powerful member of the French court, and yet he is forced to marry Helena. What does this say about relative power? Once he has married her, he leaves Helena and refuses to return home. His self-imposed exile leaves Helena a virgin wife. What does this say about the relative power of each? When he refuses to return home while she is still there, what does this say about Helena's power? When Bertram is courting Diana and falsely promising marriage, what do Mariana and the widow have to say about power? How does that reveal itself in Bertram's relationship with Diana? When the king thinks that Bertram has murdered Helena, he orders him imprisoned. Again relative levels of power should be evident. When Diana comes to claim Bertram's promises, he rejects her. He calls her a strumpet and camp follower, a liar and a prostitute. What does this say about their relative levels of power?

Throughout the play, there are many examples that could be called abuse or exercise of power. When the king offers to reward Helena, is this an exercise of power? When she takes him up on his offer and requests a noble marriage, is this an abuse or an exercise of power? When the king forces Bertram to marry Helena against her will, or when Bertram leaves Helena and refuses to return home, is this an abuse or rightful exercise of power? When the captains kidnap Parolles and threaten him, what aspects of the exercise of authority does it reveal? When Bertram rejects Diana and derides her, is this abuse? What does the play say overall about the abuse of power? About the rightful exercise of power?

Character

Analysis of a play's characters can often provide insights that can help you interpret the work's themes and meanings. In *All's Well That Ends Well*, we are presented with a number of strong characters who warrant thorough analysis. When you perform such an analysis, you want to reread the text, highlighting any passages that seem to offer insight into your chosen character. Pay attention to any monologues as well as dialogue with other characters. What are the character's motives, priorities, and values? Notice whether the character you have selected has changed in any way through the course of the play and determine both the cause of this change and whether the play portrays it in a positive or negative light. You might focus on Bertram, for example, and use your analysis to determine how the play ultimately perceives him. Is he a hero or a villain? You might examine a certain category of character, women, for example, studying Helena and Diana in order to comment on Shakespeare's depiction of female characters. Additionally, you can often make a convincing argument about the play's take on a particular idea through an analysis of one or more characters. You might investigate what the play has to say about love, marriage, or virtue through an analysis of a main character—Helena, for instance.

Sample Topics:

1. **Bertram, Count Rousillon:** Analyze the character of Bertram. Does he develop throughout the course of the play? If so, is his transformation positive or negative?

At the beginning of the play, Bertram has been called to court. When Helena is promised his hand in marriage, he runs off to war. Though he is married, he courts the genteel daughter of a widow, who has no power to hold him responsible for his actions. He fights and leads well and gains honor in the Florentine army. His foolish trust of Parolles is revealed to him, and Bertram ultimately rejects him. Once he hears of Helena's death, he returns home to marry again at the king's behest. Then he swears that he loved Helena. When Diana comes to request those things he promised her, he lies about his actions. He also slanders her. At the end, told that his wife is pregnant with his child, he swears he will love her. What do these actions suggest or reveal about Bertram? Is he an honorable man? Is he honest? Does he change throughout the story? What is the most positive reading of his character in the play? What is the most negative reading of his character in the play? Which of these two understandings do you think is most accurate?

2. **Parolles:** Analyze and evaluate the character of Parolles.

Parolles appears to be a man of the nobility. He is certainly allowed to participate in the life of the court. He says that he is a great fighter, a statement not only believed by Bertram but supposedly substantiated by others. Both Lafeu and the Captains Dumaine see through his boasts and believe him to be worse than a liar. What role does Parolles fulfill in the play? Is he the comic relief? The foil? The villain? If he is a villain, is he the main villain or a secondary one? Does Parolles change over the course of the play? At the end, is he worthy of help because of his testimony about Diana? Or does Lafeu's acceptance say more about Lafeu than about Parolles?

3. **Helena and Diana:** Shakespeare has been accused of endorsing a gender hierarchy by portraying female characters as weak and submissive. Analyze these two female characters in the work to evaluate Shakespeare's portrayal of women in the play.

Locate and analyze the passages that best describe these two characters. Do they have strong, independent personalities, or are they submissive to the men they are connected to? What do they have in common? What accounts for any significant differences in their characters? How do they interact with the male characters in the play? How are they treated or talked about by the male characters? Are they three-dimensional characters or flat? That is, do we see them as multifaceted or only as acting or thinking about or in one mode or manner. You might look at the countess in addition to or instead of Diana. Is she ruled by men, or does she rule them? How is she treated in the play? Is she shown respect? Does she support Helena or Bertram? If so, what form does it take? Based on all of this analysis, draw some conclusions about Shakespeare's portrayal of women in *All's Well That Ends Well*.

4. **King of France:** Analyze the character of the king of France and the role he plays in the play as a whole.

The king is the impetus behind the difficulties presented in the play, because it is Helena's healing him that leads to his offer of a reward and her acceptance in the form of Bertram as a husband. What do the characters say about the king while he is sick? What does Bertram say when he sees the king? How does Helena characterize her revelatory moment when she realizes that she has the medicine to heal the king? What is the king's reaction to Bertram's abandonment of Helena? Is there instant forgiveness? Quick forgiveness? Or is forgiveness withheld? Is there any justification for this reaction in the play? What do the various threats of imprisonment say about the king? What is his reaction to Bertram after he finds that Bertram is a liar? How does this differ from Bertram's reaction to finding Parolles was a liar? Is there a parallel here? What does it say about the king?

History and Context

Despite presenting a fictionalized world, *All's Well That Ends Well* takes place during a particular moment in a particular place, an identifiable historical moment. In order to understand what motivates the characters and what drives the action, then, it is vitally important to understand the play's historical and social context. Some background knowledge on Roman mythology, Christian sects, and the aristocracy would help you understand the play better and to make more informed comments.

Sample Topics:

1. **Shakespeare's sympathies in the Christian schisms:** What kind of commentary is the play offering about puritans and papists (Catholics)?

   It has been argued that the papist referred to is actually the French word for fish and that the puritan is a play on good flesh. Thus the two religionists mentioned in that section (1.3) might be a play on a French proverb that says, "Young flesh and old fish are the daintiest" (Dyce 213). What might Shakespeare referencing a proverb on eating say about his view of religion? Why is there a reference to the two groups anyway? When did the Anglican church split with the Roman Catholic church? For how many years was the split a political problem? Would it matter to the reading of the play if Shakespeare were Catholic or Anglican? There has been argument both ways, though nothing can be proved. It is clear that Shakespeare's family had been Catholic and that he was baptized in the Anglican church.

2. **Roman mythology:** What kind of religious commentary is the play making in referencing Roman gods?

   Do some background reading on Roman mythology, specifically looking at Mars, Cupid, Apollo, and Diana. Why would these four be referenced specifically? What do they tell us about the focus of the play? How would Shakespeare's references to Roman gods impact the audience? Why are Roman gods included in the play? There are multiple references to various incarnations of Mars. Why? How does this god and his associated qualities specifically suit the play? Why is Bertram's prayer to Mars relevant? What does it say about Bertram? What other references are there to Mars? Are they all about the god? What are the others about? What is Shakespeare's reasoning for using two different meanings for Mars in the play? How do the two relate to each other? Helena and the steward speak of Diana. How are their references to her similar? How are they different? To whom is Diana compared and why? How are the goddess and the mortal similar? Different? At one point, Helena refers to a span of time as "twice the horses of the sun shall bring" (2.1.771). Which of the gods does this reference? What is the significance of this reference in the body of the play?

3. **Contemporary astrology:** How does the play take advantage of an Elizabethan understanding of astrology?

Astrology is the study of the stars and planets in order to determine their effects on human life and make predictions based on them. Astrology was especially popular in Elizabethan England. Queen Elizabeth chose her coronation day based on a horoscope cast for her by John Dee, the most famous astrologer of the era. What is the point of Helena referring to Bertram as a "bright particular star"? Why do Helena and Parolles have a discussion on astrology? What are the implications of Parolles having been born under Mars? Why would Helena say that she was born under a baser star? How does the clown characterize and employ the scarcity of shooting stars? Why might these two topics be related in Elizabethan minds? What were lucky stars? How did those influence the world, according to Elizabethan understanding?

4. **War:** Who is involved in the war and why? What is the effect of the presence of war in the play?

The play is derived from Boccaccio's *Decameron*, which featured the war as well. The king speaks of the war between the Florentines and the Senoys. The First Lord argues that it might just be gossip, but the king counters that his knowledge comes from the king of Austria and is, therefore, correct. In addition, he says his cousin asks that he not send troops, so he feels unable to do so. Irrespective of his own reactions and situation, he gives leave to his vassals to support the war. The war in Florence thus offers Bertram an escape from his marriage with Helena. To what degree were other nations and citizens of other countries involved in the conflict? Why did their native countries have interest in the war? Why would noblemen go to Florence to fight? How does the war offer an honorable escape to Bertram? Why can it been seen as honorable? How does the war influence the play? How does the war help provide for or set up the resolution of the play? What place does the war have in the various relationships: Bertram and Helena, Bertram and Parolles, Bertram and Diana, Bertram and the lords?

Philosophy and Ideas

All's Well That Ends Well is a play in which philosophy and ideas play a central role. The work deals with a wide spectrum of issues, including love and marriage, honor, and chastity. To write an essay on one of these topics, it is a good idea to reread the play with this particular aspect or element in mind and to identify characters who are associated with your topic and passages that seem to give insight into the play's views on your selected issue. You will then want to analyze the characters and the passages you have identified in order to arrive at a claim to make in your essay. To discuss love and marriage, for example, you might look closely at Bertram and Helena and study their different ideas about the topics. Then, evaluate the take on these two characters. What are their fates? With which character are we more sympathetic? After performing your analysis and considering these questions, you might arrive at a claim such as the following: In *All's Well That Ends Well*, Shakespeare argues for the triumph of a feminine understanding of the importance of love and marriage over the masculine, because Helena is a far more sympathetic character. Alternatively, your analysis might lead you to a conclusion such as this: Through the characters of Helena and Bertram, Shakespeare shows the value of marriage to women and its lack of value to men. Is there any indication in the play as to which of these positions Shakespeare believes is more correct?

Sample Topics:

1. **Love and marriage:** Does the play give a negative or positive view of marriage? What part does love play in marriage? Where else in the play is love discussed?

For whom is the marriage at the beginning beneficial? Does it stay that way? How does Helena succeed in claiming her place as wife? Why is this important? What does Bertram gain from the marriage? How does the marriage change his life? Is the fact that in the end he stays married to Helena important, or is it simply an effect of the age? Do you think he has actually changed in his feelings toward Helena? What evidence in the play can you gather to support that? How did marriage help women? How did it help men? In the play, how did it constrain the two groups? What reference to marriage is made at the end of the play?

Think also about Bertram's courtship of Diana. How is it unethical? What promises does he make? What does he hope to gain from them? What proof does he give for his trustworthiness? Why is this ironic? What do Mariana and Diana's mother have to say about Bertram's courtship? What do Parolles and the First Lord have to say about it? How do their takes differ? Are the women's views significantly different than the men's? On what are the views similar? How are they different? What do you think are the reasons for this?

2. **Honor:** What is deemed as honor or as honorable in the play?

Many people have written about the masculine and feminine views of honor presented in the play. Honor is found in marriage for the women and in war for the men. These two different views give rise to many potential discussions. Marriage has been called an "honorable estate." How is this view reflected in the play? Who in the play views marriage as honorable? What other things are referred to as honorable in the play? Who refers to them as such? Are the references intended to be ironic? Truthful? There are 43 references to honor in the play, making it a central focus. Bertram seeks honor in the war and is said to have gained honor there. How is honor related to war? For whom is war honorable? In what ways? Is Bertram honorable for having sought and gained honor? Or is honor something that is given unearned? Refer to the play for possible answers.

3. **Sexuality:** What kind of commentary does the play make about sexuality?

From the onset, there is significant discussion of chastity, virginity, and maidenhood in the play. Helena says that it requires a fight to maintain one's virginity, while Parolles suggests that a sustained virginity is like "withered pears" (1.1.163). How do these two characters symbolize differing views of chastity? Do Helena and Parolles maintain these views throughout the play? Who else weighs in on the topic? To whom else is virginity important and why? When could it be lost without consequences? By whom? How does the king reward Diana's chastity? Why are there rewards for chastity? What are they? There are 20 specific references to virginity and chastity throughout the play. Read through them, and see what else comes to mind. How often do the women speak about being chaste? Do any of the male characters discuss chastity or virginity? How do they discuss it? How does Parolles describe Bertram's sexuality? What is the point?

Form and Genre

It can often be fruitful to examine a piece of literature as a constructed work of art, paying close attention to elements that inform it, such as narration, point of view, and organizational scheme. You should ask yourself why the author made the choices he did when constructing the work and how the work would be different if he had made other choices. When studying *All's Well That Ends Well,* you might explore the structure of the play and eventually use your essay to explain how the play incorporates aspects of fairy tales and morality plays. Or, you might focus on Shakespeare's decision to use a proverb as the title and use your essay to examine how the proverb, borrowed as a title from Boccaccio's story in *Decameron,* affects the meaning of the play as a whole.

Sample Topics:

1. **Fairy tale aspects of the play:** Discuss how the tropes and idioms of the fairy tale are integrated into the play.

Look again at the story of Helena. How does she meet the fairy tale definition of "persecuted heroine"? How much of the story resembles the Cinderella genre of fairy tales, in which a poor young woman endures and succeeds because of her virtue? Look at both Helena and Diana for this. How does the story support the "happily ever after" expectation of fairy tales? In many stories, there is an evil stepmother or a witch. The play has neither of these female characters. The closest semblance to a stepmother is the countess taking Helena in. How does this break from the traditional expectations associated with the fairy tale genre? According to one classification for identifying folk tales, the heroine must be persecuted by a male presence. How is Helena persecuted by a man and which one is it? How does he treat her badly? In many fairy tales, there are a series of impossible tasks set for the hero before he can triumph, and often there is an unnatural intervention of animals. Who is set impossible tasks in the play? How are they met in the play? Which character plays the role of the "helpful animal" in the play? What does that function reveal about the character overall?

2. **Morality play:** How is *All's Well That Ends Well* similar to a morality play?

Morality plays typically dramatize an individual's struggle to seek virtue and avoid vice. Who in the play seeks to maintain virtue? Who seeks to avoid vice? How are these characters rewarded in the play? What does the reward suggest about Shakespeare's adaptation of the morality play format? Usually the hero is the person who is trying to do the right thing. By that definition, who is the hero of the play? Who has the potential for heroism that remains unfulfilled? What does this say about the characters? About the play?

3. **"All's well that ends well"**: The title of the play is also a common proverb of the day. It is even quoted in the play. What does the proverb say about the focus or thrust of the work?

First, analyze the meaning of the proverb, then identify who quotes it in the play. After that, think about how it might apply to the themes of the play. What does the play have to say about the relationship between the means of achieving a desired outcome and the outcome itself? You might think about why Helena is not distraught with Bertram in the final scene. You might also examine other minor characters that seem to be heading to a bad end but instead turn their course in a positive direction. Diana and Parolles are good examples of minor characters facing challenges and threats in the play but who nevertheless end up in a strong position. Why do you think Shakespeare picked *All's Well That Ends Well* to be the play's title? Why this particular proverb? Would the focus have been as clear if he had simply had Helena say it and not emphasized it by also using it as the title?

Language, Symbols, and Imagery

An analysis of the language, symbols, and imagery in a work of literature can result in new insights that can then help you arrive at a new interpretation of the text. Note any lengthy descriptions of particular scenes or items, especially ones that appear repeatedly. If a word is important in the play, it might appear in various synonyms or connotations. A high rate of synonyms would emphasize a concept's importance, such as vow, oath, and swear. Also, as you are reading, be sure to mark passages that seem to have a special resonance, perhaps those which do not serve to further the plot so much as to reflect on an important issue, event, or character. Among the many symbols and images you might elect to focus on in *All's Well That Ends Well* are objects, items, and accessories—such as rings, feathers, food, and swords and drums or military trappings in general. In your essay, you will want to provide a new interpretation of the play based on your analysis of these symbols. You might argue, for example, that through the use of martial or militaristic imagery in the play, Shakespeare communicates that, though he has been in the war only a short time, Bertram's primary role is that of soldier.

Sample Topics:

1. **Metaphors:** Shakespeare uses multiple metaphors in the play. What is their purpose? How do they add to the play?

Look at the metaphors in the play. What do they add to the meaning? Why are they particularly used? For example, Bertram "stole from France" (3.5. 1664). What is the primary meaning of this metaphor? What other meaning might it give to the discussion? What is ironic about Parolles's statement that "virginity breeds mites" (1.1.143)? Why is this one of the first topics of discussion in the play? How is the opposite viewpoint presented at the end of the play? What is the relevance of "the hind that would be mated by the lion" (1.1.92)? What is a hind, and who does it represent in the play? Why is this a good metaphor? Who is the lion? Why is the lion an apt metaphor? What is the meaning of Helena's lines, "Yet in this captious and intenible sieve / I still pour the waters of my love" (1.3.528–29)? How is it like a sieve? How is her love like water? What does this say about her love? What does it say about the sieve?

2. **Military implements—the sword and drum:** What is the symbolic point of so many references to swords and drums in the play?

Bertram leaves France in order to avoid the responsibilities of his marriage to Helena. His mother knows that he seeks honor in Florence on the battlefield and says, "his sword can never win / The honour that he loses" (3.2.1501–02). How is his sword symbolic of honor in the play? What other references are there to the sword? A search for the word in the play will yield eight references. How many of these references are literal and how many symbolic? Historically, a sword has often been used as a phallic symbol, a physical representation of male genitalia. How might this impact your reading of the play? In what way does the Second Lord's reference to swords, "I will never trust a man again for keeping his sword / clean" (4.3.2232–33), intimate that not all swords are mighty military weapons?

Why is the drum important? There are 21 references in the play. What difference does it make to know that the phrase "following the drum" was used to describe the military? How does the reference to the drum of Mars in Bertram's prayer (2.3.1556) indicate that particular meaning? Parolles's drum plays a pivotal part in his exposure as a coward. How does the drum set the stage for the kidnapping? At what point does Parolles disavow his drum? What is the point of his doing so? Why is it significant? What does it mean for the character? For the play?

3. **Rings:** Two rings appear in the play, the physical manifestation of various goals and promises. Examine what they mean.

Shakespeare indicates the symbolic importance of rings when he has Bertram write Helena that "when thou canst get the ring upon my finger" (3.2.1458) he will be her husband. What is said about that ring throughout the play? What else is compared to a ring? How does the comparison of chastity with jewelry make a statement? What does it imply? It is referred to as a "monumental ring" (4.3.2109); how is it monumental? To what is it a monument? When the ring is offered up as proof, is it believed? Why or why not? The king arrests Bertram for owning a ring. Why is this ring so problematic? It also seems to offer proof of something. What does the king believe it proves? What does Bertram say about it? What do his words indicate about its meaning to Bertram?

Compare and Contrast Essays

Comparing and contrasting similar elements within and between plays or works often serves to sharpen one's critical focus, enabling the reader to notice features that might otherwise have been overlooked. You might, for instance, compare and contrast Shakespeare's play with Boccaccio's story, which was the original source of the play, or with William Painter's *Palace of Pleasure*, which was the first English presentation of the story. Comparing the heroines of the works might indicate what Shakespeare was trying to say about women or marriage. Comparisons and contrasts also allow an essay writer to make statements about the evolution of a particular theme across the span of an author's career. In this vein, you might compare and contrast the female characters of several of Shakespeare's plays in order to argue that his portrayal of women developed in a particular and identifiable way. To look at women and love, you might compare Juliet (of *Romeo and Juliet*) with Helena. To look at the rejected wife, you might compare *Cymbeline*'s Imogen and Helena. To examine marriage, you might compare the Macbeths with Helena and Bertram. There are really endless options when it comes to compare and contrast essays. The key is not to compare and contrast simply for the sake of doing so. Instead, be sure to use your observations and analysis to formulate a strong interpretation of and conclusion about the text.

Sample Topics:

1. **Bertram's relationship with Helena and Diana:** Compare and contrast Bertram's relationship with the two women in his life. What does it reveal about him?

   What do you know about Helena? What life experiences do she and Bertram share? How is their relationship characterized before she cures the king? What is Bertram's reaction to the king's edict that he should marry Helena? How does he inform Helena of his decision? Of his attitude? What is Helena's reaction? How does this impact Bertram? What should keep him from courting Diana? What is his excuse for courting her anyway? What is Diana's reaction? What are other characters' reactions? How does he treat Diana while he is courting her? How does he treat her when she comes to the court of France? How is this similar to how he treated Helena? How is it different?

2. **The tricking of Parolles and of Bertram:** Compare and contrast these two tricks, especially in terms of what they reveal about each of the characters.

   Both Parolles and Bertram are tricked in the play. Parolles is tricked so that Bertram may see his true nature. Bertram is tricked so that Helena might gain a husband. How are the tricks similar? What about the motivations for and the outcomes of the individual deceptions? What do the tricks and the reactions to them reveal about the two characters? Some say Shakespeare presents Parolles as a lovable scamp. Do you agree? Is this also Shakespeare's presentation of Bertram?

3. **Helena of** *All's Well That Ends Well* **and Imogen of** *Cymbeline:* Compare these two characters. What arguments can you make about Shakespeare's presentation of wronged wives?

Compare and contrast the main female characters in two of Shakespeare's romances. The husbands of both Helena and Imogen repudiate them. What does this say about Shakespeare's view of marriage? Of husbands? Of wives? Of marriage? How are their situations similar? How are they different? Are they simply clones of each other, or are the two women significantly different? Which one adopts a better approach and makes the better choices in her respective play?

Bibliography and Online Resources for *All's Well That Ends Well*

Ashliman, D. L. *Folklore and Mythology Electronic Texts.* U of Pittsburgh. Web. 21 May 2009.

"Background Information on Astrology." *Folger Shakespeare Library.* <http://www.folger.edu/documents/WhatsYourSignBackground.pdf>. Web. 21 May 2009.

Bloom, Harold. *Shakespeare: The Invention of the Human.* New York: Riverhead Books, 1998. Print.

Boccaccio, Giovanni. "Third Day: Play IX." *Decameron Web.* Brown U. <http://www.brown.edu/Departments/Italian_Studies/dweb/dec_ov/>. Web. 21 May 2009.

Bouwsma, William James. *The Waning of the Renaissance: 1550–1640.* Yale UP, 2002. Print.

Dyce, Alexander. *The Works of William Shakespeare, 4th edition.* London: Bickers & Sons, 1880. Web. 21 May 2009.

Frazier, Sir James George. *The Golden Bough: A Study of Magic and Religion, Abridged Edition.* 1922. <http://ebooks.adelaide.edu.au/f/frazer/james/golden/>. Web. 21 May 2009.

Huxley, Aldous. "Shakespeare and Religion." (*Sir Francis Bacon Web site.*) 1994. Web. 21 May 2009.

Painter, William. "The Thirty-Eighth Nouell." *Palace of Pleasure, Vol. 1.* Gutenberg Project. 2007. Web. 21 May 2009.

Shakespeare, William. *Open Source Shakespeare.* Ed. Eric M. Johnson. George Mason U, 2003. Web. 21 May 2009.

Simpson, Richard. "Was Shakespeare a Catholic?" *The Rambler* (July 1854): 19–35. *Internet Archive.* Web. < http://www.archive.org/>. 21 May 2009.

Simpson, Richard, and Henry Sebastian Bowden. *The Religion of Shakespeare.* London: Burns and Oates, Limited. 1899. Web. 21 May 2009.

PERICLES, PRINCE OF TYRE

READING TO WRITE

PERICLES (1603–08) is one of Shakespeare's more problematic plays, as it is not commonly seen as one of his better efforts, and the explanations for this are hotly debated in scholarly circles. One argument contends that the entire play is Shakespeare's original work but that he rewrote a much earlier play in which the improvements are obvious. The difficulty with this argument is that if he revised, why did he not rewrite everything? Another argument holds that Shakespeare's reading inspired him to experiment with a distant tone, which some critics proclaim is the reason that the play is uneven. Experiments are, after all, often not wholly successful. Still another argument is that the play was partially written by someone else, most likely George Wilkins, and finished by Shakespeare, who was limited in his alteration of the already extant work. Some contemporary scholars, such as Lynn Yarris, argue against the work being Shakespeare's at all. Rather than trying to read and assimilate all of the existing critical positions, however, begin much more simply. Start by selecting a particularly striking or intriguing passage to closely read in order to spur your thinking. One important element in the play is the concept of kingship. The description Pericles gives of Simonides, his future father-in-law, who is king of Pentapolis, is one telling example:

> Yon king's to me like to my father's picture,
> Which tells me in that glory once he was;

> Had princes sit, like stars, about his throne,
> And he the sun, for them to reverence;
> None that beheld him, but, like lesser lights,
> Did vail their crowns to his supremacy:
> Where now his son's like a glow-worm in the night,
> The which hath fire in darkness, none in light:
> Whereby I see that Time's the king of men,
> He's both their parent, and he is their grave,
> And gives them what he will, not what they crave. (2.3.860–70)

By saying that Simonides looks like his father, what is Pericles suggesting about appearance? Do all kings look alike or resemble one another? What argument could be made with such a starting point? Pericles discusses the king as a sun the stars revolve around. Aside from questionable cosmology, what does this say about the position and importance of the king? Does it make a difference to say that the stars were seen as satellites, much like the moon around Earth? What does such imagery suggest about the view of kingship Shakespeare is expounding? Pericles compares his father to the sun and himself to a glowworm. What is the significance of that? Why is it so important that Pericles describes the property of the glowworm as having light that is only visible at night? What does that say about the relative glory of his father and of Pericles? What does this comparison say about Simonides?

After talking about three kings, two living and one dead, Pericles branches off into a discussion of metaphorical authority. If kings are the brightest lights in the heavens but can be dimmed by time, that makes time the king and master of all, he argues. Why is time afforded this powerful and lofty position? What can Pericles do that the other kings can only do in a limited manner? What can time do that no one else can? Pericles states that time is the parent and the grave of men. If this is a description of kingship, how might it be applied to the kings in the play? Don't limit yourself to those regents under discussion here. Include also Cleon and Antiochus. How are the five men parents and graves? Are they lesser lights by this description? And if they are, what does that make those individuals who are not kings?

Based on the questions you have generated thus far, you might decide to investigate in your essay the different types of rulers discussed in the play. This would allow the topic to be expanded to discuss Lysimachus as well, since he was the governor and ultimate authority of Myteline. Which of these kings does Shakespeare offer as positive examples? Which as negative? What qualities do these different men show? What actions are described? Which qualities or actions are rewarded in the play? Which are punished? Which are neither rewarded nor punished? What does that say about those qualities or actions? Alternately, you might decide to look at the presentation of time in the play. Since time fulfills an important part in the play, though offstage, a discussion of its implications might be provoking. How did time save Pericles from an assassin? How did time favor Pericles when he was shipwrecked? What caused Pericles to leave his daughter in Tarsus for years? What was he doing during that time? What was she doing? What was happening with Thaisa? When Diana sends him straight to Ephesus, how is the timing important?

This single passage has provided several possible essay ideas. If you were to select one of the topics suggested here, use your notes to help identify other relevant passages to analyze; they in turn will lead to additional relevant passages. After you have identified and analyzed all the passages pertinent to your topic, you would then synthesize your findings and use them to help develop a thesis, the argument or interpretation of the text that your essay will present.

TOPICS AND STRATEGIES

There is a wide variety of approaches to writing about *Pericles, Prince of Tyre*. Use the sample topics and questions as a starting point. You can adopt one of the ideas, combine two, or come up with your own. When you decide on a topic, remember to spend time generating ideas and closely reading relevant passages. Only after significant preparation will you be ready to construct your thesis sentence, which states the argument that you will make in your essay. Once you have decided on your claim, you can begin writing your essay, presenting the evidence that supports your position. Not everything you come up with in your preparation will be used in the final essay. Having more information than you need can be evidence of sufficient preparation.

Themes

Looking at themes in a work of literature requires an examination of the work to find important ideas or concepts that are covered in the play. *Pericles* offers many points of departure for the examination of themes. The samples below are only a few of the possibilities. You do not have to know everything the play says about a theme when you begin. Being aware that a theme is present and important is a good starting point for examining the play to see what it says in regard to that theme.

Sample Topics:

1. **Acceptable behavior and its regulation:** How does Shakespeare show that expected behavior is rewarded and unacceptable behavior is punished?

   Unequivocally, the play states that Antiochus and his daughter and Cleon and Dionyza received the just punishment for their actions. What were their transgressions? Were there early hints that this was not acceptable behavior? How did they attempt to hide their sins? How were their sins exposed? Who announces their just reward? What does this add to the solemnity of the information? How is justice described in the play?

   Who are the good people in the play? Are they ultimately rewarded? How are these rewards meted out? Who gives the rewards? Are these superiors or inferiors? What does this say about how societal norms are enforced? Does it say anything about the social order?

2. **Fate or destiny:** The belief in fate is a belief that people cannot control their destinies: What is going to happen will happen, irrespective of what a person does to try to control life. What is the play's position on this view?

   Impersonal fate plays a large part in the play. Pericles goes to Antioch to woo the king's daughter. He is slated by the king to die, but he escapes. How is this fate? He saves the people of Tarsus as part of his escape from his assassin. How is this evidence of fate, both immediately and later in the play? Pericles ends up shipwrecked at Pentapolis. How does this further evidence of fate? His armor being retrieved from the water, what does that reveal about fate? Does fate only control the important people, or does it control everyone? How does Thaisa's coffin being brought to Cerimon illustrate fate? How does Marina being brought to cheer up Pericles an example of fate? What other instances of fate can you find in the play? In a more modern story, these effects might be seen as coincidence. How does fate differ from coincidence? Are any of these examples coincidence rather than fate? Where is coincidence seen in the play?

3. **Honor:** What does the play have to say about honor?

In the play, Antiochus is the first to discuss honor. Is this ironic? What does it tell us about honor, real and perceived? How does Pericles discuss honor and dishonor in act 1, scene 2? How does the tournament honor Thaisa? Why is it an honor for her to read the heraldic emblems on the shields? How is honor related to the gods (2.3)? Simonides invokes Thaisa's honor in a vow not to marry. Bawd and Boult refer to various people as "your honor." This was a common practice for those of lower social status when speaking to individuals of a higher social status. Is it also ironic? Lysimachus is described as honorable, and Marina disputes this descriptor. Why? Does Lysimachus prove his honor?

4. **Virginity:** The virginity of Thaisa and Marina is emphasized in the play. Why was a virginal state deemed important? Why was virginity a necessity in Shakespeare's time?

Simonides states that Thaisa will not marry for a year on the honor of her virginity. How does this action get rid of her suitors? Why is this important? Marina is sold as a virgin to the brothel owners. What economic use do they intend to make of her virginity? How does this show a different interpretation of the importance of virginity? How do the brothel owners represent or characterize virginity? Even after significant time in the brothel, Marina remains a virgin. What is the significance of this? How has it happened? What other virgins are mentioned in the play? How do they tie Thaisa and Marina together?

Character

One way to examine a text is to choose a character and analyze what the work suggests and reveals about that character. *Pericles, Prince of Tyre* encourages analysis of both major characters, such as Pericles and Marina, and more minor ones, such as Helicanus and Gower. Examining characters requires that you not only absorb what they say in the play but also what others say about them. You should also determine what type of character you have chosen. Is the character a protagonist or antagonist? Is the character static, meaning he or she remains the same throughout the work, or is he or she dynamic, meaning the character changes? Most important characters in a literary work are dynamic. If the character changes, how is that alteration indicated in the play? What is the change caused by? Is the change presented as positive or negative? Is the character you have chosen to examine three-dimensional or round—meaning that multiple facets of her or his personality are discussed—or is your character one-dimensional or flat, meaning that only one aspect of her or his life is evidenced onstage?

Sample Topics:

1. **Pericles:** Analyze and evaluate the character of Pericles.

   Pericles is the title character of the work. This immediately indicates his importance to the play. What does the audience learn about Pericles first? How does this shape their acceptance of Pericles? What goal is Pericles seen pursuing? Is he successful in the pursuit of this goal? Is the success immediate or delayed? What responsibilities does Pericles abandon? Why does he abandon them? What is the impetus for his going back to them? What do his abandonment and/or his return tell us about his character? How does Pericles react when fate intervenes in his life? Does he continue on, or does he give up? Pericles makes vows in the play. Does he keep these? Are they easy vows to honor? What does this say about his character? What finally overwhelms Pericles to the extent that he will not speak to anyone? Is this a reasonable reaction or an over-reaction? How does he shake off or transcend his depression? Does Pericles take advice? Whose advice does he take? What does this reveal about his character? What are the strengths and the weaknesses that Pericles exhibits? What do these tell us about the character?

2. **Marina:** Analyze and evaluate the character of Marina.

Reread the play focusing on the development of the character of Marina. The play follows her from birth to adolescence and adulthood, skipping over large gaps in between. How are the various presentations of Marina important? Marina's name indicates her association with the sea or bodies of water. How does this relation of the character to the sea manifest itself throughout the play? Look up the geography of the various places where she lives. How is Marina educated? How does this education cause problems for her? How does it help her? In what ways does Marina use her education to protect herself, make a living, and encourage others? When is Marina's life easy? When is it hard? What is revealed about her through her reaction to difficult times? How does Marina use story and narration to rescue her father? Was that her intention? What was her intention? How much influence does Marina have over her final disposition? Is she able to choose her husband, status, or job? Who is able to choose those things? What does this say about Marina in particular and women in general?

3. **Dionyza:** Analyze the character of Dionyza.

What is Dionyza's social status? When does she enter the play? Is she strong at this point? What problems is she facing? How does she deal with them? Later she vows to love Marina as she loves her own child. What does this show about her? Does she keep this vow, and what does that reveal about her?

After Leonine does her bidding, or says he does, how is he rewarded? What do her reactions and rewards indicate about Dionyza's character? How does Dionyza's husband talk of and to her when he learns of her actions? What is her response? How does she deal with the murders she has committed? Why is the contracted murder of Marina particularly heinous? This topic can be approached in terms of honor, debts, cannibalism, child murder, and abuse of authority. What did Dionyza gain from Pericles? What has she lost to Marina? What is her final reward? How is that discussed and presented in the play?

4. **Simonides:** Analyze and evaluate the character of Simonides.

Write down what you know about Simonides. What was his social status? How was he perceived? How is he referred to? What adjective often precedes his name? What is his relationship with his daughter? How does he treat Thaisa? Does he honor her wishes? How does he discuss her? Pericles compares Simonides to his father. What does this comparison say about Simonides? Thaisa does not return to her father after she is rescued from the sea but goes to live in Ephesus. What does this relocation reveal about Simonides?

History and Context

Shakespeare's play *Pericles, Prince of Tyre* is based on at least two earlier accounts of the prince of Tyre. In John Gower's work *Confessio Amantis*, the story is told as "The Tale of Apollonius of Tyre" and is one of the major English versions of this Latin tale, which itself may have been a retelling of an even older Greek story. Lawrence Twine's *The Patterne of Paynfull Adventures* was also a probable source Shakespeare used for the play. The play is not a seamless text, and many scholars think there were two authors (Vickers 291).

Sample Topics:

1. **Two authors:** Read the play with the assumption that there are two authors and determine which sections you think were written by each.

Note where language, style, and setting seem different. Are there sections that do not seem to fit in the play at all? Are metaphors used throughout some sections and not in others? Do you see line length differences? One way some people have argued against Shakespeare being the single author of the play is by saying that he wrote too well to have written some sections. Which sections do you think are written well? Do they remind you of other plays that Shakespeare wrote? Can you make any suppositions about the possible second author based on what he wrote about or how he wrote?

2. **Roman mythology:** Diana, Cynthia, and Lucina are all Roman goddesses named in the play. Why are they referred to, and what are the implications of their being mentioned?

The Roman goddess Diana was associated with the hunt and chastity. She is referenced 16 times in the play, 18 if you include the references to other goddesses with whom she shared many attributes or who were Greek equivalents. She is a strong female authority figure in the play. What is the significance of Thaisa wearing "Diana's livery" (2.5.1024)? Cynthia is another name for the goddess Artemis, the Greek equivalent of the Roman Diana. Is there significance in two references to goddesses in two lines in Simonides's discussion of Thaisa's vow? Pericles calls on Lucina, the goddess of childbirth and of light, but Diana was also viewed as the goddess of childbirth. So, Pericles may have been calling on another aspect of the goddess Diana. When Thaisa awakens after the storm, whose name does she call? Why did Pericles swear by Diana? What did he swear? Why was it fitting that Thaisa retired to Diana's temple? How is it ironic that Diana is served by virgins? How would Thaisa be able to be a votary there? Marina also calls on Diana. How is that appropriate? Pericles, a supreme ruler of his country, is subject to the authority of Diana. Was this an early feminist argument on Shakespeare's part? If so, what are the implications for Shakespeare's play?

3. **The Virgin Queen:** Queen Elizabeth I ruled during Shakespeare's lifetime. A female ruler was a difficult concept for many people of that age to accept or understand.

What evidence does the play offer to show how women can rule men? What about Shakespeare's presentation of Diana in the play? Does she rule men? Could this relate to the queen, whom England had been living under in Shakespeare's lifetime? Does her status as the "virgin queen" identify her with Diana? Does it influence your opinion to know that Elizabeth was identified with Diana in her various incarnations in literature, art, and music? What might this mean for Shakespeare's play? You might want to look at biographical information on Elizabeth I and see if anything else about her life indicates she is directly linked to the characterization and presentation of Diana.

Philosophy and Ideas

Pericles, Prince of Tyre introduces multiple philosophical beliefs. In order to write an essay on the philosophy or ideas expressed in the play, you need to choose one to focus on. You might be interested in what the play says about parenting among the upper class, order and disorder, use and abuse of power, virtue and vice. A good way to begin with philosophy and ideas is to read thoroughly on the subject you have chosen before moving on to your scrutiny of the text. After preliminary research to make sure you understand the concepts, you can return to the play and look for and analyze sections that deal with your topic.

Sample Topics:

1. **Vice and virtue:** Virtue has already been discussed as a theme in the play. How do vice and virtue represent ideals, both positive and negative, in the play?

In the play, Pericles says that "Kings are earth's gods; in vice their law's / their will" (1.1.152–53) and asks who can stop the gods. He is referring here to the incest of Antiochus and his daughter. How does their situation illustrate the voracious nature of vice? What cost does the vice bring to Pericles? If the title of the play is an explication of importance, then the play is about rulers. What other rulers and their vices or virtues can you detect in the play? How are vices rewarded? How are virtues rewarded? Are the rewards instantaneous, or do they take time? How does Shakespeare make connections between what actions are taken by the characters and how they ultimately end up? Is everyone who dies in the play evil? What does this say about the rewards of vice and virtue?

2. **Order and disorder:** How are the concepts of order and disorder represented in the play? What are the ramifications?

There is physical disorder at sea, when Thaisa dies, her coffin is thrown overboard, and Pericles is shipwrecked. The dumping of the body in the sea was intended to create order out of chaos: "the sea works high, / the wind is loud, and will not lie till the ship be / cleared of the dead" (3.1.1244–46). What does the quotation indicate about the importance of order for the sailors? The incest of Antiochus and his daughter is also disorder of the moral order. How is this resolved in the play? Who is able to restore order? The attempted murder of Marina was also a disruption of the moral order in several ways, since it included elements of murder, child murder, and regicide or the murder of a royal. Though Marina was not killed, the attempt created disorder. How was order restored? By whom? What is said about this particular regicide?

3. **Parenting among the upper class:** What does the play imply about the parenting philosophies of the highest socioeconomic group?

There are multiple examples of parenting, good and bad, in the play. Antiochus's parenting of his daughter, exposing her to an incestuous relationship, is portrayed in the play as clearly wrong. The results of this style of parenting are dramatic. The references to parenting include the residents of Tarsus, where parents are described as being prepared to eat "those little darlings whom they loved" (1.4.460). This is clearly not a positive view of parenting. Simonides's parenting of his daughter Thaisa, including giving a tournament in honor of her, having taught her to read heraldic devices, and listening to her preferences on a husband, is held up as the ideal, through the references to him as good, in Pericles's comparison of him to his father, and in the virtue displayed by Thaisa. Simonides is held up as a positive example of parenting. Pericles's parenting is much more problematic. His daughter is born at sea and needs care, which he secures for her as soon as possible. He then leaves her in Tarsus for 14 years. What are the results of the separation and what do they suggest about this particular style of parenting? All of these descriptions point to the importance of parenting in the play. What can be said about it? What other examples of parenting among the upper class are illustrated in the play?

4. **Luck:** Another aspect of *Pericles, Prince of Tyre* is the concept of luck. How is it represented and its influence felt in the play overall?

Both good and bad luck are each referenced in the play. Good luck comes in the form of the armor left to Pericles by his father. How useful has it been to date? Why does he need it at this point? Does it work as a talisman? Bad luck comes with the death of Thaisa at sea. The sailor insists on getting rid of the body. Does tossing the body into the sea bring calm? Is the custom shown to be useful to the sailors? Is Thaisa saved because she was thrown out? Cerimon refers to chance in terms of finding Thaisa. Dionyza says it is chance that her daughter is not with Marina. Gower suggests it is chance that brings Marina to an "honest house" (5.0.2145). Is chance another way of saying luck? Or is chance another word for coincidence? Are luck and coincidence the same thing? How can they be seen as functioning in the play?

5. **Use and abuse of power:** *Pericles, Prince of Tyre* is particularly apt for a discussion of the use and abuse of power. How does power, in its negative and positive applications, function in the play?

One approach to this topic would be scrutinizing the good examples of rulers (Pericles, Helicanus, Simonides) and contrasting them with the abusive leaders (Antiochus and Dionyza). Simonides is referred to as good by his subjects. What does this say about his use of power? How is he revealed in the play to be a good king? How is Pericles a strong ruler? Look at the ways in which he provides for his own people and for others. How is Helicanus shown to be a good ruler? Often power corrupts. Does power corrupt Helicanus? Abusive leaders factor in to the opening and conclusion of the play. Gower introduces Antiochus at the beginning and refers to the death of Cleon and Dionyza at the end. What does the use of this framing device indicate about the importance of the concept of the application of power?

Form and Genre

Literature is identified as such partially because it is well crafted. Every line indicates a choice made by the author(s). Examine how the story is organized and presented. What familiar literary patterns does it replicate or modify? To aid you in your thinking, try to imagine what the work would be like if the author had made different decisions. It might help you to know that the structure of *Pericles, Prince of Tyre* is seen as problematic and is one of the indications that Shakespeare is not the author, or at least not the sole author, of the play.

Sample Topics:

1. **Comedy:** Some critics characterize *Pericles, Prince of Tyre* as a comedy. What parts of the work support this argument?

Look at a good description of comedy (such as L. Kip Wheeler's). The comedic aspects of the play might be noted in the overall impact. Does the play stress humanity's progress? Does it show a movement from stricture to freedom? Does it present life as something to be enjoyed and celebrated? Does it censure folly? Does it suggest negativity, for example presenting the belief that humanity is foolish, but offer hope for improvement? If so, how does it do so? To what extent is Pericles a comedic hero? Is he foolish, and is his foolishness revealed? Does he change dramatically without reason? Is he self-righteous? Does he embrace the group, eschewing his individuality? Does he pretend to be more important than he is? Is he average? The comic methods are somewhat visible in the play. Is the plot intricate and implausible? Are accidents and chance the main elements propelling the plot?

2. **Structure:** Analyze the structure of the play. How does the structure help create meaning in the play?

The structure of *Pericles, Prince of Tyre* has often been found to be problematic. There is a loose chronology in which a year or a dozen can pass between one scene and the next. The sea journeys might perhaps provide structural integrity, but they are also loosely configured. Many of the journeys are to and from Tarsus. Does that make Tarsus a central site in the play? Many have argued that the first two acts of the play were written by someone else. What does this view do to alter your understanding of the structure? What is the impact on a play in which each half is written by a different author? Could the different authors explain the structural difficulties?

3. **Narrator:** What can be learned about *Pericles, Prince of Tyre* by examining the role of Gower?

In ancient Greek drama, the chorus served various functions including adding pageantry, providing time for scene and costume changes, presenting necessary information not in the play, emphasizing a theme, providing commentary (Kirkwood 182), and espousing a particular point of view (187). In what ways does Gower function like the Greek chorus? In what ways does he add to the possible roles of the chorus? What would be the point of including a single person rather than a group of people in this role? You could look at that question in several ways, from stage management issues to economic ones to its impact on the audience.

Does it make a difference to your understanding of Gower's function in the play to know that the real John Gower, a fourteenth-century poet, is one of the sources from which Shakespeare borrowed the story of Pericles?

Language, Symbols, and Imagery

Language is the fabric of a literary text. Words create the text and allow us to hear or read it. In terms of a play, the words were originally written to be read. Reading a play and hearing it are two different experiences. Part of Shakespeare's appeal is that his plays are crafted in such a way that they present a strong story even on paper. Sometimes different aspects of the play are more noticeable or identifiable when seen. The genius of Shakespeare's writing, however, is often best examined in a slow perusal of the language. Shakespeare used his talent for writing to make enduring comments on communication in *Pericles, Prince of Tyre*. While the play is at least 400 years old, its use of language, symbols, and imagery is still fresh. Something keeps *Pericles* in print, and part of that is Shakespeare's facility for language.

Sample Topics:

1. **Language:** What is the point of the heraldic devices in Latin?

Historically, many British families adopted or associated their names with Latin mottos. Some of these came from the Roman era and some from the medieval era, when the language acquired great prestige. Shakespeare could have been harking back to Britain's Roman era or could have been referencing the esteemed status afforded Latin. Look at the Latin lines and their translations:

"Lux tua vita mihi" (2.2.772).	"Your light is my life" (Stone 177).
"Piu por dulzura que por fuerza" (2.2.779).	"More by gentleness than by force" (Ray 15).
"Me pompae provexit apex" (2.2.783).	"The summit of glory has inspired me" (Stone 179).
"Quod me alit, me extinguit" (2.2.788).	"What feeds me extinguishes me" (200).
"Sic spectanda fides" (2.2.793).	"Thus is faith to be examined" (206).
"In hac spe vivo" (2.2.801).	"In this hope I live" (169).

What do these have to say about the courting of Thaisa? What do they say about the knights courting her? Is there a theme here? What is it? Why would these mottos and expressions be deemed more impressive in Latin than in English? What is ironic about the device on the shield of Pericles? How is it a foreshadowing of the play's conclusion?

2. **Oath making:** There are several oaths taken or vows made in *Pericles, Prince of Tyre*. What is the importance of this particular mode of language and its function in the play?

Some of the oaths, such as Pericles's vow not to cut his hair until his daughter's wedding, are kept. Others, such as Cleon's promise to repay the debt Tarsus owes Pericles or "The curse of heaven and men succeed their evils!" (1.4.524), are not. What is the function of the oaths in the story? Leonine says he will swear that Marina is dead and thrown into the sea, a philosophical truth if not an actual one. How does his false testimony lead to his doom? What impact do the oaths have? What rhetorical function do they serve? Are they meant to increase solemnity? Do they succeed?

3. **Sea:** What do the journeys symbolize in the play? How is the sea a metaphor?

The sea voyages that Pericles takes are important aspects of the play. They bring him into danger in Antioch, to meet Thaisa in Pentapolis, to lose Thaisa on the way to Tarsus, to pick up his daughter, and to wander, lost in his grief. What does the sea symbolize? In literature, journeys are often metaphors for growth and the process of maturing. Does this pattern apply to *Pericles?* In what ways might Pericles need to grow up? If the journeys symbolize growth, in what ways does he change with each trip? What else might they symbolize? Life as a journey is also a common metaphor. Are the sea voyages about various stages of life? If so, what stages are in the play? How might they correspond to childhood, young adult, marriageable age, parenthood, and old age? Does this work as an explanation for the sea journeys? What does such an explanation tell us about the work as a whole? Does it change the point?

4. **Allusions to Christianity and the Bible:** Even though the play is set specifically in a world of Roman mythology, there are references to Christianity integrated throughout the play. Some are more obvious than others. How do references to Christian theology affect the work's effect overall?

Is the discussion with the fisherman a reference to the book of Jonah? Jonah was swallowed by a sea creature. How would that story fit with the action presented in the play? Jonah was also spit out onto dry land. Does that establish a parallel with Pericles being cast onto the coast? Or is the casting overboard of Thaisa's body a reference to the storm in the book of Jonah? Jonah was cast from the boat to calm the storm. Jonah had disobeyed God. Had someone in *Pericles* gone against any of the gods represented there? What could these multiple similarities and comparisons to Jonah mean? The fishermen in the play become fishers of men. How is this an ironic reference to Matthew 4:19? If Pericles, by being rescued, has made them fishers of men, does this mean that Pericles is a Christ figure? How can he be seen as such? After he is rescued, the fisherman says they will have meat for holy days and fish for fasting days, a reference to the Catholic habit of eating fish on Fridays during the season of Lent. What is the point of including a reference to Catholicism? During the storm in which Marina is born, Pericles calls on the god of the sea to command the wind to be still. Is this a reference to the biblical story of Jesus calming a storm (Mark 4:35–41)? Pericles goes to Ephesus at Diana's command. In Acts 19:34, there is an uproar at Ephesus created in part by the worshippers of Diana. How would this allusion resonate with the audience? What would they be thinking as a result of this linking of the play and the New Testament story?

Compare and Contrast Essays

Sometimes looking at two similar works can reveal insights and critical positions that examining a single text cannot. Any of the romances could fruitfully be compared with the other romances, but the importance of the storm in *Pericles, Prince of Tyre* and *The Tempest* makes these two works seem likely candidates for a compare and/or contrast approach. The fact that both stories hinge on tales of intrigue occurring at the highest social levels and that a father-daughter pair are major characters in both adds to the possibilities for comparison and contrast. While you might begin by comparing and contrasting the plays in general, you would eventually want to narrow your focus, selecting a particular aspect of the plays to compare. You might focus on the storm as impetus in the plays, discussing the causes of the storms and their results. Whatever you choose to focus on, your analysis could be used to generalize about Shakespeare's writing or to point out and elaborate on the significant differences in the two plays. Of course you are not restricted to comparing and contrasting works by the same author. You might choose to compare a work with another piece of literature penned in the same period, one with similar themes or one the work itself seems to directly allude to. A good choice for a comparison or contrast essay might be to look at one of the sources for the play. Consulting a modern version of book 8 of John Gower's *Confessio Amantis* would give you insight when interpreting the poem "The Tale of Apollonious of Tyre."

Sample Topics:

1. *Pericles, Prince of Tyre* **and "The Clerk's Tale" in Chaucer's** *Canterbury Tales:* Pericles has been called a male Griselda. Look at the two texts. How accurate is the comparison?

   Are there differences besides the gender of the patient person? Who is responsible for the difficulties the two experience? How are their sufferings similar? How are they different? How long do their trials last? What is the purpose of their sufferings? Do the two main characters each mature over the course of their stories? In what ways? How are the two deaths in each text similar and how do they differ? Are there more than surface differences? Do the other characters in the tales mature?

2. **Father-daughter relationships in** *Pericles, Prince of Tyre* **and** *The Tempest:* Compare and contrast the relationships between Pericles and Marina and Prospero and Miranda.

   Was Shakespeare changing his focus in his later plays to emphasize the role and importance of family? What is the point of focusing on father-daughter relationships? Look at a biography of Shakespeare that discusses his children. It might offer one avenue of exploration. You might also want to look at cultural elements portrayed in the relationships. Was Shakespeare separated from his daughters, as Pericles was from Marina? Did he control his daughter's life, as Prospero did Miranda's? How common would these situations have been during Shakespeare's time? Might he have seen these situations in other people's lives? Alternately, you might choose to compare and contrast the romantic relationships in the two plays, specifically examining the role of the fathers of the bride in the development of the child's nuptial relationship. You might then make an argument on marriage as it relates to family obligations. What was Shakespeare suggesting about this patriarchal process of arranging marriages?

Bibliography and Online Resources for *Pericles, Prince of Tyre*

"The Classical Greek Chorus." *Southeastern Louisiana U.* n.d. <http://www2. selu.edu/Academics/Faculty/jwiemelt/classes/engl230/chorus.htm>. Web. 1 June 2009.

Davis, Suanna. "How to Write a Character Analysis." *Teaching College English.* 28 February 2008. Web. 1 June 2009.

Frazier, Sir James George. "XII. The Sacred Marriage, 1. Diana as a Goddess of Fertility." *The Golden Bough: A Study of Magic and Religion, Abridged Edition.* 1922. <http://ebooks.adelaide.edu.au/f/frazer/james/golden/>. Web. 1 June 2009.

Gower, John. "The Tale of Apollonius of Tyre." *Confessio Amantis: A Modern English Translation.* Book VIII. Ed. Richard Brodie. 2005. <http://www. richardbrodie.com/Book8.html>. 1 June 2009. Web.

Graves, T. S. "On the Date and Significance of 'Pericles.'" *Modern Philology* 13.9 (January 1916). 545–56. *JSTOR.* Web. 1 July 2009.

Hamilton, Edith. *Mythology.* New York: Back Bay Books, 1998. Print.

Hart, F. Elizabeth. "'Great is Diana' of Shakespeare's Ephesus." *Studies in English Literature, 1500–1900* 43.2 (Spring 2003). 347–74. *JSTOR.* Web. 1 July 2009.

Kirkwood, Gordon MacDonald. *A Study of Sophoclean Drama.* Ithaca, NY: Cornell UP, 1994. Print.

Moore, Jeanie Grant. "Riddled Romance: Kingship and Kinship in 'Pericles.'" *Rocky Mountain Review of Language and Literature* 57.1 (2003). 33–48. *JSTOR.* Web. 1 July 2009.

Ray, Emily Grider. *Teacher Resource Packet: Pericles by William Shakespeare.* BYU Young Company Shakespeare Troupe, 2008. Web. 1 July 2009.

Rolfe, William J. *Shakespeare's History of Pericles, Prince of Tyre.* New York: Harper & Brothers, Publishers, 1884. Web. 1 July 2009.

Schofield, William Henry. *English Literature from the Norman Conquest to Chaucer.* New York: Macmillan Company, 1906.

Shakespeare, William. *Open Source Shakespeare.* Ed. Eric M. Johnson. George Mason U, 2003. Web. 1 July 2009.

———. *The Works of William Shakespeare, Vol. VIII.* Ed. Henry Irving and Frank A. Marshall. London: Blackie & Son, 1890. Web. 1 July 2009.

Stone, Jon R. *The Routledge Dictionary of Latin Quotations: The Illiterati's Guide to Latin Maxims, Mottoes, Proverbs, and Sayings.* New York: Routledge, 2004. Print.

Thorne, W. B. "Pericles and the 'Incest-Fertility' Opposition." *Shakespeare Quarterly* 22.1 (Winter 1971): 43–56. *JSTOR*. Web. 1 July 2009.

Tompkins, J. M. S. "Why Pericles?" *The Review of English Studies, New Series* 3.12 (October 1952). 315–24. *JSTOR*. Web. 1 July 2009.

Vickers, Brian. *Shakespeare, Co-Author: A Historical Study of Five Collaborative Plays*. New York: Oxford UP, 2004. Print.

"The Virgin Queen." *Internet Shakespeare Editions*. University of Victoria. <http://internetshakespeare.uvic.ca/Library/SLT/history/virgin.html>. Web. 1 July 2009.

Wheeler, L. Kip. "Some Distinctions Between Classical Tragedy and Comedy." *Dr. Wheeler's Homepage at Carson-Newman*. Carson-Newman College. 2008. Web. 1 July 2009.

Yarris, Lynn. "From the Works of Shakespeare to the Genomes of Viruses: Berkeley Lab Scientists Create a Unique New Tool for Analyzing and Comparing Data." Berkeley Lab News Center, U.S. Department of Energy. 10 February 2009. Web. 1 July 2009.

CYMBELINE

READING TO WRITE

SHAKESPEARE'S *CYMBELINE* (1609–11, first published in 1623) presents the story of King Cymbeline's family. Even though the events of the play involve only the king's family, the variety of personalities and story lines provide a virtually limitless number of potential essay topics. In addition, since Cymbeline is king of Britain, the story line also involves his nation in a war with Rome, a war provoked by his wife. This offers another angle on the family story.

By closely reading and analyzing the text or a passage, you can identify a topic or discover evidence for a claim. When you closely read a passage, you go through multiple times. Ask yourself why Shakespeare selected and arranged the words of this passage in the precise way that he did. Imagine how the sense of the passage would change if you replaced any of the words with a synonym or reordered the sentences. Choose a passage of interest to you, perhaps one of the queen's speeches, such as this one:

> The kings your ancestors, together with
> The natural bravery of your isle, which stands
> As Neptune's park, ribbed and paled in
> With rocks unscalable and roaring waters,
> With sands that will not bear your enemies' boats,
> But suck them up to the topmast. A kind of conquest
> Caesar made here; but made not here his brag
> Of 'Came' and 'saw' and 'overcame:' with shame—
> That first that ever touch'd him—he was carried
> From off our coast, twice beaten; and his shipping—
> Poor ignorant baubles!—upon our terrible seas,

> Like egg-shells moved upon their surges, crack'd
> As easily 'gainst our rocks: for joy whereof
> The famed Cassibelan, who was once at point—
> O giglot fortune!—to master Caesar's sword,
> Made Lud's town with rejoicing fires bright
> And Britons strut with courage. (3.2.1431–45)

The references in this passage to Britain's historical involvement with Rome, to Julius Caesar and his three attempts to conquer the island, to his famous statement "veni, vidi, vici," and to the island's natural defenses all offer an interesting approach to the play's involvement with British nationalism. Since nationalism is a large theme in the play, these references offer a starting point for a discussion of nationalism. The fact that Julius Caesar, famous for his conquests, was foiled twice in his attempt to conquer England offers evidence of Britain's martial power, as does the final section, which discusses the people's rejoicing and strutting. Cassibelan was a pre-Roman conquest leader who fought against Julius Caesar. Though he lost the struggle, the queen invokes and pays homage to his resistance and spirit.

A review of the cultural history of Britain could start from this quotation, which includes references to King Lud, whose town eventually became London, and then move on to the Roman invasions that came after Lud. From the play, what can we assume that the audience of Shakespeare's time knew about these ancient kings? How might the audience respond to this presentation of Britain's history? Why are these kings discussed and not other, more recent and thus more renowned, kings? What history of the Roman invasion and occupation is invoked in this play and by this passage?

The references to the king's ancestors, including Cassibelan, offer a point of departure for discussing Cymbeline's family, perhaps starting with the queen's use of the family. She wants the king to refuse Rome tribute, so she invokes his famous ancestor Cassibelan. The queen married Cymbeline to gain power and in the hope of gaining the throne for her son. She uses her marriage to Cymbeline to work toward that end. The queen has promised to love Cymbeline's daughter as her own but plots against Imogen's happiness in order to marry her to Cloten and clear the way for his taking the throne. Thus, from Cassibelan to the queen to Imogen, we have a direct connection to the family from this one passage. Of course, we can branch out from the queen to Cloten and from Imogen to her brothers. The family connections are strong in this play, and this passage offers history as a basis for the discussion of them.

Clearly, a close reading of one passage can generate ideas for several essays. If you have analyzed a passage and generated several questions and ideas, you should then identify other passages that you think will lead you to a defendable thesis or, at the very least, help you to refine your thoughts. Analyze these subsequent passages as you did the first until you feel as though you have reached a conclusion that might function as a claim on which you can base your essay.

TOPICS AND STRATEGIES

Only a few of the possible topics that could be pursued are presented here. Use them to jump-start your imagination. Do not think of them as an outline for your paper. Instead, use the questions and observations to help you generate ideas. Once you have recorded your ideas and analyzed relevant passages in the play, you should formulate your claim, the argument you want your essay to make. Then, go back to your notes and begin to marshal evidence in support of your thesis, organizing and arranging your thoughts into a persuasive essay.

Themes

When you think about a play's theme, you are attempting to determine what major ideas or issues the work conveys or presents. Many works will share the same themes, as there are central questions that people have consistently grappled with in the form of literature. Each work will have its own slant on the themes with which it deals, and it is your job as a writer to discover and articulate this perspective in your essay. *Cymbeline* deals with themes such as love, nature and nurture, nationalism, and forgiveness and reconciliation. By isolating the most significant passages pertaining to one of these themes and then reading them closely, with an aim to analyzing their language, you can discover what the play is attempting to articulate about that particular issue; in so doing, you will have created a claim upon which to base your essay.

Sample Topics:

1. **Love:** What is the play's message about love? Who loves? How do they love?

   The main presentation of romantic love in the play is between Imogen and Posthumus. In the beginning, what does their relationship seem to be based on? What does it provide them? How are they going to maintain this relationship across distances? What does Posthumus say about Imogen to Iachimo? What does Iachimo's failure to seduce her tell us of Imogen's love? What does Posthumus's reaction to the "proof" of Imogen's unfaithfulness tell us about his love? What does it say about his willingness to believe in Imogen's infidelity? What does his vilification of Imogen say about Posthumus and his love? What does Imogen's reaction to Posthumus's orders to Pisanio tell us about her love? What does her misidentification of the body of Cloten tell us about her love? What does her reaction tell us about her love for Posthumus? What does the reunion scene say about Imogen's love? What does it say about Posthumus's love?

   A possible second and corollary example of romantic love is that between the king and the queen. What does the queen say to the king when they are with Caius Lucius? How does she address him? Is there any evidence of feeling between them other than as rulers of Britain? Does the king's reaction to his wife's deathbed confessions show anything about love? How does it demonstrate the limits of love? What does it say about false love?

2. **Nature versus nurture:** Nature is now more commonly known as genetics. Nurture is the environment in which a person is raised. How does nature influence an individual's personality and character? What part does nurture play in the formation of personality and character? Which one dominates?

   In the play, there are several competing examples of the ramifications of nature versus nurture. Examine the play, paying special attention to the scenes that offer commentary on the issue of nature versus nurture, either through example of how nature or nurture plays out in a character's life or in words, such as the discussion of the nobility of Posthumus.

Imogen was born of royalty but raised by a woman who hates her. How much do these two competing influences define Imogen's life and character? Is she virtuous because of her nature or the nurturing she receives? Analyze the scenes in which she says goodbye to Posthumus (1.1), rejects Cloten (2.3), and rejects Iachimo's seduction (1.6). Are her actions in these scenes shown as arising from the influence of her nature or her nurture? To what is her goodness ascribed? How does she discuss herself? How do Cloten and Posthumus describe her? Are these attributes of nature or nurture? Also analyze the scenes in which she meets her brothers (3.6) and is offered clemency by King Cymbeline after the battle (5.5). Are these scenes reflective of nurture, or are they some innate part of her, and thus nature? What does her brother say of her? What does her brother call her? Why is she offered clemency?

Cloten offers a different view of nature versus nurture. He is born to a scheming mother and raised as a prince. In the life of Cloten, which aspect predominates? Analyze the scene in which he has just fought with Posthumus (1.2). What do the reactions of others tell us about his life? What do others say about him? What argument does the description of Cloten minimize? How? What does his decision to rape Imogen tell us about his character? What does his fight with Guiderius tell us about his character? What does Imogen's reaction to Cloten's beheaded body tell us about the physical aspects of Cloten? How might these play into the nature versus nurture argument?

Other characters in whom nature versus nurture is a powerful argument include Posthumus, Arviragus, and Guiderius. Posthumus is born into the lower social order but raised in the royal household. Arviragus and Guiderius are royalty, raised in the wilds of Wales by a nobleman and a nurse. How do their lives bear the influences of these respective origins?

3. **Nationalism:** Nationalism emphasizes the importance of the nation, as opposed to the family, tribe, or other group. In earlier times, Britain laid claim to its nationhood through a connection

with Rome and ancient Troy. What does Shakespeare present as an argument for British sovereignty?

What is the point of giving the family lineage of Posthumus Leonatus? How does it help ground the play in British history? What arguments both for and against paying tribute are offered? On what do the arguments depend? Which arguments describe Britain as being difficult to conquer? What about Britain made it difficult? What is the basis in reality for those arguments? How do those arguments show nationalism? What argument does Cymbeline present about Britain after Caius Lucius leaves? What does the queen say about Caius Lucius's leaving? What does Cloten say about it? What does the king say? How might these statements show nationalism? What is the point of the scene in which Caius Lucius is made tribune? How does it differentiate Rome from Britain? How could this differentiation encourage nationalism? How does Imogen represent Britain? What is the significance of Posthumus removing his fancy Italian clothing and putting on British peasant's garments? How can this be seen as an argument for British nationalism? Why is the winning of the battle significant to nationalism? How does the discussion of the battle invoke a nationalistic spirit? Where in the discussion is there an emphasis on the nationalities involved?

4. **Forgiveness and reconciliation:** Forgiveness is one possible response to having been wronged. Reconciliation involves the active repairing of a rift once forgiveness has been granted. How does Cymbeline treat Imogen and Posthumus at the beginning of the play? What are his reasons? Are his reasons legitimate explanations for his actions? In the end, is there forgiveness? How does the reconciliation come about?

Look at Iachimo's relationships. What is the foundation of the bet? What are the results to be? In what ways does he attempt to tempt Imogen? When he is unsuccessful, what lie does he tell her? What request does he make of her that allows him to lie to Posthumus? What proof does he muster? How does he do this? What does he gain by the lies? What does he lose? What does Posthumus lose? How does the scene in which Iachimo confesses to the audience move the play toward forgiveness and reconciliation? Why would the scene in which Iachimo confesses to Cymbeline be included? Why does he not want to answer? Why does he say he is happy to answer? What is the reaction of Posthumus at the beginning? What is Posthumus's reaction after he finds he has not murdered his wife? What does he order Iachimo to tell? What is Posthumus's response to Iachimo at the end? How does this reaction bring about reconciliation for many?

Character

Analysis of the characters in a play can provide insights that can link or lead to an interpretation of the text's themes and meanings. In *Cymbeline*, there are a number of characters who warrant thorough analysis; both major and minor characters contribute to an interpretation of the text. When you perform such an analysis, you should revisit the text, highlighting passages that offer insight into your chosen character. Pay attention to monologues (moments when the character addresses the audience), dialogue with other characters, and places where the character is described by someone else. What are the character's motives, priorities, and values? Notice whether the character you have selected has changed in any way through the course of the play, and determine both the cause of this change and whether the play portrays it in a positive or negative light. You might examine a certain category of character, women, for example, studying Imogen and the queen in order to comment on Shakespeare's depiction of female characters. Additionally, you can often make a convincing argument about the play's take on a particular idea through an analysis of one or more characters. You might investigate what the play has to say about love, forgiveness, or fidelity through an analysis of the character of Imogen, for instance.

Sample Topics:

1. **Cymbeline:** Analyze the character of King Cymbeline. The play was originally titled *The Tragedie of Cymbeline, King of Britain*. Does he develop throughout the course of the play? If so, is this development positive or negative?

The play starts with Cymbeline angry with his daughter for marrying his foster son. What does this tell about Cymbeline as a father? Is he making a good decision? Is it rational? Any husband of his daughter will become king someday, since his sons are gone. Does this make his argument with his daughter and foster son more understandable, more reasonable?

Cymbeline is faced with being asked to pay tribute as king. What are his arguments? Does he make a good choice? Is it based on reality? Is pitting his people against Rome a good use of his authority? What benefit does Britain gain from the tax paid to Rome, and what might it lose?

Cymbeline also interacts with his wife. How does he treat her? Does it matter that his wife is evil? Is he foolish for treating her well? Is he foolish for trusting her with his daughter? What does it say about him that he thinks his wife is worthy of trust when many others in the play consider her to be dangerous?

At the end of the play, all is restored to Cymbeline. Does Cymbeline make the right decisions? He accepts Posthumus back before he knows his sons are alive. Is this growth on Cymbeline's part or simple efficiency, since he needs someone to inherit the kingdom? Are his actions those of a father or a king? Are they worthy of either appellation? Has he proved to be a good monarch for his people? Is he a good father?

2. **The queen:** Analyze and evaluate the character of the queen.

The queen is a clear villain in the play. Does the fact that she loves her son counterbalance the evil she has done as a stepmother? She says she is not the evil stepmother of stories, such as fairy tales. How is she like those extreme figures, however? How is she different? Does she change over the course of the play?

3. **Imogen and the queen:** Shakespeare has been accused by many critics of endorsing a gender hierarchy by portraying female characters as weak and submissive. He has also been said to be misogynistic, a woman hater. Does *Cymbeline* support either of these theories and assertions?

Analyze the queen and Imogen, and use them to evaluate Shakespeare's portrayal of women in his drama. Do they have strong, independent personalities, or are they submissive to the men they are connected to? What do they have in common? What accounts for any significant differences in their characters? Based on this analysis, draw some conclusions about Shakespeare's portrayal of women in *Cymbeline*.

4. **British citizens:** Analyze and evaluate the play's portrayal of the British people.

Locate the passages in the drama that describe the British people. How is this group of people represented? What connections are made between the British and fighting? Britons and courage? According to the play, what is the relationship of the British to the Romans? What kind of a person is Belarius? What are his positive and negative attributes? Are these directly linked to his status as a war hero? Cassibelan, Mulmutius, and Lud are all earlier British kings referenced in the play. Cymbeline himself is a historical ruler of Britain. How are these regents referenced in the play? What kinds of kings are they? What do we know of them? What does their inclusion say about the people they ruled?

History and Context

Though most of its characters and their actions are fictitious, *Cymbeline* takes place during a particular moment in a particular place amid an authentic historical conflict about which little is known. In order to understand what motivates the characters and what drives the action, then, it is vitally important to understand the play's historical and social context. Some background knowledge of the Roman Empire, Britain's history, the contemporary view of kingship, and the religion(s) in the play would be helpful.

Sample Topics:

1. **Shakespeare's appropriation of Roman history:** What kind of commentary is the play making about Britain's place in the world?

Cymbeline is one of Shakespeare's Roman plays. The fact that Roman history was important to Shakespeare and is used in *Cymbeline* makes it a good topic. Where are Romans (or Italians) used in the play? What is Cymbeline's connection with Rome? How is Britain connected with Rome according to the play? What references are made to Julius Caesar and to Augustus Caesar? How are these references used in the play? What is the significance of the Roman aspects of the play?

2. **British history:** How does British history impact the play?

Cassibelan, Mulmutius, Lud, and Cymbeline are all actual British kings. Histories describe Cymbeline as being king when Jesus Christ was born. How are these historical British kings referenced in the play? What kinds of kings are they? What do we know of them? What does their inclusion say about the people they ruled? What does it say about British history as understood by Shakespeare's audience? How do the references to the kings advance the play's plot? What is the significance of these references? What do Julius Caesar's two foiled attempts to conquer Britain add to the discussion of British history? Why are they referenced? At the end of the play, King Cymbeline cedes the right of tribute to Rome even though his forces have won the battle. What is the significance of that in light of British history?

3. **View of kingship:** How do political views of the day influence the play?

James I was king when *Cymbeline* was first performed. Only a few years earlier, the king had published a treatise on sovereignty, *The True Law of Free Monarchies,* in which he developed the concept of the divine right of kings. What does the play say about kings? What does it show about them? How are the king and his potential heirs presented? What does the vying for the throne show about the politicization of kingship? How does Cloten's place in the succession indicate a lack of respect for kings? How does the nature versus nurture argument impact the view of kingship? King Cymbeline refers to his subjects' unwillingness to bear the yoke of Rome, introducing the concept of the king as part of the country: "for ourself / To show less sovereignty than they, must needs / Appear unkinglike" (3.5.1951). What does this suggest about the concept of the monarchy?

4. **Religion:** How is religion used in the play? What religions are used in the play?

Roman mythology, with its gods Jupiter, Diana, and Neptune, was primarily derived from the Greek tradition. You might know these representative deities better by their Greek names: Zeus, Artemis, and Poseidon. All of these gods are referenced in *Cymbeline,* and one actually appears. The gods also send a vision to the soothsayer (4.2), and Jupiter gives Posthumus a book of prophecy (5.4) that the soothsayer explains (5.5). What is the historical significance of the Roman gods being invoked in the play? How does their inclusion change the perception of Britain? What would the contemporary audience have thought and felt about soothsayers and magic? What is the significance of including them in the play? Are there any references to Christianity in the play? Why or why not? Is it important to know that Cymbeline was popularly believed to have been king in England when Jesus Christ was born?

Philosophy and Ideas

Cymbeline is a play in which philosophy and ideas play a central role. The work grapples with a wide spectrum of concepts, including faithfulness, love, the relationship of government to its subjects, and nobility. To write an essay on one of these topics, it is a good idea to return to the play, examining it through the lens of the particular subject you have chosen and identifying characters associated with it and passages that seem to reveal the play's perspective and support your argument. Then analyze the characters and the passages you have identified in order to arrive at a claim to make in your essay. To discuss what Shakespeare asserts about women, for example, you would need to discuss Posthumus's impassioned diatribe against all women (2.5), Imogen's faithfulness even in duress, and the queen's evil in the face of a privileged life. Looking at these three points might lead you to argue that Shakespeare presents a balanced view of women in *Cymbeline.*

Sample Topics:

1. **Faithfulness:** What does the play say about the concept of being faithful and keeping faith? Does the play suggest that faithfulness is rewarded?

   There are many main scenes that deal with faithfulness, especially 3.4, 5.1, and 5.5. In addition, discussions of faithfulness on multiple levels abound in the play. Imogen, rejected for her infidelity, names herself Fidele. What does this say about her view of faithfulness? How does Posthumus describe the responsibility of a faithful servant? Does Pisanio fit this description? What has caused Posthumus's change of heart, and how does it relate to faithfulness? How does Belarius's theft of the king's children end up being an indication of his faithfulness? How is Cornelius's faithfulness to the high calling of his role as physician made evident? How does Caius Lucius calling Cymbeline's attention to Fidele demonstrate the Roman's faithfulness to his responsibility as lord? How does Caius Lucius respond to Fidele's statement that he will not request the lord's ransom? What does it say about faithfulness from the young? Is there a consistent view of faithfulness in the play?

2. **Responsibility:** What kind of commentary does the play give on the responsibility of a person for her or his actions?

   Many characters in the play give an opinion on what different people are responsible for. Pisanio states that Posthumus is responsible for believing the lies about Imogen (3.2). Why? Imogen says she is responsible for following through on her husband's wishes and asks Pisanio to kill her (3.4). Why does she believe this? What are Pisanio's grounds for disagreeing? Posthumus later argues that a servant should heed only just commands (5.1). What else does he present as necessary for a servant to do? Would the queen's deathbed confessions count as a comment on responsibility? Why or why not? What kind of responsibility is Caius Lucius displaying in pointing out Fidele to the king? What do all of these collectively say about Shakespeare's discussion of responsibility in the play?

3. **Nobility:** According to the play, is nobility innate? Are all those born to a high station inherently noble?

This topic touches again on the nature versus nurture argument. What does it mean to be noble? Is it enough that Posthumus was raised in the royal nursery? Apparently not for King Cymbeline. Cloten, though, is sufficiently noble to be a suitable match for Cymbeline's daughter and heir to the throne, so the king supports Cloten's courtship. He is noble but neither nice nor smart. What is Shakespeare saying about nobility through this character? Imogen is noble. Is her nobility the reason for her faithfulness? Does her nobility grant her anything? Belarius argues that their life in Wales is nobler than life at court (3.3). Is this a comment from Shakespeare on nobility? What does it mean that Imogen's brothers save the life of the king? Is that a result of their nobility? The king is noble, but he is not what we would call nice. He banishes Posthumus, supports Cloten, threatens Belarius, and plans to execute the Romans he has vanquished.

Form and Genre

It can often be fruitful to examine a piece of literature as a constructed work of art, paying close attention to features of the work such as narration, point of view, and organizational scheme. You should ask yourself why the author made the choices he did when constructing the work and how the work would be different if he had made other choices. When studying *Cymbeline*, you might explore the structure of the play and eventually use your essay to explain why the play dwells on some elements, such as the room in Philario's house, but leaves out others, such as the wedding of Imogen and Posthumus. Or you might focus on Shakespeare's decision to devote entire scenes to monologues, such as Posthumus's complaints against women or his lament for Imogen's death.

Sample Topics:

1. **Scenes included and excluded:** What is the point of leaving out of the play events that are described or referenced but not portrayed onstage? What is the point of including scenes that are not particularly riveting or necessary to the plot?

   Why did Shakespeare not begin the play with the wedding of Posthumus and Imogen? What would be lost if the discovery of the wedding were included? Why are we told about voyages rather than shown them? Why does Shakespeare show Posthumus's sorrow over the bloody cloth but not him receiving it? What dramatic tension is increased by this presentation of the results of Posthumus's orders?

   There are a few scenes included that are not pivotal to the plot. Why are these part of the play's final structure? What do they add in terms of character development or dramatic tension? What is the point of the scene in which Cloten recovers from the fight he almost has with Posthumus? What is the point of the scene in which Cloten brings musicians to play outside Imogen's apartments? Are these two scenes related in some way besides their presentation of Cloten? Or is that their point? What do we gain from the first scene in which Belarius, Guiderius, and Arviragus appear? What is so essential in their discussion that it could not have been left out?

2. **The monologues of Posthumus:** What is the significance of two entire scenes (2.5 and 5.1) dedicated simply to Posthumus talking?

   Both of the scenes that consist solely of one character speaking involve Posthumus. What is the point of Shakespeare giving him two separate scenes devoted to his monologues? Is it simply a showcase for a male star, as it would be if done today? Is it an opportunity to develop Posthumus as the flawed hero of tragic expectations? Remember that while, in an actual tragedy, death or serious harm comes to the main characters, this play is usually considered to be a different type of play, a tragicomedy or a romance. Are the scenes necessary for set or other technical changes? What benefit might two monologue-dominated scenes yield to a production or to the play as a work of literature?

Language, Symbols, and Imagery

An analysis of the language, symbols, and imagery in a piece of literature can result in new insights and a new interpretation of the text. In adopting this approach to developing an essay topic, be aware of lengthy descriptions of particular scenes or items, especially ones that appear repeatedly. Also, as you are reading, mark passages that seem to have a special resonance, perhaps those which do not serve to further the plot so much as reflect on an important issue, event, or character. Among the many symbols and images you might elect to focus on in *Cymbeline* are clothes and birds. In your essay, you will want to provide a fresh interpretation of the play based on your analysis of these symbols. You might argue, for example, that through the use of clothing imagery in the play, Shakespeare communicates that, though both Guiderius and Cloten seem to think that clothes make the man, it is what is inside that is really important.

Sample Topics:

1. **Dialogue:** What does the language of the dialogue tell us about the play's themes and meanings?

   Even though Caius Lucius, Iachimo, and Philario are Italians, there is no significant difference in their command of English and the linguistic abilities of the people of Britain. How does this affect you as a reader and your relationship to the characters? Does it make them seem less foreign or less of the outsider to employ English with the same facility as the nation's native speakers?

   To help you figure out the play's relation to or commentary on the role of language, identify and analyze any passages in the play that directly reference the use or concept of language. Specifically, you might look at the passage in which Posthumus remonstrates with Iachimo, saying that his language is responsible for his lack of faith in women: "This is but a custom in your tongue; you bear a graver purpose, I hope" (1.4.453). Or you might look at the scene in which Imogen learns that her husband has believed her faithless (3.4). In this scene, she asks Pisanio to read aloud what might hurt her to read on paper and remarks on the possibility of Pisanio talking his tongue weary before he is able to tell her anything worse. Pisanio also speaks of the falseness of Iachimo, saying his "tongue / Outvenoms all the worms of Nile" (1755–56). What do we learn about the softening impact of the spoken word over the written word?

2. **Clothing:** What does clothing symbolize in the play?

Look at the various passages that discuss clothing. Why is Cloten more offended by Imogen's comment on Posthumus's clothes than by others? Why does Cloten dress in the clothes of Posthumus? What does that say about his view of clothing? How true is Guiderius's comment, in regard to Cloten, that "the clothes make the man"? How are people identified or expected to be identified by their clothing? What does Posthumus say about the garments he takes off and those he puts on before the battle? How is his appearance described afterward? In what other ways is clothing used in the play?

3. **Use of "gods" and gods' names:** What is the effect of Shakespeare's use of Roman gods and either generic or specific references to deities?

Examine the dialogue in the play. Notice the way that Shakespeare's characters invoke the gods regularly. Is it significant that Imogen is the only one who references goddesses as a separate group? Is it significant that only the men refer to Diana, by name? Why do you think Shakespeare chooses to do this? What effect does it have on our perception of the characters and their exchanges? What is the point of comparing his mother to Diana, as Posthumus does, or Pisanio saying that Imogen is "goddess-like?"

What is the significance of the various characters' reference to the gods as expletives? What is the significance of these exclamatory remarks? Do you think they replace some other, less acceptable utterance? Why is there not a problem with this usage of the gods' titles?

Specific gods are named: Diana, Jupiter, and Neptune, as well as the anthropomorphic Nature. What is the importance of the use of these gods in the play? (See topic 4 under the "History and Context" section of this chapter.) Were these gods worshipped in Shakespeare's day? What does their invocation accomplish or contribute to the play?

4. **Birds:** Shakespeare often uses birds in his work, and *Cymbeline* references several birds specifically. What is the role and function of birds and the allusions to them?

In *Cymbeline,* eagles are referenced nine times. In 1.1, Imogen refers to Posthumus as an eagle and Cloten as a puttock, which could be any one of a diverse group of birds of prey. What do these symbols say about the two men, at least as far as Imogen is concerned? The soothsayer references the Roman eagle (4.2, 5.5), and Posthumus echoes this when he calls those who have fled the battlefield chickens and "stoop'd eagles" (5.3.3068). Jupiter descends on an eagle, as the stage directions dictate, in 5.4 and, later in that scene, orders his eagle to fly away. In that same scene, Posthumus's dead father talks of "the holy eagle," "the royal bird," and "the immortal wing" (3265–70). What do these references to eagles mean for the play? Are they primarily Roman references, or are they religious references, since it is "Jove's bird" (4.2.2758)?

In addition to these references, Imogen is described as the "Arabian bird" (1.6.622), which is the phoenix. How accurate is this in the play? In what ways does she symbolically die and return to life? Does it help the allusion to know that Arviragus, after finding Imogen's body, says, "The bird is dead" (4.2.2577)?

There is also a reference to the caged singing bird by Arviragus, who says, "We make a quire, as doth the prison'd bird, / And sing our bondage freely" (3.3.1647–48). Does this relate to Imogen as the phoenix? Is this some other bird? What does Shakespeare intend Arviragus to suggest in employing this imagery? Why is it employed rather than some other visual referent?

Compare and Contrast Essays

Comparing and contrasting similar elements in and between or among plays often serves to sharpen an essay's focus, enabling the writer to notice features that might otherwise have been overlooked. You might, for instance, compare and contrast Iachimo and Posthumus in order to determine what the play has to say about betrayal or Imogen and Cloten to illustrate what it takes to live a meaningful life. Comparisons and contrasts also allow us to make statements about the evolution of a particular theme over the span of an author's career. In this vein, you might compare and contrast the female characters of several of Shakespeare's plays in order to argue that his portrayal of women developed in a particular and definable way. There are limitless options when it comes to compare and contrast essays. The key is not to compare and contrast simply for the sake of doing so. Be sure to use your observations and analysis to make an argument that offers an original interpretation of the text.

Sample Topics:

1. **Iachimo and Posthumus:** Compare and contrast Iachimo and Posthumus.

   What do you know about Iachimo? How was he similar to Posthumus? Why does Posthumus argue with and then bet with Iachimo? What significant differences are there between Iachimo and Posthumus? What are the differences in their betrayals? Based on your analysis of the play's hero, Posthumus, and his nemesis, Iachimo, what generalizations can you make about the play's depiction of betrayal? What makes a bad man? What constitutes an unforgivable action?

2. **Imogen and Cloten:** Compare and contrast these two characters, particularly in regard to living a meaningful life.

   Analyze those passages that reveal the inner workings of Imogen and Cloten. What do the two have in common? In what ways are they different? How does each character view the situation in her or his family? How about outside her or his family? How does each imagine a positive ending to Cymbeline's anger? Based on this information, which of these two has a more reasonable expectation? What differences between the two change these expectations? How are the diverse endings of their experience in the play an argument for the legitimacy of their roles or their actions?

3. **Imogen of *Cymbeline* and Helena of *All's Well That Ends Well:***
   Both characters are virtuous and have husbands who abandon them. What insight into each work do these similarities yield?

What do Imogen and Helena have in common? How are they different? You might look at the relative status of the women and their husbands, their relationship to those who separate them, and their attitudes about the separation. How are their situations similar? How are those different? You might have a look at how Helena resolves her situation versus Imogen's acceptance of hers for most of the play. How is Helena's role as trickster different from Imogen's role as instigator of revelations?

Bibliography and Online Resources for *Cymbeline*

Bergeron, David M. "*Cymbeline:* Shakespeare's Last Roman Play." *Shakespeare Quarterly* 31.1 (Spring 1980): 31–41. *JSTOR.* Web. 1 July 2009.

Forsyth, Jennifer. "Playing with Wench-like Words: *Copia* and Surplus in the Internet Edition of *Cymbeline.*" *Early Modern Literary Studies* 9.3/Special Issue 12 (January 2004): 3.1–27. Web. 1 July 2009.

Harrison, William. *An Historicall Description of the Lland of Britaine, An Electronic Edition.* Ed. Henry Ellis. 2008. <http://www.perseus.tufts.edu/>. Web. 1 July 2009.

Hazlitt, William. "Characters of Shakespeare's Plays: Cymbeline." *University of Toronto English Library.* 1817. Web. 1 July 2009.

History of Roman Britain. HistoryWorld.net. 4 June 2009. <http://www.historyworld.net/wrldhis/PlainTextHistories.asp?historyid=ac71>. Web. 1 July 2009.

Hoeniger, F. D. "Iron and Romance in *Cymbeline.*" *Studies in English Literature, 1500–1900* 2 (1962): 219–28. *JSTOR.* Web. 1 July 2009.

Holinshed, Raphael. *The Chronicles of England, Scotland and Ireland.* London: Henry Denham, 1587. < http://dewey.lib.upenn.edu>. Web. 1 July 2009.

James I. *The True Law of Free Monarchies and Basilikon Doron.* Ed. Daniel Fischlin and Mark Fortier. Toronto: Victoria UP, 1996. Web. 1 July 2009.

Mikalachki, Jodi. "The Masculine Romance of Roman Britain: *Cymbeline* and Early Modern English Nationalism." *Shakespeare Quarterly* 46.3 (Autumn 1995): 301–22. *JSTOR.* Web. 1 July 2009.

Shakespeare, William. *Open Source Shakespeare.* Ed. Eric M. Johnson. George Mason U, 2003. Web. 1 July 2009.

Stewart, Andrew. "Some Uses for Romance: Shakespeare's *Cymbeline* and Jonson's *The New Inn.*" *Renaissance Forum* 3.1 (Spring 1998): n. pag. Web. 1 July 2009.

Sullivan, Garrett A. "Civilizing Wales: *Cymbeline,* Roads and the Landscapes of Early Modern Britain." *Early Modern Literary Studies* 4.2/ Special Issue 3 (September, 1998): 3.1–34. Web. 1 July 2009.

THE WINTER'S TALE

READING TO WRITE

THE PLOT of *The Winter's Tale* is derived from the work of Robert Greene, whose pastoral romance *Pandosto* Shakespeare adapted almost in its entirety. *Pandosto* was popular both with British audiences and abroad; it was the first English novel to be translated into French (Salingar 50). Shakespeare's play is noteworthy for the degree to which Shakespeare relied on the source material and because the changes he introduced were made primarily to imitate medieval plays, with a harking back—as in *Pericles, Prince of Tyre*—to old tales (5.2.3136).

The play is not entirely taken from Greene's work; the assault of the bear does not take place in *Pandosto.* However, a similar scene occurs in a comedy about Mucedorus published in 1598, which Shakespeare might have used as an additional source. In that scene, a man identified with the tag "the Clowne" comes running onstage talking about a bear (Brooke 109). Since both plays feature clowns talking about a bear, this earlier play seems a likely source.

Shakespeare's version is half tragedy and half comedy. The main tragedy of the play centers on the actions of Leontes and how they lead to disaster for many people. Antigonus becomes somewhat an oracle when he declares to the king:

> Be certain what you do, sir, lest your justice
> Prove violence; in which the three great ones suffer,
> Yourself, your queen, your son. (2.1.749–51)

In *Pandosto*, Hermione remains dead, and Leontes commits suicide. *The Winter's Tale* is less tragic than its source. Despite this lightening of the tragedy, there is suffering in the play nonetheless. Antigonus's words suggest looking at the tragedy in terms of how the three highest-ranking figures in the kingdom suffer. How and why do they suffer? Tragedies involve death, and at least one major death in this play is permanent. What does this add to the seriousness of the play? What has the kingdom lost as a result of the death?

In addition, while the three royals suffered severely, others join them in misery as well. Looking at who else in the play experiences suffering offers a different approach to the work while still using the quotation as the same point of origin. Antigonus and the sailors might not have been important to the kingdom, but they left behind families. What suffering might Antigonus's loss have brought to his family? Camillo had to leave his home. Though he prospered in Bohemia, he was homesick. Is this suffering? Who else suffered?

Another approach to the quotation would be to look at the ways in which the justice of Leontes goes awry or wrong. The king is the ultimate judge in a monarchy. Was Leontes making a good decision when he first determined that Polixenes and Hermione had an affair? Did he listen to the various character witnesses? Was he willing to look for evidence? What does this tell you about the king's failure in one of his most important duties?

Any of these approaches, or others, might give you an opening into a discussion of the work. You could look at additional passages that relate to and support the particular approach you have taken. Usually these passages will present more questions before they lead to any answers. Once you have arrived at a definitive or conclusive statement, a point that you think is worth sharing about judgment or suffering, for example, then you can begin to develop your essay.

TOPICS AND STRATEGIES

Think of the topic suggestions as streetlights illuminating part of the path to a good essay. They do not reveal the only path or the whole path, but they help you figure out what direction you might want to go in. Or, seeing what is in that path, you might decide to go an entirely different way. Peruse the suggestions for ideas that catch your attention and curiosity. If an idea has grabbed you, then you can probably seize a reader's attention discussing that topic. Don't use the suggestions as a list of points to cover. Instead use them to generate your own questions. Look for the holes in the plans as they are presented. What questions were left out? What ideas could be combined to form a more complex or layered topic for your essay? If you employ the topic suggestions and discussions in this way, your essay will be fully your own and more intriguing because it will have come from your thoughts on the topic and your experiences with the text. As you approach and confront the text, take notes, using them to determine a thesis, a statement, on which your essay will rest. Your essay will be a presentation of your analysis and the evidence you find in support of it. It should be a definitive and original look at the topic you chose.

Themes

Part of the reason *The Winter's Tale* is still read today, and commonly produced onstage as well, is that it introduces and comments on several universal themes, such as love, the cycle of life, maturing, and friendship. If your essay is going to explore a thematic vein, you will want to select a single theme to scrutinize, and you may need to narrow it down even further, to focus on a specific aspect of the theme you have chosen for your essay. If you select love, for instance, you might want to focus on the effects of jealousy on love or the effects of being raised in a loving home on being willing to love. Whatever you choose, you need to look for passages that are relevant to your topic in order to answer the question— what does *The Winter's Tale* say about love, or growing up, or friendship? Once you have found relevant passages, you can analyze them in terms of that central organizing question.

Sample Topics:

1. **Love:** How does *The Winter's Tale* discuss love? Love and jealousy, love and faithfulness, being in love, and romantic love are some of the ways this theme is exhibited in the play.

   King Leontes is the most overt representation of the conflation of love and jealousy in the play. Who does Leontes love? Don't limit yourself here to simply romantic love. He also loves his childhood friend. What incident triggers Leontes's turn from a positive love to a jealous one? Of whom is he jealous? Is there any reason for his jealousy? What is his reasoning? How does this jealousy impact the life of other characters? Look at how it changes one or two other lives: Hermione, Polixenes, Camillo, Mamillius, Perdita, Antigonus, or Paulina. These characters were not jealous, but their lives are changed by jealousy nonetheless. What does this say about the nature of jealousy? What was Shakespeare trying to show?

There are several characters in the play who are loving. Queen Hermione is described as being good, even by her husband when he is upset with her, and she is shown to be loving. How is her love exhibited in the play? How is it expressed to her children? To her husband? To Polixenes? To Paulina? Perdita is also shown as a loving character. She loves her father, Old Shepherd. How does she show this? She also loves Florizel. How does she express this affection? When she hears about her mother's death, what is her response? How does her reaction indicate a loving nature? Paulina loves the queen. How does she show it? She also loves the king. How does she show that? How does she make evident her love for Perdita? Is Shakespeare saying anything about love when the most visibly caring characters are primarily women? What might he be suggesting? Why might he not mean anything at all by this?

Florizel follows a falcon across Old Shepherd's land and falls in love with Perdita. How does he reveal his love to her before the scenes when we see them together? How does he show his love during those scenes? Look at his exchanges with Perdita. What do they say about the nature of his love when he describes what the Roman gods did for love (4.4.1883–94)? When he speaks at length about how he is enraptured by her (4.4.2016–27), what does this suggest about his love? Also examine his response to his disguised father's rebuke for not buying her trinkets from the peddler. What does this indicate about Florizel's love for Perdita? When his father reveals himself, how does Florizel's response show his love for Perdita?

2. **Maturing:** Who grows up metaphorically in the play?

On a literal level, Perdita grows up in the play, but we do not see this growth. The play shows her as a baby and then 16 years later as a girl of marriageable age. Her father, however, an adult already when he becomes irrationally jealous of Hermione and Polixenes, is portrayed as changing and maturing. How is his lack of maturity initially established in the play? Are later portrayals of him the same? How does he display a sense of maturity in his relationship with Paulina? His responses to her are good indicators of his maturity level in the play, so read their interactions carefully.

3. **Cycle of life:** How does *The Winter's Tale* show the importance of the cycle of life?

The cycle of life theme is most closely associated with Perdita and her situation, growing up in distant Sicilia and then returning. The theme is also suggested in the discussion of Prosperina (Persephone of Greek mythology). How does the course of Perdita's life resemble the shift from winter to spring? What does the Greek reference add to this metaphor?

The cycle of life is also shown in the structure of the play. The beginning is associated with harvest time, a period of fruitfulness. Then death comes ushering in the tragic portion of the play and echoing the barrenness of winter. The play's pattern then progresses to a renewal of life as typified by the relationship of Florizel and Perdita. Their love blossoms, equated to the flowering of spring. What does the escape to Sicilia add? How is the end once again a fruitful time?

This same cycle of life is also evident in Bohemia's natural order. The cycle begins with a horrible storm in the desert. What time of year or season is most likely to witness storms? The cycle then continues with the desert blooming during the sheepshearing scene. The long discussion of flowers, along with the shearing, gives an indication of the time in which the action is occurring. Look up when sheep are sheared. Then read again the discussion Perdita has with Polixenes. In what ways does the exchange reference the cycle of life?

The cycle of life is also made manifest in the changing circumstances of the Old Shepherd. He begins as a fairly poor shepherd and eventually becomes, after finding Perdita, a prosperous farmer. How might these stages relate to the seasonal cycle of life? Does the threat of death add another part to the cycle? When he reveals Perdita's origins to Polixenes, the shepherd reassumes the status of a gentleman. What season might this relate to?

4. **Friendship:** How does *The Winter's Tale* portray friendship?

The play begins with the friendship of Leontes and Polixenes, a longstanding bond between the two. How long have the two kings been friends? What changes their friendship? Is the source of the change one- or two-sided? How do the two men respond to the change? If this were the only friendship in the play, what view of friendship would be supported? What other friendships are shown in the play? What about the friendship of Paulina and Hermione? How does their friendship change the friendship dynamics represented in the play? Do they remain friends throughout? How is this friendship seen? What is the end result of this friendship? How is the broken friendship between the two kings finally redeemed? Will this repair last? Does it say anything about friendship that there are so few friends in the play? Or is it simply a function of the level of society the play is primarily about? What does the Clown's discussion of how gentlemen act to their friends tell us? Does it add a nuance or different aspect to Shakespeare's presentation of friendship?

Character

Plays are especially suited to character analysis. The characters are the vehicle propelling the play forward, and their words are what shape the play and detail the plot. One of the challenges some plays present is that there are so many interrelated characters, it is difficult to isolate those most relevant to your thesis. Should you analyze all the characters as a group? No. You can't do that well in an academic essay. Such depth of character analysis would require a book. So how do you decide on a character? One way is to look at the character you find most compelling. This does not have to be a character you like, just one that catches your attention. If you are appalled by Leontes yet find yourself rereading his lines trying to figure him out, then he would be a good character for you to examine. If you love Paulina, with her brash response to the king's authority and her strength in standing up for her beliefs, then she would be a good character to explore in greater depth. Another way to approach character analysis is to take two of the characters from the play and see how their similar attributes are developed differently. Both Polixenes and Old Shepherd are fathers whose lives are threatened. An examination of the ways in which they are similar could help you develop a character analysis of one or the other or of both. Finally, you might pick a minor character such as Camillo or the Clown and write about that character's significance to the play and how he or she supports and contributes to the development of the play's various themes.

Sample Topics:

1. **Leontes:** Analyze and evaluate the character of Leontes.

Look in particular at passages in which Leontes talks about his emotions and actions. Begin in act 1, scene 2, when Leontes asks Mamillius if he is his son. Then follow the speeches of Leontes in the next scene and then in act 2, scene 3. What do his words tell you of the character and attitude of Leontes? What is he thinking? What does he do and why? The court of justice in act 3, scene 2 has a purpose, the king says. What was it? Does he use it for that explicit purpose? Is there irony associated with the court? What happens there? What is Leontes's response to the oracle's proclamation? When is justice served? To whom is it served? The play leaves Leontes for a time and returns to him again in the final act. Look there for examples of how he has changed. Is he impetuous? Is he easily angered? Does he make oaths? Does he keep them? Is he a friend? Is he mourning? What are his actions, and how do they match his words? Then take the two sets of ideas about Leontes and compare them. Has Leontes changed? Has he improved? What is the cause if he has? What is the point? You might make a list of the personality attributes of the king, marking where these aspects surface or are suggested, and see which are emphasized. Are these the traits that you noticed the most? If not, what makes them more noticeable? How does the king contribute to themes in the play? How is he a bad example? A good one?

2. **Hermione:** Though she is absent through much of the play, Hermione is a major character. How does she retain this central status through absence?

Characters can be analyzed by what they say and by what others say about them. Sometimes the two paint different pictures. In *The Winter's Tale*, Hermione is a consistent character. She does not change. However, the king, her husband, views her as being different or altered. Look at what he says about her compared to how the other characters represent her in the first part of the play. No one seeing the play would believe Leontes's point of view is accurate. Why not? How does Shakespeare show us that this is ridiculous? What adjectives are used to describe Hermione? Are her looks described? In what way? How do the descriptions of her character and her looks compare? The Greeks believed that beauty was equated with goodness. Is Shakespeare supporting this contention through Hermione? If Hermione is really not dead, what does her disappearance from her home and her husband's life for 16 years say about her? Why would an audience be sympathetic? Why wouldn't they? If she is really dead, what does it say about her that her spirit animated the statue when her daughter came into the chapel?

3. **Autolycus:** What is the significance of this character, who is based on a figure from ancient Greek literature, to the overall themes and meaning of *The Winter's Tale*?

Autolycus in the play says he is named for the Greek Autolycus (4.3.1747ff). That Autolycus is described by Hyginus in his *Fabulae* as a skillful thief with an uncanny ability to change what he stole. He is also the grandfather of Ulysses of *Odyssey* fame. What might these Greek literary connotations tell us about the character Shakespeare creates? Look at his first song. It is marked by references to sex and sexual adventures. What does this tell us of Autolycus, and how does it relate to themes in the work? Since the first act in the play is about sexual misconduct presented in a serious way, what are the ramifications of the introduction of sexual misconduct through song? Is it important? How does it help develop the play? Why is it Autolycus who performs the song? How does his character contribute to the play overall? How does he define good and bad? What does he do that is good? What does he do that is bad? Is Autolycus a truthful person? Is he truthful when he is talking to the audience? When he is talking to other characters in the play? What does this reveal about him? He lies and knows he lies. How might this make him a foil to Leontes? If you look at him as a foil, what else can you see?

History and Context

John Donne said, "No man is an island," and the same can be said of works of art, particularly Shakespeare's plays. None of them was created in isolation. Each sprang from something else and borrowed from both life and art. The debt *The Winter's Tale* owes to *Pandosto* and *The Comedy of Mucedorus* has already been discussed. In addition, some critics have detected a political theme in *The Winter's Tale*, through reading Hermione as Henry VIII's wife Anne Boleyn. These are just a few of the historical, textual, and cultural contexts of the play.

Sample Topics:

1. **Henry VIII and Anne Boleyn:** One of Henry VIII's wives, Anne Boleyn, was imprisoned, and a good friend of Henry VIII's was executed for having an affair with her.

   Shakespeare was born after Henry VIII died. However, his parents had lived under this infamous king. Their lives and world had been influenced by his break with the Roman Catholic Church. Shakespeare lived most of his life under the reign of Anne Boleyn's only daughter, Elizabeth I. Familiarize yourself with the history of Henry VIII, Anne Boleyn, and Elizabeth I. How is their story similar to the one enacted in the play? How is it different? How might the Delphic oracle's note be interpreted with this in mind? How is it accurate? Is it inaccurate in any detail? Did a son of Henry VIII's die? When? Are there any other parallels in the play to this political history?

2. **Social standing:** Birth determined your station in life during Shakespeare's time. How do social standing and class consciousness inform and influence the play?

While there was still some flexibility in social class, during Shakespeare's lifetime, class was increasingly becoming a rigid, unchangeable status. Polixenes argues for flexibility in social class in his discussion of the flowers but argues against it in his reaction to Perdita as a future daughter-in-law. Eventually his choices uphold the mobility he argued in the horticulture discussion, because he and Leontes ennoble Old Shepherd and Clown. At the end of the play, they are gentlemen.

One way to look at social standing in the play is to examine the arguments and actions of Polixenes. Why does he apply an argument of social mobility to flowers yet reject the possibility for people? What is the point of his horticulture argument? Is what he says just as valid for people? If it is, then why does he reject it? What would the acceptance of that argument mean to his rank? The social status of others? How do his later actions match his argument for flowers? For people? Looking at the play, what did Shakespeare support?

Another way to examine social standing is to look at the Clown's final discussion with his father and Autocyclus. What does the Clown say about gentlemen? How do they act? What do they say? How is this different from how he and his father would have previously acted? How do you know? This discussion is contained within the comic section of the play. What does that add to the discussion? What is Shakespeare saying? Would the audience have agreed with him? Why might he have been saying it?

Philosophy and Ideas

Not only did the history and context of the play affect its creation, but so did the philosophy and ideas of the day. Many of the ideas prevalent in Shakespeare's time made it into the play. They include the concept of divine retribution, the role of fate in life, the insulation of the aristocracy, and the place of the aristocracy through birth or advancement. Examining, in particular, the aristocracy's role in the play can provide a greater understanding of its place in the cultural life of Shakespeare's time.

Sample Topics:

1. **Divine retribution:** Divine retribution is usually when the gods punish humans for their wrong choices. It can also be the gods rewarding someone for his or her right choices.

Divine retribution is a major factor throughout the play. The death of Mamillius is a strike against Leontes by the gods. He recognizes this when he says, "Apollo's angry; and the heavens themselves / Do strike at my injustice" (3.2.1373–74). Paulina presents Hermione's death as a punishment for the tyranny and jealousy of Leontes (3.2.1410ff). The destruction of the ship and the mauling of Antigonus are payback for their part in the abandonment of Perdita. Old Shepherd believes he has been rewarded for taking in a changeling.

What is the purpose of divine retribution in the play? Is it a way of representing or a manifestation of the philosophy that anything bad that happens has a purpose and intention? This has long been a belief in various parts of the world. What other functions do divine retribution serve in the play? Is it an important aspect of the play? Do the gods get involved in the action on a regular basis, even though they are never seen? What does this say about life in general? Who is affected by the divine retribution? Leontes said he is repaid for the death of his son. Why must Mamillius, who is innocent of any wrongdoing, be required to pay the price? What does this mean for the hurt and injured in a belief system that expects and accepts divine retribution? Antigonus offers to do anything to potentially save the child's life. That is why the king sends Antigonus to abandon her. The ship and Antigonus, it could be argued, are simply doing their duty as Sicilians, but they are destroyed. How does this contrast with Camillo, who did not carry out his duty as it was given to him by Leontes? What does this tell us about the guilt of Antigonus and the sailors? Is Old Shepherd being rewarded for raising Perdita by the money left with her? Would he have still had the money if he took it and left her in the desert? What does this suggest about his character? How would his fate have changed had he left her? How is his care for her again rewarded in the end? Is this also divine retribution?

2. **The role of fate:** How does fate play a role in the play?

Is there an element of fate in Perdita's situation? Perdita means "lost." The oracle states that Leontes will be without an heir until that which is lost is found. Is this an example of fate? Perdita is seemingly "left to her fate" to die in the desert, and yet she does not. Is this fate? The prince of Bohemia falls in love with her, even though he thinks she is a commoner. How might this be a form of fate? Would Polixenes and Florizel have ever been reconciled without the Clown having heard the name of the man consumed by the bear? Was that fate? Was it fate that the statue came to life? That Paulina is given in marriage to Camillo? That Autolycus was able to prove beneficial to the prince? What other aspects of fate are there?

3. **Sex:** Sex is important in the play, and rules for appropriate sexual expression and attitudes toward sex pervade the play. How do such considerations add to a richer understanding of the play overall?

In what way are the birds in Autolycus's song associated with sexuality? "[T]umbling in the hay" is a metaphor for having sex. Where did this metaphor come from? Is it correctly applied here in the play? With whom is Autolycus tumbling? Do you think this is a literal use of that phrase? Or is it a figurative term used to describe sexual partners? Does this usage still exist today? Does Autolycus's reference to wandering by moonlight refer to sex? How might it? Why might it not? The juxtaposition of tinker and sheets is intended to create the impression that Autolycus sells sheets. While that may be true, what else might trafficking in sheets mean?

  After having read this section, you might look at what the song reveals about Autolycus. Who did he serve? What does he do? What are his expectations? What does it say about his view of sex? What does it say about hanging or the gallows? What does it say about theft? Is there any connection between the sex discussed, the thefts, and the gallows? How might those references be related? How are these views presented in the play in other ways? What does this speech say about Autolycus? About the status of the play? What does it say about Autolycus's status? Is there something shady in his history? What is it? How might it affect the course or outcome of the play? Is this a serious song? Does it mean anything that it is not? Is it a signal to the audience of something? What is it an indication of?

Form and Genre

Examining *The Winter's Tale* as a romance, as part tragedy and part comedy, can help you see things in the play that you might not have noted otherwise. Analyzing and attempting to define the genre of a text can help you. What parts are funny? Why are they comical? When is the comedy introduced? Since the play represents a carefully crafted work, why was humor introduced when it was? What aspects of the play are tragic? How are they tragic? Does any aspect of the play remain consistently tragic? Is this a main issue in the play by the end? How is the play, in its setting and concerns, far removed from the audience of Shakespeare's time? How is it a romance in the modern usage of the word?

You can also examine the form of *The Winter's Tale* as a piece of dramatic writing. What are the limitations of a play as compared to a novel, for example, or a sonnet? How is the play different from the stories from which it is derived? Is this a factor of the form of the play or something else? The play is also divided into acts and scenes. Looking at which scenes are tragic and which comic might tell you that the play is about half tragedy and half comedy. Was this a deliberate division in the play? How can you tell? Examining the use of the character of Time could also tell you something about the form of the play. So could the use of songs and music in the play. This musical component was not common in Shakespeare's plays, yet in *The Winter's Tale* there are multiple songs. How does the music impact the form?

Sample Topics:

1. **Time:** Examine Time's role in the play and how it impacts the structural form of the work.

Time has been equated to a Greek chorus in the play. Gather additional information and insight on the function of the Greek chorus to support this claim. Does Time add to the spectacle? In what way? Does he provide literal time for the actors to change costumes? Does he give relevant summary information? If so, what information does he impart? Is this important information? Does he provide otherwise unknown background? If so, what does he provide? How is it relevant to the play? Does his speech emphasize any themes? How? Which ones? He is a presence who appears once, tells us what has happened, then disappears. What does this tell us about his importance? Is his appearance necessary? How else might the 16-year span of the play be made clear to the audience? What does Time's appearance as a character contribute to the structure of the play? How does it make the play more coherent? How does it intrude on the experience of the tale?

2. **Structure:** The play is half tragedy and half comedy. What are the ramifications of Shakespeare adopting this hybrid form?

The play can be divided almost in half, the first part of the play containing the tragedy, with Antigonus being devoured by a bear as the final tragic incident in the play. From there on, the play transitions to its comic mode.

What aspects of the play are tragic? How are they tragic? Does any part of the play remain tragic? Is this a main issue in the play by the end? Why or why not? If tragedy is not permanent, does that lend the tragic strain of the play less of an impact? Does tragedy's impact on the lives of the characters change? How or why not? When do you see the comedy introduced in the play? Why would Shakespeare choose to introduce it when he does? What could Shakespeare have been trying to say? How does the introduction of the comic impact the play? Does the rest of the play remain comic? Or is the comedy interrupted or relieved, depending on your viewpoint, by other genres and which ones? How does their presence change the play?

3. **Love story:** This play is several different love stories blended together. What conclusions can you draw about the play's handling of the convention of romantic coupling?

What love stories are present in the play? Who loves? Who is loved? How is love shown? How is love discussed? How is love described? Especially look at Florizel's description of love by the Roman gods. Who is vindicated by love? How does this vindication take place in the play? As this play is one of the earliest examples of the love of children repairing the harm done by the misguided or qualified love of a previous generation, this aspect might warrant a second look. How does the love story of Perdita and Florizel ease the situation between Polixenes and Leontes? How was this situation caused by a love story?

Language, Symbols, and Imagery

Shakespeare is considered one of the most accomplished purveyors of the English language, partially because of his use of language and the impact of his images and symbols. Shakespeare contributed many words to the English language. He also introduced many symbols and images that continue to enchant audiences today. How do you identify a literary symbol? You should read the text looking for objects or entities that take on significance in the text or that recur frequently. It is not enough to find symbols; you then need to determine what Shakespeare was attempting to convey by employing and integrating that symbol into his work.

Sample Topics:

1. **Flowers:** What do the flowers in the play symbolize?

Revisit the text, noting the play's use of flowers. There is an entire discussion between Perdita and Polixenes on flowers. What is the nature of this discussion? How is it ironic? What does Polixenes say about flowers that he does not believe about people? How do we know? Is this important? What is the symbolism of spring, summer, and winter flowers? How is it discussed? To whom are winter flowers given? Think of those characters in relation to Perdita. How were they involved with her wintering experience?

2. **The statue:** What part does the statue play?

The critic Andrew Gurr argues that there is no statue; Paulina has simply sequestered Hermione until a time that her reappearance is guaranteed to bring about a reconciliation. What in the play supports this view? What does not? If the statue is literal, how does the discussion of the wrinkles and the fact that it seems to breathe add to its symbolic import and impact? If the statue is really just Hermione, what is added to the play by the reference to the famous artist who created it and to the paint drying? Could the statue be intended to be both literal and metaphoric? What would it bring to the play in these two guises?

3. **Sheepshearing:** A pivotal scene in the play is the one that takes place at the sheepshearing festival. Why does Shakespeare choose this particular setting and this particular agricultural activity?

Shearing sheep is a metaphor for trickery. Who is being tricked during this celebration? How are they being tricked? Autolycus is clearly a trickster figure. What about Polixenes? Is he also attempting to mislead or deceive others? Who thinks they are being tricked during the sheepshearing festival? How do they think this trickery is being brought about? Look at the Old Shepherd and Perdita. Also look at Polixenes and Camillo. Are there layers of trickery present in their actions or interactions? Who is tricking whom? How? How does this add a farcical aspect to the play?

Compare and Contrast Essays

Pursuing compare and contrast essays can simplify your task by presenting you with two sources or topics to look at. This gives you a wider range of texts with which to work and helps you brainstorm. If, for instance, you decided to compare *The Winter's Tale* with *Pandosto*, you could read both works and look for ways in which they are similar and ways in which they differ. Some of those similarities might be obvious, since *Pandosto* is a source for the play, but others may require interpretive work to link and establish them. *Pandosto* was an innovative work, so perhaps you could look at ways in which *The Winter's Tale* is similarly novel or groundbreaking. Some of the differences would be obvious, too, in that *Pandosto* is a prose narrative while *The Winter's Tale* is a play. Discussing those differences might be too obvious, but if you looked at what is possible to do in a story versus what is possible to do in a play, this might be a fruitful line of inquiry. Whatever you choose to compare and contrast, determine the conclusion or implication of the notion of similarity or difference. Simply saying something is like or unlike something else is not a strong thesis for an essay.

Sample Topics:

1. ***Pandosto* and *The Winter's Tale:*** Shakespeare did not adopt the entire story as Greene wrote it. Look for differences and try to postulate a possible reason for these.

   Read *Pandosto* in light of your reading of the play. What did you notice? The names in the two texts are different. What might be an explanation for that? Why would Shakespeare change the names of a popular story in its retelling? What names were abandoned? What names were retained? Look up the meanings or uses of those names. Do the meanings of the names explain or suggest why they would be changed? The inclusion of the bear becomes one of the most famous stage directions of all time. Obviously it is an addition to the original story, both in form and content. What could be the point of this? Why is it necessary to add the bear? Is there a symbolic meaning to the animal's pursuit of Antigonus? Is it simply added for comic relief? What does it say about the nature of comedy that a bear attack could be used for such purposes? Two deaths from the original story are altered and staged in a very different manner. What is the point of that? What does it add to the story? What does it remove from the story? How does it potentially shift the play from a tragedy to a romance? There are other differences and similarities in the two works. These are just some basic ideas to get you started. What other differences can you see in the two texts? What things did Shakespeare not change? What might have been the reason?

2. **Parenting in *Pericles, Prince of Tyre* and *The Winter's Tale*:** Both tales include fathers and daughters as major characters. How does one play's situation illuminate the familial relations presented in another?

Return to these texts with a particular focus on the father-daughter relationships. How are Pericles and Leontes similar as fathers? How are they different? How do their parenting decisions strike you as a modern reader? While her biological father is Leontes, how is Perdita's adopted father more of a parent to her? What does this have to say about belonging? Is there an argument being presented against adoption? What might be the source of that? Both daughters lose their mothers to "death" and are abandoned by their fathers. Are there any other similarities between the two girls? What differences do you see, in terms of the intended outcomes and the reality? Perhaps the father-daughter relationships point to the reality that parents may attempt to do their best, as Pericles did, and still fail. What does it say about fate or chance? How can this same idea be shown in *The Winter's Tale*? In the end, both girls are married. One chooses her spouse, and the other has her spouse chosen for her. How do these choices reflect the father-daughter relationships already established in the two plays?

Bibliography and Online Resources for *The Winter's Tale*

Bloom, Allan. *Shakespeare on Love and Friendship.* Chicago: U Chicago P, 2000. Print.

Brooke, Tucker. *The Shakespeare Apocrypha.* Oxford: Clarendon Press, 1908. Web. 12 August 2009.

Donne, John. "Meditation XVII." *Devotions Upon Emergent Occasions.* 1624. Web. 12 August 2009.

Greene, Robert. *Pandosto, Or the Historie of Dorastus and Fawnia.* London: Thomas Cadman, 1588. Web. 12 August 2009.

Gurr, Andrew. "The Bear, the Statue, and Hysteria in *The Winter's Tale*." *Shakespeare Quarterly* 34.4 (Winter 1983): 420–25. *JSTOR.* Web. 12 August 2009.

Hamilton, Edith. *Mythology.* New York: Back Bay Books, 1998. Print.

Hyginus, Gaius Julius. *Fabulae.* Trans. Mary Grant. *Theoi E-Texts Library.* 2007. Web. 12 August 2009.

Mahood, M. M. *Shakespeare's Wordplay.* New York: Taylor & Francis, 2007. Web. 12 August 2009.

Nicoll, Allardyce. *Shakespeare Survey: The Histories.* New York: Cambridge UP, 2002. Print.

Salingar, Leo. *Shakespeare and the Traditions of Comedy.* New York: Cambridge UP, 1976. Print.

Shakespeare, William. *Open Source Shakespeare.* Ed. Eric M. Johnson. George Mason U, 2003. Web. 1 July 2009.

———. *The Winter's Tale.* Ed. Stephen Orgel. New York: Oxford UP, 1998. Print.

THE TEMPEST

READING TO WRITE

*T*HE *TEMPEST* was written around 1610, and it was most likely the final complete play that William Shakespeare wrote. In its original presentation, the play was labeled a comedy; however, most people now identify it as one of Shakespeare's late romances. It was a popular play in its day and was performed at the court of James I.

Many modern performances circumvent a strict reading of the play to present Caliban as a Caribbean or African character whose slavery is a commentary on the colonialism of Britain. While this is an interesting and popular reading of the play, it is not true to the play's content. Often in literature, there is the figure of the "other," the outsider, often represented by a member of an ethnic or racial minority. Caliban is the minority figure in *The Tempest,* not in terms of race, however, but of species and experience.

Caliban's mother, Sycorax, was a "blue-eyed hag" (1.2.405), indicating he is half-European, his "otherness" not coming from his mother. Despite his racial heritage, Caliban is described as a "freckled whelp" (I.ii.419) who does not possess a human shape. Prospero says Caliban's father was a devil, and many early performances portrayed him as half-animal. Read the discussion between Caliban and Prospero in which they talk of their common history:

> *Caliban:* When thou camest first,
> Thou strokedst me and madest much of me, wouldst give me
> Water with berries in't, and teach me how
> To name the bigger light, and how the less,

That burn by day and night: and then I loved thee
And show'd thee all the qualities o' the isle,
The fresh springs, brine-pits, barren place and fertile:
Cursed be I that did so! All the charms
Of Sycorax, toads, beetles, bats, light on you!
For I am all the subjects that you have,
Which first was mine own king: and here you sty me
In this hard rock, whiles you do keep from me
The rest o' the island.

Prospero: Thou most lying slave,
Whom stripes may move, not kindness! I have used thee,
Filth as thou art, with human care, and lodged thee
In mine own cell, till thou didst seek to violate
The honour of my child. (1.2.483–500)

What does the passage say was the original relationship of Caliban and Prospero? How did the two treat each other? Was this a short relationship? If you are unsure, read more of their discussions. Exploring a little further in the play, you will find Prospero telling him:

I pitied thee,
Took pains to make thee speak, taught thee each hour
One thing or other: when thou didst not, savage,
Know thine own meaning, but wouldst gabble like
A thing most brutish, I endow'd thy purposes
With words that made them known. But thy vile race,
Though thou didst learn, had that in't which
good natures
Could not abide to be with . . . (1.2.506–13)

Prospero not only taught Caliban astronomy and perhaps astrology in return for being taught about the island, but he also taught Caliban to speak. Caliban, at least according to Prospero, could not even be understood, nor did he understand himself. How do these descriptions represent Caliban? Is he a "noble savage"? Why did he attempt to rape Miranda? Before that attempt, what had been his relationship with

Prospero? What evidence is there of his relationship with Miranda? How do these potentially label him as other?

What does Caliban look like? Trinculo describes him as looking like a dead fish with human legs and fish arms (2.2). How does this physical description betoken his otherness? How does Caliban smell? What does Caliban worship?

Identify additional dialogue in the play that addresses the issue of the other and analyze it, such as when Caliban first meets Stephano and Trinculo. How is Caliban treated? How does he react to them? These additional analyses will bring more questions before you arrive at your own conclusion. Once you have formulated a strong, defendable thesis about the role of the other in the play, then you have arrived at your claim and are ready to begin drafting your essay.

TOPICS AND STRATEGIES

Several possible topics are presented here to give you a point of departure for your discussion of *The Tempest*, but they are not complete. More than likely, they will suggest other ideas you can explore and develop. If you select one of the sample topics discussed, think of it as a springboard that propels you more deeply into your topic, allowing you to brainstorm, generate ideas, and plan. You will need to extend your line of inquiry and expand the scope and extent of your ideas in order to create your essay. You can start with one of the topics, then continue to explore and think about the idea until a conclusion has been reached. This will become your thesis, and you can then select from your notes and analyses the appropriate supporting evidence to include in your essay.

Themes

Justice, the supernatural, nature versus nurture, and forgiveness are some of the central themes of *The Tempest*. Each of these offers different approaches to an essay on themes in the play. One of the more difficult aspects of writing an essay on theme is avoiding simply stating that the play presents arguments about the reality of justice. The essay will need to make a point about the role of justice in the play and not simply state that justice is one topic discussed. For example, you might examine the entire play and see how often evil is punished and good rewarded. An analysis of such instances might indicate that Shakespeare is arguing that some evils are forgivable while others are not. Or you might look at the tale and examine which character's sense of justice is being served. Prospero is not happy that his brother has taken over his kingdom, though he originally handed him the reins. How is this injustice? How is it just? In the end, Prospero regains his kingdom, and nothing negative happens to Antonio. Is that justice? Is there justice in the situation with Ariel? Is it justice that Prospero freed Ariel from a prison so that he can enslave him? How does justice enter the play with the figure of Caliban? You need to use your essay to describe what the play says about the topic of justice. For example, you might say that the play shows justice is an illusion and use the experiences of Antonio, Ariel, and Prospero to establish that. Or you might say that in the play Shakespeare makes the point that justice will prevail and use Alonso, Ferdinand, and Caliban in support of that contention.

Sample Topics:

1. **The supernatural:** Much in the play revolves around the supernatural. Prospero searches for occult knowledge but in a rational manner, which is contrasted in the play with Sycorax, who consorted with at least one devil. Caliban is half-human, half-demon. Ariel, a spirit, is a major character. The storm is created by magic. The survivors are separated by magic.

   While a significant aspect of romances is often the supernatural, some romances avoid it entirely. That *The Tempest* includes it may add to the argument that the play is a romance, but supernatural elements are not included for that purpose alone. What else does Shakespeare argue through the supernatural? Does he say that all spirits are evil? Does he argue that sometimes justice can only be obtained through supernatural means? Does he suggest that magic is useful? Does he state that magic is good, evil, or neutral? What does the play say about the study of magic in terms of Prospero? Is he a good character? Does he use magic for good? Was his study of magic good? If it was, why does he abandon it? Is this a commentary on magic or on something else?

You might read about the history of the occult in Shakespeare's day, looking at John Dee and others who were seen as involved with the supernatural realm. What would the audience have known and how might it have impacted their understanding of the play? Is Shakespeare arguing for a particular response to non-Christian supernatural action? Does Christianity have any part in the play? Most of the audience would have been Christian. What might account for the lack of emphasis on that particular belief system?

2. **Nature versus nurture:** One could argue that Prospero raised both Miranda and Caliban. One was the daughter of a "piece of virtue" (1.2.152) and the other of a witch (5.1.2343). He taught both of them (1.2), yet one was properly obedient and the other tried to hurt both Miranda and Prospero.

If this is Shakespeare's commentary on nature versus nurture, what does it say about which part of the divide is more important? Why would audiences of the day agree? Think not only about the royal succession and its accompanying problems with Henry VIII but also about social class. How would an emphasis on nature over nurture support the hierarchy of social class? How would it explain those things that were not readily alterable or changeable? How would it help to keep them from changing? Is this an argument that encourages fatalism or the acceptance of the status quo? How might it be integrated into a belief system? Is there any indication of that in the play?

Other aspects of the play also include elements of nature versus nurture. Ariel was enslaved but still served Prospero well. What does that say about the argument? Was Ariel powerful? Was his life experience during the play powerful? Why or why not? Prospero planned for Ferdinand to fall in love with Miranda, and he does. Without knowing her status, Ferdinand commits to her. What does this say about nature versus nurture? Do you think Shakespeare was saying that nobility recognizes nobility? Consider his introduction of Fidele to Arviragus and Guiderius in *Cymbeline*. The three immediately bond, and the older two call the younger one brother. They are, in fact, siblings. Is the relationship of Ferdinand and Miranda another example of this?

What does it say of nature versus nurture that both Prospero and Alonso's brothers plotted against them? Did Prospero steal anything? If so, is it on the same level or to the same degree as Antonio's theft of the dukedom? If not, what makes the difference between the actions of the two who are biological brothers and, presumably, raised in a similar household? Sebastian and Antonio decide to murder Alonso. How is this related to nature versus nurture? Or is it?

3. **Forgiveness:** Locate and analyze passages that comment on forgiveness, such as when Prospero talks to Ferdinand (4.1) or when Alonso and Prospero reconcile (5.1). Look at Prospero's discussion of his forgiveness of his brother, though his brother does not ask for it.

What is Shakespeare saying about forgiveness through *The Tempest*? Is it important? Is it good? Is it necessary? Is it healing? How could these be argued? Is it really forgiveness of his brother when Prospero says that calling Antonio his brother would infect his mouth (5.1)? Is that forgiveness, or is it something else? If it is not forgiveness, how is it related to forgiveness? Are there other similar examples in the play? Who forgives in the play? Who is forgiven? What is their comparative social standing? What is their relationship to each other? Does this impact your understanding of what Shakespeare is saying about forgiveness?

Character

The Tempest has many characters that offer interesting points of entrance into a discussion of the play. Prospero, the main character, is a popular figure with many; he is in control, and he triumphs in recovering his position as Duke of Milan. Others dislike him intensely for his disregard of his duties and his promise to Ariel. The spirit Ariel is another popular character. The dependence on the man who set him free and yet his independence in determining how to fulfill his master's instructions offer a telling juxtaposition. Miranda, as the only female in the play, offers a different perspective. Since she is young but clearly of marriageable age, and she is manipulated into falling in love with Ferdinand, she is an example of the compliant daughter revered in Shakespeare's day. Choosing one character to look at, or comparing two, can prove a revealing way of looking at *The Tempest*.

Sample Topics:

1. **Prospero:** You might choose one relationship that Prospero is involved in and examine what it reveals about his character. What does that relationship add to the play?

   Formerly the Duke of Milan, Prospero lost his title and status due to the political machinations of his brother. His brother would never have had an opportunity to betray him, however, had Prospero not turned over the responsibilities of running the kingdom in order to devote himself to his studies. What does this say about Prospero? How does he behave responsibly in the play? How has he been irresponsible? Was he a good ruler? Was he a good student? How have his studies hurt him? How have they helped him? To what use does he put his studies in the play? How have learning and intellectual activity benefited him? What does Caliban say about Prospero's books? What does Prospero eventually promise to do with his books?

   Is Prospero a sympathetic or unsympathetic creature? Why? Is he a good father? What does he say about Miranda? How does he treat her? How does he educate her? How does he talk to her? Is he a good friend? How does he treat Gonzalo, who helped him? Why would he do this? Are there extenuating circumstances? Is Prospero smart? Is he intellectually savvy, socially savvy, or both? How can you tell? What in the play makes you think that?

Is he good? Look at James Wyatt's introduction of the subject of good: "Being good requires a certain quality of temperament, the sense of virtues that spur a character not just to avoid evil or its appearance, but to actively promote good" (1). Does Prospero promote good? If so, how? Does he avoid evil? Does he avoid the appearance of evil? Is Prospero moral? Why or why not? Is he cruel? If so, to whom? Is he evil? What in the play shows this? Does he keep his promises? Does he do so immediately? Why does he treat Caliban badly? Is this warranted? How does he treat Ariel? Is this warranted? As a ruler, he would be expected to be in charge of those around him. Does this add anything to your understanding of his character? Does it mitigate his actions?

2. **Ariel:** This character is a powerful spirit in the play who interacts with almost everyone. What are the implications for Shakespeare integrating yet another nonhuman presence into *The Tempest*?

Analyze what you know of Ariel's background. How did he become a prisoner? How is he freed? What does he agree to? Does he keep his promise? Does he do so willingly or grudgingly? What does this tell you about Ariel? Is the spirit good or evil? How is what he does good? How is what he does not good? How do his actions influence a discussion of who he is?

Look at the physical actions Ariel performs in the play. What does he do? Does Prospero give him exact directions all the time, or is Ariel able to make his own decisions in fulfilling Prospero's requests? How do the choices Ariel makes show intelligence? What else do they show about Ariel? Is Ariel powerful? Is he more powerful than Prospero? Whose power is Ariel using? What do we learn about Ariel's talents, musical abilities, and physical capabilities from the various actions he performs?

3. **Miranda:** Miranda has little memory of the time before her 12 years on the island. While there, human contact has been

limited to her father and Caliban. What are the far-reaching effects of this isolated existence?

Think about how old Miranda is. What does this tell you about her abilities? Her knowledge? How did she learn on the island? What has her time been spent learning? What does this prepare her for? What does it fail to prepare her for?

What is Miranda's relationship with her father like? How does he treat her? He calls her both a wench and a cherubim. What are the circumstances in which he refers to her with each of these descriptions? What is the significance of these namings? How does he speak of her? How does she respond to him? What does this tell us about their time on the island?

Prospero sets Miranda up to meet and fall in love with Ferdinand. How reasonable was it of her father to expect her to love the prince of Naples? What causes her to love him? How long does that take? Does he love her? How do you know? What is the basis of their love? Will such a basis last a lifetime? How does Miranda defend Ferdinand? What does she say about him? What do her own words reveal about her? Is the passion she develops for Ferdinand displayed elsewhere in the play? Why does Prospero force Ferdinand to work? How does Miranda react to this? What do we learn about Miranda from these actions?

Miranda interacts with other characters on the island: Ariel, Caliban, Alonso, and others. What do her interactions and responses to these people tell us about her? Is Miranda a well-developed character? Does she change in the context of the play? Is she typical of Shakespeare's heroines? Is she typical of what was expected from a daughter of the aristocracy in that time? She is innocent, but is she naïve? Does she trust her own judgment? Is her judgment correct?

History and Context

During the time that *The Tempest* was written, life was much different from what it is today. The black plague had recently swept through the population of vast parts of Europe, reducing it by as much as 50 percent.

Smallpox was a scourge on the people of that era, killing many. Marriages among the nobility were often arranged for political or financial gain, while marriages among other classes might be contracted for any number of reasons. A few years before the play was written, Queen Elizabeth I, who had reigned for many years, died childless, leaving the throne to James I. Christianity was still a sensitive issue since England had forcibly left Catholicism under Henry VIII. Thus references to Christianity would be politically and emotionally charged. Looking at how some of these facts might have influenced the play would be an excellent strategy for creating an essay.

Sample Topics:

1. **The plagues:** At the time *The Tempest* was written, the threat of the black plague was diminishing outside London, where outbreaks still recurred regularly. The red plague, which Caliban attempts to curse the others with, is usually identified as smallpox but could also simply indicate the physical symptoms associated with the plague.

   If Caliban learned language and about the outside world from Prospero, why would he know about the plagues? Why would people in the audience know about the plagues? What would they think of them? Would it be an effective curse? What does Shakespeare gain by having Caliban reference it?

2. **Marriage in Shakespeare's time:** Miranda is 15. Was this an acceptable marriage age in Shakespeare's day?

   During Shakespeare's time, women were usually in their twenties when they married (see the article "The Age of Marriage" referenced in the bibliography). While girls could marry as young as seven, 12 was considered to be the age of consent. If a young woman was married earlier than 12, she could contest her marriage until she was 14. So in the play, Miranda is older than the age of consent. In addition, nobility often married younger than the lower classes, because marriage was a way to strengthen family fortunes or enhance political ties. Does

Ferdinand know how old Miranda is? Would he care? Does the audience know how old Ferdinand or his sister are?

Marriages were usually arranged by the parents, and thus Prospero's matchmaking was normal. How does Prospero bring Miranda and Ferdinand together? How does he attempt to encourage them to stay together? Usually both sets of parents were involved in a betrothal. Why does this not happen in the play? What does it mean for the betrothal? Why is Prospero not concerned? How does Alonso react?

3. **Roman mythology:** Iris, Ceres, and Juno come to the island to celebrate Ferdinand and Miranda's wedding. They speak of Cupid and Venus.

Shakespeare invokes Roman mythology in the play. Why would Iris, the Greek mythological personification of rainbows, have been an appropriate inclusion for the play? What other references to rainbows might this invoke? Think about the Old Testament story of Noah and the flood. Why would Juno's presence in the play be appropriate? Reread her lines and see if they mean more to you now that you know what particular aspect of life she was associated with. Why would Ceres be appropriate for the play? What kind of harvest is hoped for in the play? Ceres does not want to see Venus and Cupid, because they are responsible for her daughter living with Pluto. What does Shakespeare say they were plotting for Ferdinand and Miranda? Were they successful? Was there a discussion of this earlier in the play, without the gods mentioned? How were they foiled? This part of the play is relatively short, yet it contains several allusions that enrich the work. Think about these references and formulate what you think they add to the play.

4. **Performed for James I:** Since the play was performed for the king, the presentation of what it means to be a ruler is particularly important. What effect does performance history have on an understanding of the work as literature?

Ruling is an important concept in the play. James I had been king for several years before the play was written, so his history might have been intentionally or unintentionally incorporated into the play. Is it? If so, how? Why might this play have been appropriate to present before King James? What positive lessons might it offer? What negative actions does it caution against? Are there any parallels between Prospero and James I? What might they mean? Why would a king be inclined to view this play positively? How might the king who wrote on the concept of the divine right of kings see the presentation of rule in the play?

Philosophy and Ideas

An essay that deals with philosophy and ideas must evaluate the philosophical basis or ideological position of the text. Looking at philosophy and ideas in *The Tempest* might involve examining the concept of justice, forgiveness, romantic love, chastity, or rule. Part of what makes Shakespeare's work timeless is the multiplicity of ideas presented in his works. These philosophical preoccupations, as made manifest in action and word, create an ideological framework that you can examine in an essay. If you choose to look at justice, you might focus on discussions of justice in the play as well as the repercussions of actions. Are these just? You might look at the ways justice is involved in the relationships of Prospero and Ariel, Prospero and Caliban, and Prospero and Alonso. You might look at justice in conjunction with revenge. Prospero seeks justice and the return of his crown but does not seek revenge. Often seeking justice and seeking revenge are conflated. Is this true in the play? While justice is an issue in the work and provides the play with philosophical grounding, it is only one of several ideas presented by Shakespeare in *The Tempest*.

Sample Topics:

1. **Romantic love:** According to critic Edward I. Berry, Shakespeare is "exceptional in providing a convincing psychology behind the convention" of love at first sight (46). This convention is common in Shakespeare's works and appears in

The Tempest. Why would an audience be unsurprised that Miranda and Ferdinand fall in love?

Why would Miranda be likely to love Ferdinand? What has her experience taught her? Why would Ferdinand be likely to love Miranda? What has he recently lost? Why could Miranda help fill that gap?

Look at the words Miranda uses when she first sees Ferdinand (2.1). Is Prospero's plan to marry Miranda to Ferdinand being successfully advanced in Miranda's view? Is it going well from Ferdinand's standpoint? Examine Ferdinand's first words to Miranda. Just a few lines in this one scene bring Miranda and Ferdinand together and cause them to fall in love. What is it about each other that attracts one to the other? What are the indications as to the basis of their mutual attraction? Does knowing this make it more understandable that Prospero causes them problems immediately? Why does his plan make sense? Look at the rest of the conversations Ferdinand and Miranda have. From them, what else can you learn about Shakespeare's view of romantic love?

2. **Chastity:** Chastity, abstaining from sexual relations, was required of women before marriage. The issue is an important one in the play as well. Does Shakespeare's representation of chastity reflect the views of his times?

Start with Ferdinand's commentary on chastity: "O, if a virgin, / And your affection not gone forth, I'll make you / The queen of Naples" (2.1.623–25). These lines make clear that Ferdinand is interested in marrying Miranda, but only if she has been chaste. Miranda says that if he does not marry her, she will not marry anyone. "I am your wife, if you will marry me; / If not, I'll die your maid" (3.1.1376–77). A maid, or maiden, was an unmarried woman and often also a virgin.

Other characters are also concerned about the chastity of the couple. Prospero says that there will be negative consequences to the relationship if they have sex outside marriage. What are those consequences, and why might they be the result? He returns to the concept after a brief discussion of other matters with Ariel. What does Prospero say might be the cause of the promises being broken? How likely is that? How common was it? You might look at Shakespeare's own life for some illumination on the matter.

Form and Genre

The Tempest is a romance yet contains significant comic and tragic aspects as well. L. Kip Wheeler offers a useful comparison of tragedy and comedy that could prove valuable background for an essay on genre. Examining *The Tempest* as a romance, as partly tragedy and as partly comedy can help you see elements or aspects of the play you might not have otherwise considered. This is one way a thorough consideration of genre can enhance your exploration of a work. Also, since *The Tempest* is a play, you might want to think about the ways in which the form of the play impacts the work. Unlike a novel, a play cannot directly or as easily present a character's unspoken or inner thoughts. What does the heavy reliance on dialogue and action add to the play? In what ways does it detract or limit the author?

Sample Topics:

1. **Comedy:** Some scholars have categorized *The Tempest* as a comedy.

Do you agree that this is a legitimate categorization of the play? What parts are funny? Why are they comical? Are there comic characters in the play, characters whose primary function is to make the audience laugh? Who are they? What makes them comic? How do they look, talk, and act that is different from the more serious characters? How does the play reveal a sense of humor? Where are there lighthearted approaches to serious subjects? Where is there absurdity? Is it ridiculed or accepted? How can the play be seen as a celebration of living? How does the play offer hope that life will improve? What values conflict in the play (Wheeler)?

2. **Tragedy:** A tragedy is a form of art in which the protagonist is defeated in his or her life because of a flaw in the character. Tragedy often involves death. How does *The Tempest* fit this formula?

   What aspects of the play are tragic? How are they tragic? Does the experience of Prospero qualify as tragedy? Is a situation explicitly tragic if the characters only think that death and loss are involved? Alonso thinks his son is dead. The group with Alonso discusses why he is at fault for the loss of his son. Read that section of the play again. How do Alonso's decisions lead to what is erroneously perceived to be a tragedy? Why do the other characters dislike his decisions? Often tragedy is somber, with grim circumstances. How are the struggles in the play serious and painful for the characters? Why are they less so for the audience? Tragedy often involves characters going against societal norms and the tremendous punishment for this, even when they do it unknowingly. How are societal expectations shown in the play? Where are they disregarded? Does this bring problems? If so, why? If not, why not? Often tragedy illuminates the inability of the characters to forge their own destiny, shown through a situation that is forced on them. Why do the characters in the play think they are straining against the inevitable? How accurate are they? Does this contribute to the idea of the play as a tragedy or diminish it?

3. **Romance:** In the introduction to *The Scarlet Letter*, Nathaniel Hawthorne says romance is "a neutral territory, somewhere between the real world and fairyland, where the Actual and the Imaginary may meet, and each imbue itself with the nature of the other" (38). What are the implications of this statement when applied to *The Tempest*?

   How is the situation in *The Tempest* like the real world? Do mothers sometimes die and brothers turn against brothers? Think of the play and try to list 20 or 30 ways in which *The*

Tempest mirrors reality or integrates aspects of realism. How is the play like an imaginary world? Do spirits traipse about the Earth taking on different forms? Do they play music? Do they repair ships or destroy them? Can a man learn how to control the weather? Are people commonly imprisoned in trees? Romances often take place in unfamiliar territory. How does the play reflect that particular aspect of the romance? What about the play's setting and subject matter make it far removed from the audience of Shakespeare's time? Was Italy close to England? How many early modern Brits would have traveled to the continent? What about to Tunis or another part of North Africa? How does the location factor into the world of the play? Is it near England? What do we know about the island that Prospero lives on? Do we know where it is? A modern romance is usually defined as a love story. How is it a romance in the modern usage of the word? How is the play modern with the love presented? How is it archaic? Is the love story a major part of the story? Was it because he wanted to have his daughter become queen of Naples that Prospero wrecked the ship? How large a part does the love story occupy in the play?

Language, Symbols, and Imagery

Essential elements of literature include symbols and imagery. Closely examining a work's symbols or language can produce compelling or unexpected claims for an essay. Generating a lot of material as you read and write about the play is a good way to begin. The more analysis you perform, the more likely your ideas will be strong and workable. This means that you may come up with far more information than you can use in your essay. This excess a good thing, because it allows you to pick the best ideas to then develop. Symbolism in *The Tempest* is present from the onset; Shakespeare provides a symbol in the title. Focusing on the storm, literally and metaphorically in the play, might serve as a good starting point for your essay. While the literal impact of the storm should be clear to you after a single reading of the play, metaphorical meanings for it might continue to surface as you revisit, analyze, and refine your critical position.

Sample Topics:

1. **The storm:** What commentary does Shakespeare offer about the literal and metaphorical presence of storms and storm imagery in the play?

   The play is titled *The Tempest.* Does the title make the storm a central, essential symbol? If so, what is it a symbol of? How is that interpretation supported by the play? What drives the storm? What literally creates it? What figuratively creates it, or why was it created? How is the storm ironic? Look at Prospero's arrival on the island versus Alonso's. How do the various characters react to the storm? What do those involved think has happened? How do they become separated?

   The play's literal storm also takes on metaphorical import: Difficult times often reveal the true character of people. Is that an accurate description of what happens in the play? Whose facades are washed away in the storm? Whose true natures are revealed in a positive light? The tempest ends Miranda's isolation, Prospero's exile, and Antonio's rule of Milan. What might these various transitions have in common metaphorically with the storm? Are there other things the storm changes?

2. **Drowning:** The word *drown* or *drowning* is used 20 times in the play. Even after the survivors make it to shore, drowning is used as a metaphor.

   The first mention of drowning is as a macabre joke when Gonzalo says the sailor does not have the mark of drowning but of hanging on him. He takes this to mean they will not drown. It might refer to a literal mark, which early phrenologists thought would identify the fate of the person, or it might simply be a joke. What do you think? Since Shakespeare included the comment, it must have some significance, even if only as an attempt at comic relief. Why is it important?

   When Ferdinand hears Ariel playing music, he says it is a lament for his drowned father. Ferdinand just lost his father (or thought he did), so the timing might be the only association. But why specify that his father was drowned? The audience already knows that. Reexamine each of the references to drowning in the play and see if they are literal or symbolic. If they are symbolic, what do they mean? How would one drown in alcohol, as Stephano says of Caliban? Caliban says dropsy, or alcoholism, will drown Stephano and Trinculo; how would that happen? Toward the end of the play, Prospero promises to drown his book. It is an unlikely symbol. Usually we would think of books burning. Why use drowning? Why is the switch in terminology important?

3. **Sounds:** Caliban says, "Be not afeard; the isle is full of noises, / Sounds and sweet airs, that give delight and hurt not" (3.2.1533–34). Shakespeare uses sounds, music, and songs throughout the play. What are the ramifications of these audio inclusions?

The play begins with the sounds of a storm and the ship breaking up. What is the point of those sounds? Why are they ominous? What do they symbolize? For his part, Ariel uses sounds, which Gonzalo refers to as a humming, to wake Gonzalo and Alonso before they can be murdered in their sleep. Antonio and Sebastian lie about the sound, saying it was a herd of wild beasts, because they need to explain their drawn swords. Here the quiet sound is salvation and the loud sound deception. Is there symbolism in this reversal? What does it mean?

Music is also often used. When Ariel leads Ferdinand to Miranda, he does it with music, which Ferdinand says is for his father. Was that the purpose of the tune? If it was not, why does Ferdinand say it is? What is the difference between a song and a tune? Is it symbolic that music can mean multiple things? Look through the play for other uses of noise, music, and song. Does this emphasis on aurality point to the importance of listening or the breakdown of communication in the play?

Compare and Contrast Essays

A good way to come up with ideas for essays is to examine two elements side by side to help you identify features in each that you might not otherwise have noticed. You might compare two characters, such as Ferdinand

and Caliban. Understanding their similarities and differences might help to explain Miranda's immediate attraction to Ferdinand, since she has previously only been exposed to Caliban. You do not have to limit your comparisons to what is in a single text, though. For instance, you might want to compare the experience of Ferdinand and Miranda's love with that of Florizel and Perdita from another Shakespearean romance, *The Winter's Tale*. Both couples are young and in love. In both, the father of the young woman supports the match. From there, however, the romances diverge significantly. Other literature or popular culture manifestations could also be compared. The point is to find two works that you know have something in common and compare them, looking for more than surface differences and similarities. In doing so, you will often be able to say something more insightful about the play you were offered as a topic.

Sample Topics:

1. **Ferdinand and Caliban:** Both men are interested in Miranda, but their approaches are significantly different. Compare and contrast each character's relation to and views of the play's female protagonist.

   Begin by listing what you know about the two characters. How were they raised? Where? What was their parentage? How are they referred to in the play? A key element to examine is their difference in physical appearance. However, you must remember that Miranda grew up around Caliban. So their physicality and looks, while very different, might be less significant than you would think at first. Or they might not be. After all, what does Miranda first say about Ferdinand? How does she speak of him, and what does she say?

   Prospero supported Ferdinand in his courtship of Miranda and was not happy with Caliban for desiring Miranda. What were the differences? What was the difference in approach? What is the difference in their education and experience? What is the difference in their family background? What is the difference in their attitudes toward working for Prospero? What do those differences say about them?

There are many other ways to compare and contrast Ferdinand and Caliban. Use those points that are most useful and develop them into your essay.

2. **Ferdinand and Miranda in *The Tempest* as compared to Florizel and Perdita in *The Winter's Tale:* Both** women have a lot in common, as do the men. Their similarities actually make the differences between them as couples even more striking. What conclusions can you draw about the representation of love and courtship in Shakespeare's romances?

Perdita and Miranda are both exiled nobility, young women marked by their beauty and goodness. Look at how their fathers talk about them and to them. Both fall in love with royalty. In what other ways are the two women similar? Perdita was banished by her father, while Miranda was banished with her father. In what other ways are they different?

Ferdinand and Florizel are both princes. Both fall in love quickly. Neither consults his father before the betrothal. Examine the reasoning behind this. In what other ways are the two men similar? Different?

As a couple, Ferdinand and Miranda have her father's blessing. They gain immediate acceptance of his father for the match, once Alonso hears of it. Florizel and Perdita also have her father's approval of the match. However, when his father learns of it, he not only disapproves, but he threatens Old Shepherd with a painful death and says he will scratch up Perdita's face. What does this say about what he thinks is the basis of their relationship? What are the circumstances that made these two reactions different? What did the fathers know or not know? How would that impact the reactions? In what other ways can you compare and contrast the couples?

Bibliography and Online Resources for *The Tempest*

Adams, Robert M. *Shakespeare: The Four Romances.* New York: W.W. Norton, 1989. Print.

"The Age of Marriage." *Internet Shakespeare*. University of Victoria, Canada. <http://internetshakespeare.uvic.ca/Library/SLT/society/marriage.html>. Web. 15 June 2009.

Bennett, Susan. *Performing Nostalgia: Shifting Shakespeare and the Contemporary Past*. New York: Routledge, 1995. Print.

Berry, Edward I. "Rosalyne and Rosalind." *Shakespeare Quarterly* 31.1 (Spring 1980):42–52. *JSTOR*. Web. 15 June 2009.

Bieman, Elizabeth. *William Shakespeare: The Romances*. New York: Simon & Schuster Macmillan, 1990. Print.

Bloom, Harold. *Shakespeare: The Invention of the Human*. New York: Riverhead Books, 1998. Print.

Chambers, E. K. *William Shakespeare: A Study of Facts and Problems*. New York: Oxford UP, 1989. Print.

Crystal, David and Ben Crystal. *Shakespeare's Words*. Complete texts of Shakespeare with glossary. May 2008. <http://www.shakespeareswords.com/>. Web. 15 June 2009.

Davis, Lloyd. *Sexuality and Gender in the English Renaissance*. New York: Routledge, 1998. Print.

Frazier, Sir James George. *The Golden Bough: A Study of Magic and Religion, Abridged Edition*. 1922. <http://ebooks.adelaide.edu.au/f/frazer/james/golden/>. Web. 15 June 2009.

Hamilton, Edith. *Mythology*. New York: Back Bay Books, 1998. Print.

Hawthorne, Nathaniel. *The Scarlet Letter*. New York: Penguin Classics, 1983. Print.

"Historical Background of Marriage Customs." *Folger Shakespeare Library*. <http://www.folger.edu/documents/marriagenew.pdf>. Web. 15 June 2009.

James I. *True Law of Free Monarchies*. <http://www.fordham.edu/halsall/mod/james1-trew2.html>. Web. 15 June 2009.

Linebaugh, Peter and Marcus Rediker. *The Many-Headed Hydra: The Hidden History of the Revolutionary Atlantic*. New York: Verso Books, 2002. Print.

McDonald, Russ. *Shakespeare: An Anthology of Criticism and Theory 1945–2000*. Hoboken, NJ: Wiley-Blackwell, 2004. Print.

Nixon, Rob. "Caribbean and African Appropriations of 'The Tempest.'" *Critical Inquiry* 13.3 (Spring 1987): 557–78. *JSTOR*. Web. 14 June 2009.

Shakespeare, William. *Open Source Shakespeare*. Ed. Eric M. Johnson. George Mason U, 2003. Web. 14 June 2009.

———. *The Tempest: A Case Study in Critical Controversy*. Eds. James D. Phelan and Gerald Graff. New York: Bedford/St. Martins, 2008. Print.

Smith, Hallett. "Shakespeare's Romances." *The Huntington Library Quarterly* 27.3 (Mary 1964): 279–87. *JSTOR*. Web. 14 June 2009.

Wheeler, L. Kip. "Some Distinctions Between Classical Tragedy and Comedy." 2008. <web.cn.edu/kwheeler/documents/Tragedy_Comedy.pdf>. Web. 1 June 2009.

Wyatt, James. *The Book of Exalted Deeds*. Renton, WA: Wizards of the Coast, 2003. Print.

THE TWO
NOBLE KINSMEN

READING TO WRITE

WRITTEN IN 1613 or 1614, *The Two Noble Kinsmen* was most likely a collaboration between William Shakespeare, the probable author of the first and last acts of the play, and John Fletcher, the playwright who followed Shakespeare as the main playwright with his acting company. It is also Shakespeare's final play. While many recognize it as Shakespeare's work, it is not fully accepted as such by everyone. For example, the Cambridge edition of Shakespeare's collected works does not include the play, though the Oxford edition does.

Even those who accept that *The Two Noble Kinsmen* is Shakespeare's final play find it problematic. There is a significant change in style in the play, accounted for by the two authors, and there are no memorable lines, as there are in almost every other play. The play is similar to others in Shakespeare's corpus in theme and borrowing—the play is taken from Chaucer—but it does not have the strength of the other plays. Theodore Spencer has an interesting introduction to the play in which he says that Fletcher's section succeeded, while Shakespeare's failed, being "static and, though with splendor, stiff . . . slow, and dense" (257).

Choose a passage that is particularly germane to the play and examine it closely to see what it tells you about the work. Try to determine why Shakespeare chose to express the thoughts the way he did. What was Shakespeare saying? What would change if synonyms were used? What would change if the order of the passage changed? An example of a relevant passage from the play that would be good for a close reading is Palamon's discussion of honor.

Our services stand now for Thebes, not Creon,
Yet to be neutral to him were dishonour,
Rebellious to oppose. Therefore we must
With him stand to the mercy of our fate,
Who hath bounded our last minute. (1.3.99–103)

Let's to the King, who, were he
A quarter carrier of that honour which
His enemy come in, the blood we venture
Should be as for our health, which were not spent,
Rather laid out for purchase. But, alas,
Our hands advanced before our hearts, what will
The fall o'th'stroke do damage? (1.3.108–13)

Palamon has quite a bit to say about the honor they want to keep. You might go through the work line by line, examining the points he makes. What services do the two men give? Why are they now for Thebes? How is that different from being for Creon? Why is it dishonorable to be neutral? How would their honor fare if they did not follow him? Why are they at the mercy of fate? Why must they stand with him? How has he bound them? Think about how a person became a knight. How much honor does Palamon say Creon has? Why? What does he say would happen if Creon were honorable? What would happen to them? Because he is not, what is going to happen? Why will their hands be advanced before their hearts? To which does Shakespeare tie honor? Why will the fight do damage to them? To whom is a stroke of the sword usually damaging?

Instead of examining each line, you might want to look at the overall discussion. How does Palamon regard their honor? What must they do for honor? Does he feel that this is a good thing? Is honor equivalent to doing good? If it is not, what is it equivalent to? How is he defining honor? What are its limitations and its parameters?

The story of Creon comes originally from the plays of Sophocles, beginning with *Oedipus Rex.* You might want to reread the plays and note which parts Shakespeare used and which he did not. The educated in the audience would have known the earlier plays. What references would they bring to this discussion of honor by Palamon? How would it impact their understanding of the work? How does it make this section of the play richer?

Obviously a close reading of a play can lead to several different essay topics. Once you have read through the passage and generated questions, you can then return to the text and look for other related passages. These should be passages that help you develop a particular line of thought you are interested in pursuing. Examine these passages as you did the first and continue this process until you have developed a thought sufficiently to base your essay on it.

TOPICS AND STRATEGIES

In this chapter are various essay topics on *The Two Noble Kinsmen*. While there are many good topics suggested, the suggestions are not exhaustive. There are many good topics not included in this chapter. As you examine the topics suggested, you may want to adapt the suggestions or you may come up with an entirely different topic on your own. Should you decide to use one of the chapter's topics, make sure you avoid simply answering the questions for the essay in order. The questions and the comments are intended to help you generate your own ideas and analyze the work more productively. They are not organized for an essay nor are they complete. Thinking about the questions and the reading, taking thorough notes, and rereading the play will help you craft an exemplary essay. Once you have chosen an approach, as a good student you will want to focus your findings into an interpretation that then becomes the basis for your essay. If you are having trouble coming up with an argument, continue working with the play until you find one. Be aware that all the work that is done in the prewriting phase of the essay, including note taking and brainstorming, helps make the written essay stronger, so don't think that you aren't working on the paper as you read, take notes, and think. Do make sure, though, that you allow sufficient time to actually draft and revise the essay itself. Hurried writing will not typically result in a powerful essay, even if you have thoroughly prepared for composition.

Themes

The Two Noble Kinsmen addresses many themes, including the nature of romantic love, friendship, and innocence and experience. Whether you choose to write about any of these themes or another that you identified in your reading, it is a good idea to reread the play with your theme in mind, looking for particular passages applicable to your topic. Having identified these elements, analyze them in order to form a conclusion or argument about the precise intention of the play in its discussion of that theme.

Sample Topics:

1. **Love can cause enmity:** Examine *The Two Noble Kinsmen* for its portrayal of romantic love and its impact on other relationships.

In your rereading, pursue a thorough understanding of Palamon and Arcite's relationship prior to Emilia. How did they talk about each other? How did they react to each other? What did they do with each other? Were they close? How close were they? Did they believe that anything could come between them? How do you know? Immediately, though, their love for Emilia caused a rift. Why? What does this say about love? Which relationship proves stronger? How do you know? What shows that their commitment to being with Emilia is strong? What do they do that is dishonorable? How is that resolved? What do they agree to? Why? What are they expecting as a result? Will each one accept it if he does not win? Why? What is their vision for this fight? How is friendship limited or diminished by male-female romantic relationships? Which is harder? Which survives?

2. **Friendship triumphs over rivalry:** How does *The Two Noble Kinsmen* portray friendship throughout the play?

The Two Noble Kinsmen deals very robustly with the limitations and implications of friendship. At the beginning of the play, Arcite and Palamon are as close as two people can get. Palamon says, "I do not think it possible our friendship / Should ever leave us" (2.2.113–14). What is their familial relationship? How much of their lives have they spent together? What is their mutual response to King Creon? How do they preserve their honor? What is said about them as warriors? How do they abide in the prison? Are they content? What does this show about them? What fractures their friendship? Why is it broken? What arguments do they make over which of them has a better claim to Emilia? What do those claims say about their friendship? What does the rivalry show about the strength of their friendship, which before this was presented as strong? How do Shakespeare and Fletcher contrast the relative importance of the two relationships? Are they willing to forgo their romantic feelings for their love? The two men do reconcile at the end of the play. How are they reacting toward the situation in which they find themselves? Are they friends again during the processional? What is happening to Palamon while Arcite is riding through the streets in triumph? What brings about their reconciliation? Does either hold a grudge? What does this say about the strength of their friendship?

3. **Transition from innocence to experience:** What does the play say about the maturation process? Looking at the play's theme of the transition from innocence to experience is a fruitful enterprise. This topic can be approached using different characters.

One way to discuss this transition is through Palamon and Arcite. The play takes the two male leads, who are great friends in their innocence, and leads them into romantic love, usually a more mature experience, which breaks their youthful friendship. Why does the friendship break? What indicates that it is a brittle friendship? What indicates that it is strong? How do they treat each other before Emilia enters the play? If the entrance of Emilia is the beginning of the maturation process for these two characters, they have a long way to go. What shows that they are not mature in their discussions of Emilia? How is their lack of maturity shown in their actions with each other and with others? What experiences cause them to change? At the end of the play, are they still innocent? Have they learned from their experiences?

Another way to discuss the transition from innocence to experience is through the jailer's daughter. She is a naïve young lady at the beginning. She believes that the two men are not active participants in life because they suffer so well. She has no experience with men such as these. The young suitor who woos her is not a soldier, nor is he discussed as particularly mature. Do we see her interact with him at the beginning of the play? Who talks of their relationship? What do they say? Quickly following the release of Arcite, the jailer's daughter puts her father's life in jeopardy to help Palamon escape. Has she become less innocent here? Why does she do it? What expectations does she have? Are those expectations met? How do these unmet expectations change her? Eventually the doctor prescribes sex with the suitor as a way to bring her to her right mind. This is often considered the ending of innocence for both men and women. Has she gained any useful experience in this play? Is her experience a positive process? How does Shakespeare intend for you to think of the transition in her case?

Are there any other transitions in the play between innocence and experience? Who else is naïve at the beginning and more worldly wise at the end? How was this process accomplished for them?

Character

Characters are one of the easier topics to choose for an essay. Who the characters are in the play is obvious. You can choose from a plethora of characters involved in multiple scenes throughout the play. However, one of the criticisms people have made about *The Two Noble Kinsmen* is that the characters are one-dimensional and do not change. Because of this, you might look for ways that you see the characters being developed fully and how they change, thus arguing that they are dynamic. Or you might look to see what the individual characters mean for Shakespeare and Fletcher. As you get ready to write your character analysis, you will want to compile everything you know about the character. Examine what the character says, how the character acts and reacts, and how other people talk about and react to the character. Make sure you note if or when the information might be unreliable and why. For example, if you are writing on Palamon, how reliable is what the jailer's daughter says about him? Why? Using all this information, you will be able to put together a coherent and in-depth character analysis that accurately interprets the play.

Sample Topics:

1. **Palamon:** Analyze the character of Palamon. Since he wins the fair lady, he is the romantic hero of the play. Does he act like a hero throughout the work?

   How is Palamon introduced in the play? What does he say? What are his interactions with others like? Why is it somewhat ironic that he ends up in jail because of his loyalty to Thebes? How does he fall in love with Emilia? Why do he and Arcite have a falling out? What do their words say about their character? What does the jailer's daughter say about Palamon? How does he get out of jail? Does he seem grateful or does he simply believe it is his due? How do you know? What shows his insensitivity to the jailer's daughter? Is her love for him relevant to his character? How does he react to Arcite when they meet? What does he say? Why does Theseus say that Palamon is less in the wrong? Do you agree? Why does Palamon think a fight over Emilia is worthwhile? What is at risk? To whom does Palamon pray? What does this say about him? What does he ask? Does he receive it? How does he receive it? Since he is the answer to Emilia's prayers, Palamon must love Emilia best. How do Shakespeare and Fletcher show this in the play?

2. **Arcite:** Analyze and evaluate the character of Arcite.

   How is Arcite first presented? What is he discussing? What do he and Palamon decide to do on that topic? How do the two regard their prison sentence? According to other characters, what does this say about Arcite's character? What changes Arcite's attitude? How does that impact his relationship with Palamon? Why is Arcite chosen to be released? Honor would require that he leave Athens; why does he do something dishonorable? How does he react to Palamon when they meet in the woods? What does he want to happen? Why is he willing to fight Palamon? What is his expectation? To whom does Arcite pray? What does he ask? Does he receive this? Why does Arcite reconcile with Palamon? What do the actions he takes tell you about Arcite's character? In tragedies, the hero has a fatal flaw that leads to his demise. What would be Arcite's fatal flaw? Do you think that he is the tragic hero in the play? Why or why not?

3. **The jailer's daughter:** Analyze the jailer's daughter and her role in the play.

The jailer's daughter says in her first appearance in the play that the two cousins must not be able soldiers, because they are too calm about their suffering. What does this say about the worldview of the character? What does she believe about the relationship of doing and suffering? How does she describe the cousins originally? What do you know from other characters about her situation before the action presented in the play? After Arcite is released, the jailer's daughter releases Palamon. Why does she wait till then? What consequences does she expect because of her actions? Why does she act as she does? What does this say about her view of love? In her monologue she begins by saying that there is no point to her loving Palamon because of their social differences. What is their relative social standing? How does she view those differences? Does she think he will marry her? What is the other alternative? Does she want to do that? She discusses the progression of her emotions. Reread the section and see if it makes sense that by the end she says, "ere tomorrow he shall love me" (2.4.33). At what age does she say women become enamored of men? How old is she? In her next monologue, she talks of her freeing Palamon. How does she respond to his actions? Does she become more disillusioned? Why or why not? What sends her into madness? How does she act? Who takes advantage of this? Who tries to help her? What does she say about Palamon while she is mad? Are those things true? Is she a reliable character witness? How is she cured? What is required? Does it work? What is she given for her release of Palamon? Is it timely? What difference does that make? Is it what she was expecting? What happens to her by the end of the play? What situation is she in? Has her character changed? Has she grown?

4. **Emilia:** Analyze Emilia as both a sister and the beloved.

At what point does Emilia show up in the play? She is the duke's sister in the sense that she is his sister-in-law. How does she take advantage of that position for other people's welfare? What does she request? What is her response to the request to choose a mate from the two fighting Thebans? To whom does she pray? What does she request? How does she react when she is betrothed to Arcite? What does she say when she is given to Palamon? How do all these actions and speeches show her character? What do they show about her? Is she intended to be the ideal woman or does she have some personality? Is there any part of the play that refers to or shows her Amazonian heritage? If so, what is it? How does it display her heritage? Why is this relevant?

History and Context

Examining cultural, social, and historical contexts can often impact your understanding of a literary work. With Shakespeare and Fletcher's *The Two Noble Kinsmen*, an understanding of ancient Greek history might impact your reading. Also reading Chaucer's "The Knight's Tale" might give you a fresh perspective. Understanding Roman mythology is particularly relevant to this play, since three of the central characters appeal to different gods and multiple other gods and generic gods are invoked in the play. In addition, the social ramifications of marriage in the nobility at the time the play was written also might change your perception of the play. With this knowledge, you would be much less likely to misinterpret the play by analyzing it using twenty-first-century assumptions and social mores. From a positive perspective, you would also be better prepared to notice small details and to recognize where Shakespeare is making social commentary and where he is simply presenting social experiences. Because of this, the time you take to learn about the context is well spent as it allows you to form reasonable interpretations of the play for your essay. Researching the cultural and historical contexts might be essential to your analysis of the play, particularly if you deal with Shakespeare and Fletcher's development of a topic with significant cultural or historical implications.

Sample Topics:

1. **Greek history:** Analyze how the play presents the historical experiences of Theseus and Hippolyta. Are these accurate?

There are various stories of Theseus and Hippolyta. In some, Theseus comes to the Amazons with Heracles (the Greek version of Hercules); this reinforces Theseus as a Greek hero, which status he gained on destroying the Cretan minotaur. In some, Theseus battles Hippolyta and wins, thus gaining her agreement to marriage. In others, he kidnaps her and she is forced into marriage by her situation. In others, he does not marry her. Clearly the different approaches offer Shakespeare latitude in what he presents. Look up the various myths of Theseus and Hippolyta and create an argument of which one Shakespeare was using most extensively. A popular source is Joel Skidmore's *Encyclopedia of Greek Mythology* Web site. Consult as well Chaucer's "The Knight's Tale." How does Shakespeare change the story? What does he keep? What is he trying to present that could explain these adaptations? How does his portrayal of Theseus and Hippolyta reinforce various themes in the play? How does it influence the plot? Shakespeare is returning to these characters, whom he featured earlier in *A Midsummer Night's Dream*. What appeal do these characters have that he used them again? How are they developed differently in the two plays? Is there some point in using Greek history with Roman mythology?

2. **Amazons:** Why does Shakespeare set the play in a time when the queen of the Amazons was involved? What does he say about Amazons or women warriors?

Begin with some background reading, such as Celeste Turner Wright's "The Amazons in Elizabethan Literature." This gives you not only a literary introduction but also a historical one. While it does not focus on Shakespeare, several of the points made in the article are apropos. Or you might read Lorna Hardwick's "Ancient Amazons—Heroes, Outsiders, or Women?" Why might Amazons be particularly appealing to those of Shakespeare's time? What Amazonian woman has been influential in English history in their lifetime? Is there any connection between the Amazons of the story and Queen Elizabeth? How are Hippolyta and her sister Emilia portrayed sympathetically? What do they do or say that makes the audience like them? When Emilia cannot make a decision, is this a factor of Elizabethan expectations of women? Does it take away from her stature as an Amazon? How does Shakespeare's presentation of the women differ from the historical presentation of Amazons? What might have been his purpose in doing this?

3. **Roman mythology:** Shakespeare invokes Roman mythology more than 50 times in the play. How does he use Roman mythology?

Shakespeare has his characters refer to Roman deities throughout the play. Three of them are actually prayed to in the final act of the play and their actions, not the actions of the characters, control the outcome of the play. Frazier's work has an interesting presentation of Roman mythology, as does Hamilton's. Which characters pray to which gods? How are the gods relevant to those characters? Juno, the goddess of marriage, is referenced by Theseus in a manner that may be foreshadowing of the problems he and Hippolyta will have, since he tells her that she is more beautiful than Juno, a typical way to evoke the gods' wrath (I.i.63). How does knowing the story of Theseus make this more likely? Why would Theseus do this? Both Theseus and Emilia call on Bellona, the Roman goddess of war in the first act. How does she serve as an impetus in the play? Why do they call on her then but not in the rest of the play? The gods most often referenced in the work are Mars (among others in 1.1.63, 1.1.181, 2.2.21, 5.1.35, and 5.6.106) and Diana (1.3.52, 2.5.52, 5.3.1). Cynthia (4.1.151, 4.2.58) is often conflated with Diana, since in Greek mythology the attributes of the two goddesses are found in Artemis. Venus is also referenced multiple times in the final act of the play. How do the three gods stand for the characters who pray to them? What do the aspects of the gods tell you about the characters? How do the choices of gods to pray to illuminate the characters? Theseus and Emilia mention Bellona, but Arcite refers to Mars. Both are gods of war; what are the differences between them and how might that illustrate something about the characters? Ancient stories are also referenced, besides the ones in which the characters star, including those of Daedelus (3.5.117), Hercules (1.1.66, 2.5.2, 5.5.119), Narcissus (2.2.120), and Prosperine (4.3.24). How do the mentions of these stories add to the play? What do they add to the play? What reasons might Shakespeare have had for choosing these stories and not others? Emilia is called a goddess (2.2.132, 2.2.134, 2.2.166). Usually such an action in mythology would provoke the gods to wrath and end the story badly for the person using the appellation. Instead of that happening in the play, Palamon wins the lady. What is the purpose of the naming? What does it say about Emilia? About Palamon? Why do the playwrights use Roman mythology in a story about Greek history?

4. **Marriage:** What do Shakespeare and Fletcher say in *The Two Noble Kinsmen* about marriage?

The Two Noble Kinsmen has been referred to as the repudiation of Shakespeare's more optimistic final works (Berggren). How might the presentation of marriage in the play show this? The jailer's daughter begins her first monologue by saying that Palamon cannot love her because she is from a different social class, but she ends by hoping that he will. What does this say about her understanding of marriage? If marriages were usually arranged by the family (Alchin), what does the jailer's attitude show? How does the fact that marriages were arranged for advantage make Emilia less ridiculous for being unable to choose between the two men? Do marriages work out well in the play? Whose marriage begins the play? How is it interrupted? What has been those three women's experience with marriage? Theseus refers to his marriage as "this daring deed / Of fate in wedlock" (1.1.163–64). How is marriage, or the engagement to marry, a tempter of fate in the play? Are the betrothals happy? Are the weddings joyous occasions looked forward to? Does the beginning of the play with the interruption of the wedding by the three widows foreshadow disaster for the marriages in the play? Can you see Palamon and Emilia being happy? We know that Theseus and Hippolyta ended badly. What will be the experience of the jailer's daughter and her suitor? What does the wooer gain by marrying her? Will it be a successful relationship? Who speaks of marriage in the play? What do they say? Two gods of marriage are invoked in the play, Juno and Hymen. Why are they referred to? How are they referred to? What might this mean for the play and its characters?

Philosophy and Ideas

Interpretations of *The Two Noble Kinsmen* can be made through various philosophical and ideological approaches. Perhaps you wish to examine how the play portrays madness, a topic that is difficult to discuss and often avoided as a social taboo by polite society.

Sample Topics:

1. **Madness:** What kind of commentary does the play make about madness?

A major motif in the play is madness. Clearly the jailer's daughter goes mad during the play. What causes her insanity? How do you know that is the cause? What manifestations of madness can be seen in her character? How does she act? What does she say? Where does she go? How do others treat her? Is there significance to the fact that her last act before she is obviously mad is releasing Palamon from jail? Was this an act of madness? Why might it be seen as such? How does her first monologue set up her madness? What other things indicate she will go mad? Littledale suggests that the mad songs are adaptations of childhood poetry (201); if this is correct, what does this say about the jailer's daughter's mind-set? Does it offer a different approach to her descriptions of Palamon if they are examined in terms of a child's perception? The countrymen who are dancing describe her as "mad as a March hare" (3.5.74). Why do they say she is mad? Would you agree with them? The doctor says that in order to cure her, those around her must act as if her view of reality is correct. What does he recommend that the various friends and family members do? What is their reaction to his suggestions? Do his suggestions work? How do you know? Does it seem that they would? Why or why not?

Though the jailer's daughter is the clearest example of madness in the play, there are other discussions of madness as well. When Emilia is in the garden, before Palamon and Arcite see her, she sees a narcissus flower and remarks that the man the flower was named after "was a fair boy, certain, but a fool / To love himself; were there not maids enough?" (2.2.120–21). Narcissus fell in love with his reflection in a pool and, in trying to embrace it, drowned; after his death, he was turned into a flower. Are his actions mad? Who would fall in love with themselves? Is this a reference to Palamon and Arcite's self-assurance that they are perfectly happy in jail? What does it mean that Emilia says, "men are mad things" (2.2.126) just before Palamon sees her? Is this the playwrights' way of saying that love is madness? Are there other passages that indicate this?

What other ways are in the play that indicate that men are mad? Is Theseus mad to put off his marriage to take care of Creon? Are Arcite and Palamon mad to let a woman they have never spoken to break up their friendship? Arcite accuses Palamon of madness (2.2.203) and he agrees that he is mad. Is he? What is madness according to their discussion? Later on, Arcite asks if it is mad to live in the woods (3.3.23), which, by implication, would imply that whoever is living in the woods is mad. Since this is Palamon, is this another allusion to his madness? Is the jailer mad to let the suitor have sex with his daughter before marriage? Is the doctor mad to say that madness can be cured by indulging the mad fancies?

2. **Romantic love:** What does *The Two Noble Kinsmen* say about romantic love?

Palamon is in prison and looking out at the gardens when he falls in love with Emilia. Arcite looks out the window and does the same. What does this say about love? Is it based on anything other than physical attraction? What are their arguments for which one loves her best? What are they for who should be able to love her? Palamon and Arcite later discuss their earlier sexual adventures (3.3). There is no hint of love there. When the jailer's daughter releases Palamon because she loves him, Palamon feels no responsibility to her. What do these events say about love in relation to social class? Look at what the jailer's daughter says about loving Palamon and the possibility of his returning her love (2.4). She says she shouldn't love him because he will not return her love. Then she says why he won't. What is the reason? Does that fit with the rest of the play's presentation of love being in social classes? If it does, how might Palamon and Arcite have known that they could love Emilia? What about Emilia showed her social class even as they watched her walk in the garden? Examine the discussions of the two men when they agree to fight to the death for the opportunity to marry Emilia. What do they say about love? How does this reinforce or change the rest of the play's presentation of romantic love?

Other relationships that can be looked at in the play are the jailer's daughter and her suitor, Theseus and Hippolyta, and the three queens' relationships with their husbands. How are these discussed? What do the various couples do to show love? How does the inclusion of these couples make the play a richer discussion of romantic love? What does it show about romantic love?

Form and Genre

The Two Noble Kinsmen is a romance but can be viewed as part tragedy and part comedy. Wheeler offers a handy comparison of tragedy and comedy online that you might take advantage of. Thinking of the play as a romance, as partly tragedy, and as partly comedy can help you see things in the play that you might not have otherwise. This is how thinking of the genre of a text can help you. Also, since *The Two Noble Kinsmen* is a play, you might want to think about the ways in which the form of the play impacts the work. Look at when people are talking in the play when in a novel they would be thinking, for example. What does this add to the play? What does it take away?

Sample Topics:

1. **Comic elements:** To what extent are comic elements integrated into the play, and what is the effect to the work overall?

   Which parts of the play reflect or reference elements of comedy? What makes them less serious? Are there comic characters in the play, characters whose job is to make the audience laugh? Who are they? What makes them comic? How do they look, talk, and act differently from the more serious characters? How does the play show a sense of fun? Where are there lighthearted approaches to serious subjects?

2. **Tragic elements:** Which parts of the play are the most serious? How are they dealt with differently than the comic elements?

   Tragedy often involves characters going against societal norms and the tremendous punishment for this, even when they do it unknowingly. How are societal norms shown in the play? Where are they disregarded? How does this bring problems? Often tragedy shows the inability of the characters to overcome their fate or destiny. Which characters are involved in a tragic situation from this perspective?

3. **Romance:** One of the features of a romance is that it often occurs in an alternatively imagined or unfamiliar place. This could mean that it takes place in a foreign or unreal locale or that the characters are out of the ordinary. How is this definition reflected in *The Two Noble Kinsmen*?

Where do the playwrights use uncommon characters? Do you know three queens? Have you chatted with Amazons? What others are uncommon? How are the locales exotic? This story is set in ancient Athens and Thebes. Is the time setting also exotic? Why would the playwrights use the exotic in the play? What does it add to the story?

Language, Symbols, and Imagery

Approaching Shakespeare's *The Two Noble Kinsmen* in terms of symbolism and imagery could create an intriguing essay. Critics and readers interpret symbolism in various ways; you could use your interpretation of them to develop an analysis for your essay. You might identify a single symbol or a group of symbols and examine what they add to the play. What does the symbol you have chosen stand for? How can you tell? Does Shakespeare use the symbol in a traditional way, or does he use it in an innovative way? How does an analysis of the symbol offer you a means of interpreting the play? There are several kinds of symbols that Shakespeare tends to use frequently, including natural elements. In this play, both birds and flowers are frequently referenced.

Sample Topics:

1. **Flowers:** What is the significance of flowers in the play?

Flowers are introduced immediately following the prologue. The boy sings about roses, daisies, thyme, maiden pink, primrose, oxlips, marigolds, and larkspur, while strewing flowers about. The boy's song is the longest list of flowers in Shakespeare, though he uses them a lot in his plays. Flowers have been endowed with meaning throughout history. During Shakespeare's era, roses were associated with royalty and Venus, the goddess of love; daisies were associated with innocence; thyme was associated with faithfulness; and maiden pinks were associated with purity and virginity (Hoeninger and Brender a Brandis 92). Why would the play begin with these flowers? What is their relevance to the immediate scene? What is their relevance to the entire play? Look up the meaning of flowers online. You may want to look through several Web sites to see if the reported meanings differ. How do the meanings for the other flowers also fit the play? How do they fit the immediate context? Flowers are mentioned other places in the play. What flowers are mentioned? In what context are they mentioned? How do the playwrights use the language of flowers to add to what their words say?

2. **Birds:** What do they mean in the play and how do they invoke more than the literal birds?

Shakespeare was very knowledgeable about animals and plants, and in this play birds are discussed in various places. Turkeys, wren hawks, owlets, hawks, swallows, and ravens are among the actual birds mentioned in the play. The play also introduces the phoenix, an imaginary bird that immolates itself and is reborn every 500 years. What is the point of mentioning the birds? What do these birds have in common? How are they different? Several of these are mentioned in connection with folk beliefs or ancient stories associated with them. Look online to see what associations you can find. For example, in the Elizabethan era, turkeys were thought to be jealous (Shakespeare 3227), thus making sense of the line "To have my wife as jealous as a turkey" (II.iii.31). Hawks and owls are predators. How are they discussed in the play? Does such a mention match their actions? Ravens were associated with war in Old English literature and early medieval writings, though in later times ravens were viewed as harbingers of bad luck. How does this match up with the use of ravens in the play? What does the inclusion of the different birds say about the awareness of the audience? If they did not understand the allusions, how much would have been lost from the sense of the play? If they did, how much richer would the play have been?

3. **Sexual imagery:** Analyze and interpret the various instances of sexual imagery in the text.

There is quite a bit of sexual imagery in the text, including homoeroticism, evoked through Palamon and Arcite's relationship, their description of it, and Palamon's description of the deeds he would do that would inspire Emilia to "take manhood to her / And seek to ravage me" (2.2.262–63). Look at the passages describing their relationship. How does that description evoke homosexuality? Are there other instances of homoeroticism in the play? Is Emilia's invocation of Narcissus another example? Why or why not?

Another aspect of sexual imagery involves maidenhood or virginity. When the boy sings of flowers at the beginning of the play, he mentions "Maiden pinks, of odour faint" (I.i.4). The name itself can be seen as sexual imagery. When Emilia is in the garden, she also speaks of roses and says that a woman is like a rose:

> For when the west wind courts her gently,
> How modestly she blows, and paints the sun
> With her chaste blushes! When the north comes near her,
> Rude and impatient, then, like chastity,
> She locks her beauties in her bud again,
> And leaves him to base briers. (2.2.138–43)

What do the flower equivalents say about women and sex? Are they strong and hardy? Fragile? Beautiful? Why is virginity compared with flowers? The earlier discussion in this chapter on flowers may give you other ways of thinking about the flowers. Can the meanings of the flowers also be seen as sexual?

In addition to the allusions to sex and the symbols for sex, there are also frank discussions of chastity and virginity. In the prologue, plays are compared to maidenheads (an earlier word for hymen). The jailer's daughter, before she becomes quite mad, says, "To be his whore is witless" (2.5.5), and while she is talking about madness there, she is also mentioning the sex act. Later she speaks of it again, "Let him do / What he will with me—so he use me kindly" (2.6.28–29). When Palamon and Arcite are trying to avoid discussing Emilia, they mention women with whom they have previously had sex, including the lord steward's daughter (3.3.29) and the marshal's sister (3.3.37). The jailer's daughter says she "must lose my maidenhead by cocklight" (4.1.112). And the doctor recommends sex as the cure for her madness (5.4). What other discussions of sex are in the play? Why are they there? Is this a risqué play? Or is the sex included to make it more realistic? Why is there such a discussion of sex? Is it because sex is associated with love and marriage? Or is it for some other reason? What support for your ideas can you find in the play?

Compare and Contrast Essays

When you compare and contrast two works, you gain scope of material and a broader perspective as well. Since Shakespeare and Fletcher borrowed from Chaucer's "The Knight's Tale," you might look at how the two texts are similar and different. You might even look at how the first and last acts differ from Chaucer's work and see if the middle acts are more or less similar to Chaucer. This would allow you to see if Shakespeare borrowed more heavily or made more changes to the text than Fletcher did.

Sample Topics:

1. **Chaucer's "The Knight's Tale" and *The Two Noble Kinsmen:*** Compare and contrast these two literary works.

Chaucer's *The Canterbury Tales*, from which "The Knight's Tale" comes, was one of the leading literary works during the Elizabethan era, even though the work was written 200 years earlier. Shakespeare and Fletcher adapted the story into a play format. Analyze the changes that are made to the play from the story. What simple changes were made? What major changes were made? Go through this chapter looking at themes, philosophy, and symbols. See which are in the play and not the story. What accounts for the differences? How have the differences changed the story? What have they added? What have they diminished? How have the characters changed? How were their circumstances changed? What might be some of the advantages of these changes for the playwrights? What was kept the same? Why might those decisions have been made?

2. ***The Two Noble Kinsmen* and *A Midsummer Night's Dream*:** Both of these plays were inspired in part by Chaucer's "The Knight's Tale." Look for similarities between the two plays and how the differences are expressed.

Theseus and Hippolyta appear in both plays. How are they involved? Why does Shakespeare invoke the same time in their lives twice? What two parts do they play in both plays? How do these fit the two very disparate stories? What other similarities are there in the two tales? How do they contribute to the comedy? Since *A Midsummer Night's Dream* is a comedy and *The Two Noble Kinsmen* is a romance, there must be some differences between the plays. What are the differences? What differences specifically separate the two plays' categorizations? How do these impact the reception of the play? How do they impact the categorization of the play? Which play is more popular? Why? What types of characters are missing from *The Two Noble Kinsmen*? What types of characters are missing from *A Midsummer Night's Dream*? Does the absence of these characters significantly change the seriousness of the play? What else creates the differences between the plays?

Bibliography and Online Resources for *The Two Noble Kinsmen*

"The Age of Marriage." *Internet Shakespeare.* University of Victoria, Canada. <http://internetshakespeare.uvic.ca/Library/SLT/society/marriage.html>. Web. 15 June 2009.

Alchin, L. K. "Elizabethan Marriages and Weddings." *Elizabethan Era* Web site. 20 March 2008. Web. 15 June 2009.

Berggren, Paula S. "'For What We Lack, / We Laugh': Incompletion and 'The Two Noble Kinsmen.'" *Modern Language Studies* 14.4 (Autumn 1984): 3–17. *JSTOR.* Web. 15 June 2009.

Chaucer, Geoffrey. "The Knight's Tale: Middle and Modern English." *Librarius.* <http://www.librarius.com/canttran/knighttrfs.htm>. Web. 15 June 2009.

Davis, Suanna. "How to Write a Character Analysis." *Teaching College English.* 28 February 2008. Web. 15 June 2009.

Frazier, Sir James George. *The Golden Bough: A Study of Magic and Religion, Abridged Edition.* 1922. <http://ebooks.adelaide.edu.au/f/frazer/james/golden/>. Web. 15 June 2009.

Hamilton, Edith. *Mythology.* New York: Back Bay Books, 1998. Print.

Hardwick, Lorna. "Ancient Amazons—Heroes, Outsiders, or Women?" *Greece and Rome* 37.1 (April 1990): 14–36. *JSTOR.* Web. 15 June 2009.

Hoeniger, David and Gerard Brender a Brandis. *A Gathering of Flowers from Shakespeare.* Ontario, CA: Porcupine's Quill, 2006. Print.

Littledale, H. "The Mad Songs in 'The Two Noble Kinsmen.'" *The Modern Language Review* 5.2 (April 1910): 200–01. *JSTOR.* Web. 15 June 2009.

"The Meaning of Flowers." *Internet Florist* website. 2009. Web. 15 June 2009.

Nicholson, R. H. "Theseus's 'Ordinaunce': Justice and Ceremony in the 'Knight's Tale.'" *The Chaucer Review* 22.3 (Winter 1988): 192–213. *JSTOR.* Web. 15 June 2009.

Shakespeare, William. *Two Noble Kinsmen. The Norton Shakespeare Based on the Oxford Edition.* Ed. Stephen Greenblatt, Walter Cohen, Jean E. Howard, and Katharine Eisaman Maus. New York, 1997. 3195–278. Print.

Skidmore, Joel. "Theseus." *Encyclopedia of Greek Mythology.* 18 March 2009. Web. 15 June 2009.

Spencer, Theodore. "The Two Noble Kinsmen." *Modern Philology* 36.3 (February 1939): 255–76. *JSTOR.* Web. 15 June 2009.

Wheeler, L. Kip. "Some Distinctions Between Classical Tragedy and Comedy." *Carson-Newman College: Dr. Wheeler's Website.* 2008. Web. 15 June 2009.

Wright, Celeste Turner. "The Amazons in Elizabethan Literature." *Studies in Philology* 37.3 (July 1940): 433–56. *JSTOR.* Web. 15 June 2009.

INDEX